T0338520

Analyzing the Role of Risk Mitigation and Monitoring in Software Development

Rohit Kumar
Chandigarh University, India

Anjali Tayal
Infosys Technologies, India

Sargam Kapil
C–DAC, India

A volume in the Advances in
Systems Analysis, Software
Engineering, and High Performance
Computing (ASASEHPC) Book Series

Published in the United States of America by
    IGI Global
    Engineering Science Reference (an imprint of IGI Global)
    701 E. Chocolate Avenue
    Hershey PA, USA 17033
    Tel: 717-533-8845
    Fax: 717-533-8661
    E-mail: cust@igi-global.com
    Web site: http://www.igi-global.com

Library of Congress Cataloging-in-Publication Data

Names: Kumar, Rohit, 1986- editor. | Tayal, Anjali, 1991- editor. | Kapil,
   Sargam, 1992- editor.
Title: Analyzing the role of risk mitigation and monitoring in software
   development / Rohit Kumar, Anjali Tayal, and Sargam Kapil, editors.
Description: Hershey, PA : Engineering Science Reference, an imprint of IGI
   Global, [2018] | Includes bibliographical references and index.
Identifiers: LCCN 2017061170| ISBN 9781522560296 (hardcover) | ISBN
   9781522560302 (ebook)
Subjects: LCSH: Application software--Development. | Computer software
   industry--Risk management.
Classification: LCC QA76.76.A65 A538 2018 | DDC 005.3--dc23 LC record available at https://
lccn.loc.gov/2017061170

This book is published in the IGI Global book series Advances in Systems Analysis, Software Engineering, and High Performance Computing (ASASEHPC) (ISSN: 2327-3453; eISSN: 2327-3461)

British Cataloguing in Publication Data
A Cataloguing in Publication record for this book is available from the British Library.

All work contributed to this book is new, previously-unpublished material.
The views expressed in this book are those of the authors, but not necessarily of the publisher.

For electronic access to this publication, please contact: eresources@igi-global.com.

Advances in Systems Analysis, Software Engineering, and High Performance Computing (ASASEHPC) Book Series

ISSN:2327-3453
EISSN:2327-3461

Editor-in-Chief: Vijayan Sugumaran, Oakland University, USA

MISSION

The theory and practice of computing applications and distributed systems has emerged as one of the key areas of research driving innovations in business, engineering, and science. The fields of software engineering, systems analysis, and high performance computing offer a wide range of applications and solutions in solving computational problems for any modern organization.

The **Advances in Systems Analysis, Software Engineering, and High Performance Computing (ASASEHPC) Book Series** brings together research in the areas of distributed computing, systems and software engineering, high performance computing, and service science. This collection of publications is useful for academics, researchers, and practitioners seeking the latest practices and knowledge in this field.

COVERAGE

- Computer graphics
- Performance Modelling
- Storage Systems
- Distributed Cloud Computing
- Enterprise Information Systems
- Parallel Architectures
- Engineering Environments
- Network Management
- Metadata and Semantic Web
- Computer Networking

IGI Global is currently accepting manuscripts for publication within this series. To submit a proposal for a volume in this series, please contact our Acquisition Editors at Acquisitions@igi-global.com or visit: http://www.igi-global.com/publish/.

Titles in this Series

For a list of additional titles in this series, please visit:
https://www.igi-global.com/book-series/advances-systems-analysis-software-engineering/73689

Formation Methods, Models, and Hardware Implementation of Pseudorandom Number...
Stepan Bilan (State Economy and Technology University of Transport, Ukraine)
Engineering Science Reference • ©2018 • 301pp • H/C (ISBN: 9781522527732) • US $180.00

Aligning Perceptual and Conceptual Information for Cognitive Contextual System...
Gary Kuvich (IBM, USA)
Engineering Science Reference • ©2018 • 172pp • H/C (ISBN: 9781522524311) • US $165.00

Applied Computational Intelligence and Soft Computing in Engineering
Saifullah Khalid (CCSI Airport, India)
Engineering Science Reference • ©2018 • 340pp • H/C (ISBN: 9781522531296) • US $225.00

Enhancing Software Fault Prediction With Machine Learning Emerging Research...
Ekbal Rashid (Aurora's Technological and Research Institute, India)
Engineering Science Reference • ©2018 • 129pp • H/C (ISBN: 9781522531852) • US $165.00

Solutions for Cyber-Physical Systems Ubiquity
Norbert Druml (Independent Researcher, Austria) Andreas Genser (Independent Researcher, Austria) Armin Krieg (Independent Researcher, Austria) Manuel Menghin (Independent Researcher, Austria) and Andrea Hoeller (Independent Researcher, Austria)
Engineering Science Reference • ©2018 • 482pp • H/C (ISBN: 9781522528456) • US $225.00

Large-Scale Fuzzy Interconnected Control Systems Design and Analysis
Zhixiong Zhong (Xiamen University of Technology, China) and Chih-Min Lin (Yuan Ze University, Taiwan)
Information Science Reference • ©2017 • 223pp • H/C (ISBN: 9781522523857) • US $175.00

Microcontroller System Design Using PIC18F Processors
Nicolas K. Haddad (University of Balamand, Lebanon)
Information Science Reference • ©2017 • 428pp • H/C (ISBN: 9781683180005) • US $195.00

For an entire list of titles in this series, please visit:
https://www.igi-global.com/book-series/advances-systems-analysis-software-engineering/73689

701 East Chocolate Avenue, Hershey, PA 17033, USA
Tel: 717-533-8845 x100 • Fax: 717-533-8661
E-Mail: cust@igi-global.com • www.igi-global.com

Editorial Advisory Board

Table of Contents

Preface..xvii

Acknowledgment.. xix

Chapter 1
Risk Mitigation Planning, Implementation, and Progress Monitoring: Risk
Mitigation...1
    Yadwinder Kaur, Chandigarh University, India
    Satvir Singh, Chandigarh Engineering College, India

Chapter 2
Risk Management Metrics 21
    Rimsy Dua, Chandigarh University, India
    Samiksha Sharma, Chandigarh University, India
    Rohit Kumar, Chandigarh University, India

Chapter 3
Software Vulnerability Management: How Intelligence Helps in Mitigating
Software Vulnerabilities...34
    Rimsy Dua, Chandigarh University, India
    Samiksha Sharma, Chandigarh University, India
    Abhishek Sharma, Chandigarh University, India

Chapter 4
Risks Assessment in Designing Phase: Its Impacts and Issues..............................46
    Ankita Sharma, Chandigarh University, India
    Vipin Pal, National Institute of Technology Meghalaya, India
    Nitish Ojha, Chandigarh University, India
    Rohit Bajaj, Chandigarh University, India

Chapter 5
Problems, Threats in Software Development Life Cycle and Their Analysis 61
Deepika Rana, Chandigarh University, India
Manisha Malhotra, Chandigarh University, India

Chapter 6
An Analysis on Risk Management and Risk in the Software Projects 83
Rajshree Srivastava, Chandigarh University, India

Chapter 7
New Classification of Security Requirements for Quantitative Risk
Assessment..100
Neila Rjaibi, ISG, Tunisia
Latifa Ben Arfa Rabai, ISG, Tunisia

Chapter 8
Estimating Risks Related to Extended Enterprise Systems (EES) 118
Jasleen Kaur, Chandigarh University, India
Rajinder Kaur, Chandigarh University, India

Chapter 9
Meta-Heuristic Approach for Software Project Risk Schedule Analysis...........136
Isha Sharma, Chandigarh University, India
Deepshikha Chhabra, Chandigarh University, India

Chapter 10
Development and Enhancing of Software and Programming Products by
Client Information Administration in Market..150
Abhishek Sharma, Chandigarh University, India
Lokesh Pawar, Chandigarh University, India
Manjot Kaur, Chandigarh University, India

Chapter 11
Risk Management in Web Development..188
Anu Priya Sharma, Chandigarh University, India
Sugandha Sharma, Chandigarh University, India

Chapter 12
Use of Software Metrics to Improve the Quality of Software Projects Using
Regression Testing 204
Arshpreet Kaur Sidhu, Chandigarh University, India
Sumeet Kaur Sehra, GNDEC, India

Chapter 13

Gamification: An Effectual Learning Application for SE.................................219

    Samiksha Sharma, Chandigarh University, India

    Rimsy Dua, Chandigarh University, India

Chapter 14

A New Approach for Reinforcement of Project DEMATEL-FMCDM-
TODIM Fuzzy Approach 234

    Rajshree Srivastava, Chandigarh University, India

    Shiv Kumar Verma, Glocal University, India

    Vikas Thukral, Charles River Development, USA

Chapter 15

Role of Attacker Capabilities in Risk Estimation and Mitigation....................244

    Deepshikha Chhabra, Chandigarh University, India

    Isha Sharma, Chandigarh University, India

Chapter 16

Risks Analysis and Mitigation Technique in EDA Sector: VLSI Supply
Chain 256

    Lokesh Pawar, Chandigarh University, India

    Rohit Kumar, Chandigarh University, India

    Anurag Sharma, Chandigarh University, India

Chapter 17

Why India Should Make It Compulsory to Go for BIM 266

    Bhupinder Kaur Srao, Punjab Technical University, India

    Hardeep Singh Rai, GNDEC, India

    Kulwinder Singh Mann, GNDEC, India

Compilation of References 278

About the Contributors 299

Index 306

Detailed Table of Contents

Preface... xvii

Acknowledgment xix

Chapter 1
Risk Mitigation Planning, Implementation, and Progress Monitoring: Risk
Mitigation..1
    Yadwinder Kaur, Chandigarh University, India
    Satvir Singh, Chandigarh Engineering College, India

This chapter describes how any event or condition that might affect your work is termed as a risk. All risks are not harmful. Identifying easier options to complete a task are not harmful events at all. Events can be classified in two parts: threats and opportunities. A Threat event is one which can cause problems for the expectations of the developer. An opportunity is also a risk, but one which can be turned to an advantage. If these opportunities which arise can be handled carefully and implemented properly they can lead to extraordinary results in reducing cost, time and can provide a boost to effectiveness of the project. When work on a needed project started, it requires an error proof planning. Undoubtedly every project is carried out with great planning; even then carefully planned project can bring trouble. In all, the appropriate steps taken to examine possible project risks can lead to new avenues to improve company productivity.

Chapter 2
Risk Management Metrics 21
    Rimsy Dua, Chandigarh University, India
    Samiksha Sharma, Chandigarh University, India
    Rohit Kumar, Chandigarh University, India

This chapter describes how risk management deals with the detection, the evaluation and the precedence of the risks in the process of project management. There is always an uncertainty factor related to the decisions of an investment while managing a project. Risk management is a proactive approach to deal with such future events that can lead to slow performance of the software project management. For successful risk management; there are different metrics that have been used in the past and are being getting used in the present for inspecting the progress of a project at specific points in a timeline that help in reducing the amount of risk. For the adoption of effective metrics for risk management, data is required. All of the metrics can be applied to the different domains of project, process and product. The chapter also covers strategies to advance, distinguish, estimate, and forecast the risk management process. A review of the key point indicators (KPIs) are also integrated along with the project metrics to signify the future and the present renderings.

Chapter 3
Software Vulnerability Management: How Intelligence Helps in Mitigating
Software Vulnerabilities..34
Rimsy Dua, Chandigarh University, India
Samiksha Sharma, Chandigarh University, India
Abhishek Sharma, Chandigarh University, India

This chapter describes how with the proliferation of internet users, internet-related security threats are also increasing rapidly because of the software vulnerabilities that arise in software. Basically, there are two terms: bug and vulnerability. No doubt, bug and vulnerability are due to programming errors but vulnerabilities are more dangerous than bugs. Software vulnerability is a kind of flaw that arises in software or is a hole in the security of the software that allows an attacker to exploit that flaw. Unlike bugs, software vulnerability can affect a whole network thereby allowing unauthorised access to the database itself. Integrity and confidentiality of the software product is compromised due to the software vulnerability. These flaws must be patched in order to minimalize the impact of software vulnerability on an organisation. This chapter familiarises the methods of managing software vulnerabilities and discusses mitigation of the risks of different vulnerabilities in a software.

Chapter 4
Risks Assessment in Designing Phase: Its Impacts and Issues...........................46
Ankita Sharma, Chandigarh University, India
Vipin Pal, National Institute of Technology Meghalaya, India
Nitish Ojha, Chandigarh University, India
Rohit Bajaj, Chandigarh University, India

This chapter describes how risk analysis is a phenomena or methodology which is considered to be an amalgamation of various contexts to analyze and reach upon a conclusion about the fragility, vulnerability, flaws, defects, possible threats and dangers, which a particular software or system is prone to. It is an organization-level decision support tool which helps in gathering all sorts of data. That data, further, helps in arriving at a conclusion about how fragile or vulnerable a particular system is. Being a risk analyst, possessing deep knowledge, requires that one will analyze all possibilities of any risk, possible in any form, limitations of every risk assessment technique being applied and finally, the practical possibility or possible outcome of a particular risk-calculation strategy applied in a real-time environment.

Chapter 5

Problems, Threats in Software Development Life Cycle and Their Analysis 61
Deepika Rana, Chandigarh University, India
Manisha Malhotra, Chandigarh University, India

This content has been removed at the discretion of the publisher and the editors.

Chapter 6

An Analysis on Risk Management and Risk in the Software Projects 83
Rajshree Srivastava, Chandigarh University, India

Controlling risk in software project is considered to be a major contributor for a project success. This chapter reconsiders the status of risk and its management in the science and literature. The survey is supported by the recent study of risk practices in government agencies in India, thereby contributing to a gap in research in the public sector. After the study, it is found that the risk is barely been conceived in research. The findings which were found are considered to be a challenging situation for risk management and to project management. Further, it was noticed that software projects do not follow a uniform structure which introduces variations in the risk and projects. Risk management research is not efficient in terms of practice. Directions and implication for the research and practice are discussed in this chapter.

Chapter 7

New Classification of Security Requirements for Quantitative Risk
Assessment..100
Neila Rjaibi, ISG, Tunisia
Latifa Ben Arfa Rabai, ISG, Tunisia

Objective assessment metrics are continuously recommended and a financial analysis of the risk is required in order to justify the security improvements. It is, thus, critically important to validate the security applications as trustworthy and to generalize this research work to other systems. The chapter addresses firstly the problem of quantifying the security of large scale systems, originally the level of e-learning systems. The risk analysis model considers the variability between the system's stakeholders, the requirements, the components and the security attacks. But, in case of large systems, other security challenges are crucially important to be considered. Indeed, our risk analysis model is strengthened to include the development of new requirements classification.

Chapter 8

Estimating Risks Related to Extended Enterprise Systems (EES) 118
Jasleen Kaur, Chandigarh University, India
Rajinder Kaur, Chandigarh University, India

This chapter describes how risks are inherent in all systems. Risk is the ability of losing or gaining something of value. Values, like social status, financial wealth, or physical health, may be won or lost while taking threat as a result of a given movement. Risks also can be termed as the intentional interaction with ambiguity or uncertainty. Uncertainty is a capability, unpredictable, and uncontrollable final results; risk is an effect of action taken regardless of uncertainty. Extended Enterprise Systems (EESs) are defined as a complex structure of unique but interdependent and distributed organizational systems which are related in an autonomic manner to acquire goals beyond the reaching capacities of each. The purpose of this chapter is to estimate a set of critical risks that come across in proper logistics and the functioning of EESs. Identifying, analyzing and managing the risk in the EESs will result in an increase in the overall effectiveness and efficiency of the system. So, estimating risk could serve as the most important and powerful weapon in the hands of a decision maker of an EES.

Chapter 9

Meta-Heuristic Approach for Software Project Risk Schedule Analysis...........136
Isha Sharma, Chandigarh University, India
Deepshikha Chhabra, Chandigarh University, India

This chapter illustrates a technique to shorten the time duration using structured method. This is done by considering multiple resource constraints apart from time for the software project. The resource constraints are due to limited availability of resources (hardware, software, people, etc.). The difficulty is to locate minimal duration schedule. This is done by assigning the start time for each activity with the clear representation of precedence among them and resources available. There are various optimization approaches available but authors have selected a genetic algorithm. This method emulates the concept of biological evolution that is based on natural selection. This chapter concludes that additional research is needed in this area to provide better outcomes.

Chapter 10

Development and Enhancing of Software and Programming Products by
Client Information Administration in Market 150

Abhishek Sharma, Chandigarh University, India
Lokesh Pawar, Chandigarh University, India
Manjot Kaur, Chandigarh University, India

This chapter describes how client information administration (CIA) assumes a vital part in the creation of high-quality programming items or software products. As CIA in enterprise software (ES) advancement is relatively new, this raises inquiries on how CIA empowering agents can be utilized to help ES advancement organizations enhance their product quality. In this study, human, authoritative and mechanical CIA empowering influences were recognized from prior literature. The weights of these elements were dictated by specialists from the ES advancement organizations. In view of the essential factors, a hypothetical model was created. The proposed display was assessed by circulating an overview survey to chiefs in ES advancement organizations. The outcomes demonstrated that "client inclusion" together with "trust" were the most powerful factors, followed by the "CRA innovation framework" and the "cross-useful participation." The proposed processes demonstrated in this investigation can be utilized as a rule for the use of CIA in ES advancement organizations to enhance product quality.

Chapter 11

Risk Management in Web Development 188

Anu Priya Sharma, Chandigarh University, India
Sugandha Sharma, Chandigarh University, India

This chapter describes how risk management is the identification, assessment, and prioritization of risks followed by coordinated and economical application of resources to minimize, monitor, and control the probability or impact of unfortunate events or to maximize the realization of opportunities. The National Institute of Standards and Technology, actuarial societies, and ISO standards has developed various risk management standards. The standards (methods, definitions and goals) are created in the context of project management, security, engineering, industrial processes, financial portfolios, actuarial assessments, or public health and safety.

Chapter 12

Use of Software Metrics to Improve the Quality of Software Projects Using
Regression Testing 204

Arshpreet Kaur Sidhu, Chandigarh University, India
Sumeet Kaur Sehra, GNDEC, India

Testing of software is broadly divided into three types i.e., code based, model based and specification based. To find faults at early stage, model based testing can be used in which testing can be started from design phase. Furthermore, in this chapter, to generate new test cases and to ensure the quality of changed software, regression testing is used. Early detection of faults will not only reduce the cost, time and effort of developers but also will help finding risks. We are using structural metrics to check the effect of changes made to software. Finally, the authors suggest identifying metrics and analyze the results using NDepend simulator. If results show deviation from standards then again perform regression testing to improve the quality of software.

Chapter 13
Gamification: An Effectual Learning Application for SE...................................219
Samiksha Sharma, Chandigarh University, India
Rimsy Dua, Chandigarh University, India

This chapter describes how gamification is a technique which is used to bring the gaming methods and elements into the working environment of the company to make the allocated tasks more interesting for the user. Gamification helps in improving the performance, interest, involvement and motivation towards a specific goal. In software engineering, while applying gamification, all the software projects are made into challenges that require certain skills to get fulfilled with the integrated effort of the working team. This chapter will introduce the structure of the gamification application used in software engineering. A real scenario is presented where the gamification is applied in a company for different working fields like project management, testing and management of requirements. As a result, after applying the gamification technique, the performance has been improved to a greater extent, improved design and increased development effort by the user team. The chapter will bring out the insight of gamification in software engineering and how it helps in creating the intellectual working atmosphere.

Chapter 14
A New Approach for Reinforcement of Project DEMATEL-FMCDM-
TODIM Fuzzy Approach 234
Rajshree Srivastava, Chandigarh University, India
Shiv Kumar Verma, Glocal University, India
Vikas Thukral, Charles River Development, USA

This chapter describes how an effective work towards software project risk plays a vital role in determining the accomplishment of any project. In this chapter, the aim is to associate fuzzy criteria decision-making based on the approaches for the development of an assessment framework. This framework will be helpful in terms of identification and ranking the software risk according to its characteristics which will be helpful in decision-making of a software lifecycle. For the assessment for the risk of a project, there is an integration of fuzzy decision-making trial, evaluation laboratory trial and fuzzy multi-criteria decision. This new method proposed will be effective in terms of ranking and as well as to measure the software risk factors.

Chapter 15

Role of Attacker Capabilities in Risk Estimation and Mitigation.....................244
Deepshikha Chhabra, Chandigarh University, India
Isha Sharma, Chandigarh University, India

This chapter describes how the impacts of risk, or we may say risk exposure, are dependent upon the losses already occurred by the risk and probability to occur. There are various methods for estimating the risks and its impacts. The loss created by the threat can be reduced if the attacker does not have access to the system's objects or resources which are vulnerable to the risk. Attacker capabilities play the major role in the risk estimation and mitigation approach. Use of appropriate knowledge, skill and time to exploit the system or to create the threat comes under Attacker Capability. In this chapter, we will discuss how to include attacker capabilities when the risk estimation or mitigation plan is made. We will conclude the chapter with an appropriate study of various examples which indicate that impacts of risks can be minimised or reduced if we include the attacker capability while estimating the risk impacts and preparing the risk mitigation approach.

Chapter 16

Risks Analysis and Mitigation Technique in EDA Sector: VLSI Supply
Chain..256
Lokesh Pawar, Chandigarh University, India
Rohit Kumar, Chandigarh University, India
Anurag Sharma, Chandigarh University, India

This chapter describes how as the semiconductor industry is growing at a streaming pace, it comprises a number of global business entities. The industry includes the designing of the VLSI chips, manufacturing of those chips, system integration and the distribution of the VLSI chip. With this the industry has raised the bar among its vendors to provide best possible IC solutions and a highly secure product. The authors thus present this chapter in calculating views on risk involved in this area which are prone to security risks and at the same time focuses on the VLSI supply chain with references to a recent survey that illustrates various ways to handle those risks. In the absence of an effective security mechanism, a varlet here viz. an intellectual property (IP)provider or an integrated circuit design industry, an EDA company, a foundry lab, a distributor of chips or a system integrator, may easily lead to design IP theft or tampering with a designed IC. Since these risks compromise the security system for the VLSI chips, this leads to have a sound security system for an apt risk management.

Chapter 17

Why India Should Make It Compulsory to Go for BIM 266

Bhupinder Kaur Srao, Punjab Technical University, India
Hardeep Singh Rai, GNDEC, India
Kulwinder Singh Mann, GNDEC, India

This chapter describes how the effective tool for scheduling and controlling costs, calculating time periods and managing the technological enhancement of a construction project is project risk assessment. Projects under construction usually encounter a lot of uncertainties at different stages of work, which leads to increase of risk in terms of the expected cost of construction, delays in handing over and a poor quality of the project. The Indian built environment sector is ruined by delays and cost overruns as projects are not completed within time and within quality guidelines. Due to the increasing complexity of the design, operation, construction maintenance of modern built environmental assets, traditional construction has become an outdated paradigm. Building Information Modelling (BIM) is a multi-dimensional tool. It is a process that puts all the team members together to build a virtual design and construction methodologies all through the complete design. This extends to the full life of the project, entailing all the construction processes and maintenance of the building.

Compilation of References 278

About the Contributors 299

Index 306

Preface

Biggest challenge faced by software industry is cost control and schedule control. Other big challenge is to control and minimize the risk of software failures. With the development of large scale software's the essence of quality, robustness and zero tolerance to software failures have increased, which necessitates effective risk management of software. Risk management is a key and very important project management process. Risk management varies from software to software and different practices are used for different phases of software development. Number of tools and techniques are available for risk management of various software development phases. Risks are inherent and cannot be avoided easily so work should be done to minimize the harm caused by them and there comes the importance of risk analysis and risk mitigation.

The management of risk in projects is currently one of the main subjects of interest for researchers and practitioners working in the area of project management. Risk management has been designated as one of the eight main areas of the Project Management Body of Knowledge (PMBOK) by the Project Management Institute, which is the largest professional organization dedicated to the project management. Further, most training programs for project managers include a course on risk management. Within the currently accepted view of project management as a life cycle process, project risk management (PRM) is also seen as a process that accompanies the project from its definition through its planning, execution and control phases up to its completion and closure. A number of variations of the PRM process have been proposed. Boehm suggested a process consisting of two main phases: risk assessment, which includes identification, analysis and prioritization, and risk control, which includes risk management planning, risk resolution and risk monitoring planning, tracking and corrective action. The Software Engineering Institute, a leading source of methodologies for managing software development projects, looks at project risk management as consisting of five distinct phases (identification; analysis; response planning; tracking and control) linked by an ongoing risk communications effort.

In this book number of tools, methods, processes alongside theoretical concepts have been mentioned and discussed in detail to manage and control software development risks. This book captures the latest research and innovations and case studies in the field of software development risk management. The contents of this book will be an ideal reference source for researchers, teachers and practitioner who are working or willing to work in the field of software risk management.

Acknowledgment

First and foremost, I want pay deepest tributes to the God for completion of this project, its' with his blessings that I have seen this day. Secondly, I also want to pay immense tributes to my father Late Sh. Balwan Singh Bhullar who taught me the essence of love, care and compassion.

I am highly thankful to Maria Rhodes, Assistant Development Editor, IGI Global for constant help, encouragement, mentoring and valuable suggestions. I never felt alone under the passionate support of Maria Rhodes. I am also thankful to Ms. Jan Travers, Director of Intellectual Property and Contracts, IGI global for timely completion of all initial formalities regarding this project. I also want to pay special thanks to my highly reputed publisher IGI global for providing me the opportunity for authoring this book.

I would like to express my gratitude to many people who saw me through this book; to all those who provided support, talked things over, read, wrote, offered comments, allowed me to quote their remarks and assisted in the editing, proofreading and design.

I would like to thank all the authors and colleagues who enabled me to publish this book. Alongside it I want to thank my mother, Sheela Devi Bhullar, my charming son, Dhairya Bhullar, my wife, Richa Bhullar and brother Vikram Singh Bhullar who supported and encouraged me in spite of all the time it took me away from them. It was a long and difficult journey for them.

I would like to pay special thank to Dr. Kavita Taneja, Dr. Harmunish Taneja for their constant motivation, love and care and their faith in me. I owe a special thanks to my friend Lokesh Pawar for his deep faith in me and unconditional support. I am thankful to the god for providing me such wonderful friends like him. When they are around my problems, worries disappear in a loud laughter.

Rohit Kumar
Chandigarh University, India

Chapter 1
Risk Mitigation Planning, Implementation, and Progress Monitoring:
Risk Mitigation

Yadwinder Kaur
Chandigarh University, India

Satvir Singh
Chandigarh Engineering College, India

ABSTRACT

This chapter describes how any event or condition that might affect your work is termed as a risk. All risks are not harmful. Identifying easier options to complete a task are not harmful events at all. Events can be classified in two parts: threats and opportunities. A Threat event is one which can cause problems for the expectations of the developer. An opportunity is also a risk, but one which can be turned to an advantage. If these opportunities which arise can be handled carefully and implemented properly they can lead to extraordinary results in reducing cost, time and can provide a boost to effectiveness of the project. When work on a needed project started, it requires an error proof planning. Undoubtedly every project is carried out with great planning; even then carefully planned project can bring trouble. In all, the appropriate steps taken to examine possible project risks can lead to new avenues to improve company productivity.

DOI: 10.4018/978-1-5225-6029-6.ch001

INTRODUCTION

A project can always face surprising problems; about a developer cannot think about or anticipate. Sometimes, when work cannot be brought into right track, it can make team members get frustrated and they might think to give-up. Sometimes, while work in progress and it is not right track and team members devoting their time and ability to make it succeeded, resources may be turned out to be unavailable which are required for project development. To avoid this scenario risk planning can be used to identify likely to be present troubles and all reasons behind the existence of troubles. This chapter includes the process which explains that how risks can be determined. Once risks are found then which vital steps can be taken to prevent the occurrence of the risks which can be either avoided or minimized. If risks cannot be eliminated then what modes of operand can be opted for to reduce the effects of potential troubles? Reduction of Risks is done through a process, which is termed as Risks Mitigation Process. In Risk mitigation, first, proper planning is carried out and then implementation of the plan is done. During this process actions are developed to boost-up opportunities and to reduce threats to project goals. Actions to reduce or eliminate threats are taken in Risk mitigation implementation. While risks are being reduced or eliminated it is mandatory to keep record of done changes. This can be achieved through proper documentation of the amendments. So, keep track of identified risks, identifying new risks, and evaluating risk process effectiveness throughout the whole project is done in Risk mitigation progress monitoring.

Risk can be defined as the chances of something going wrong and the generation of negative outputs as consequences of the risk. Most tedious task is to spot the risk. If spotting task is ignored on the risk, later it can bring reputation, money and time on the verge of ending. These reasons make Risk Analysis an important phase when someone's work can involve risk. Risk analysis is used to identify and understand the risks which can occur during development after implementation phase. It provides necessary support to either manage risks or to reduce their impacts. The process of identifying risks and analyzing is done for the preparation for risk mitigation. Mitigation process involves steps to reduce the adverse effects of a risk if it encounters. In this chapter, discussion on the reasons of doing risk mitigation planning and on the numerous mitigation approaches has been done.

BACKGROUND

Planning of risk management has been shown in Figure 1. Basic steps are shown in the *Figure 1* depicts risk identification, its consequences assessment, risk analysis, Mitigation planning, implementation, and progress monitoring. It is an iterative

Figure 1. Basic steps taken during Risk Management

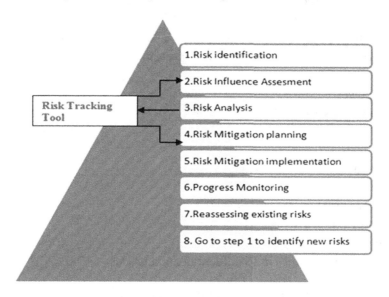

process, to meet with the desired goal the risk tracking tool is used to keep record of the results of risk analysis which feeds input to risk mitigation implementation and risk consequences assessment.

In the risk mitigation planning plans are designed to handle, eradicate, or to reduce the impact up to an acceptable level. Once a plan is executed, it is required to be monitored continuously to assess its effects with the intention to revise the steps for management if it is required.

MAIN FOCUS OF THE CHAPTER

Risk Identification

To identify a risk is a creative as well as a disciplined task. A creative process always involves brainstorming sessions. In those sessions, team members are asked to prepare a list of everything which can lead to troubles. All given ideas are entertained and compilation of various ideas and evaluation on the ideas is performed after the end of the session. In disciplined process checklists of expected risks are prepared. Few companies and industries prepare risk checklists based on past experiences on a project. The project manager and project team can take the help of these checklists to identify some specified risks and to enhance the thinking of the team without wasting much time. The past experience working under same management and past experience on a project and experts in the company are the precious resources for identifying risks on a project.

The foremost tasks to identify the reasons behind risks are exploring categories of risks. Below are some examples of categories for risks:

- Manpower
- Technical issues
- Cost risks
- Deadlines
- Customer
- Contracts
- Weather problem
- Funding problems
- Political pressure
- Environmental issues in Risk Identification process

Second task can be selection of the tools and techniques which are essential to achieve the objective. Few Risk Identification tools have been shown in *Figure 2*.

REQUIREMENT COLLECTION TECHNIQUES

To collect requirements following are the basics techniques which can be opted to meet the objective:

Figure 2. Risk Identification tools

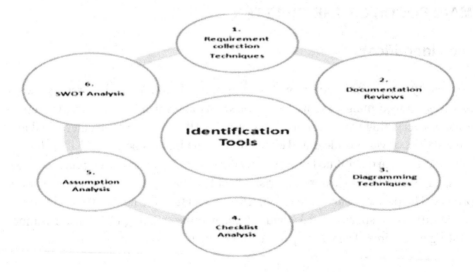

Interviewing

An interview session is usually conducted with project team members, stakeholders and outside/inside experts to work on a common goal to identify potential risks.

Identify Root Causes

Root causes are searched for existing which can help to determine other potential risks. It is a specific technique to find a problem, to unearth the underlying causes which can lead to risks and to develop preventive measures.

Brainstorming

The prime objective of brainstorming with a group of people who aims on identification of risk is to prepare a list of potential risks for underlying project. Brainstorming is usually performed with a number of experts who belong to various disciplines and are not the part of the project team. In the framework risk breakdown structure can be used. Risks are determined, categories are framed and risks' definition is made more sharpened.

Delphi Technique

In Delphi technique a team of anonymous experts are consulted. It a fine way to approach up to consensus of an expert A list of questionnaire is prepared and sent to experts, inputs from experts are compiled, and sent back to them for further comments until a consensus is achieved. Consensus might be obtained in a few rounds. This technique reduces data biasing and restraining from only a few people undue influence on project.

Documentation Reviews

The standard practice to identify risks is a structured review performed on project documentation. It includes reviewing project related documents such as plans, assumptions, old project files, contracts, previous failures, articles, organizational process assets etc. Indicators of risk in projects can be determined from quality of the plans, correctness between those plans and the project requirements.

Diagramming Techniques

Diagramming Techniques are used to identify risks in a project. Generally included diagrams are: Cause and affect diagram, System /process flow charts and influence diagrams.

Cause and Effect Diagram

This diagram is also called as Ishikawa diagram or Fish-bone diagram. It known as 'Ishikawa diagram' named after its developer Dr. Kaoru Ishikawa, a Japanese quality control statistician. The diagram resembles with a fish skeleton, as shown in *Figure 3*, so it is also name as 'fishbone diagram'. The diagram explains the main reasons and sub-reasons which results in negative effects. It is used to identify uncertain root causes of the risks.

System /Process Flow Charts

System flow charts are used to show interrelationship among different elements of a system. Structure of the diagram can be seen in *Figure 4*. These are used to analyze thorough process consisting of few logical steps to attain an output. Flow charts are the simplest way to identify bottlenecks and superfluous processes.

Figure 3. Fish-bone diagram

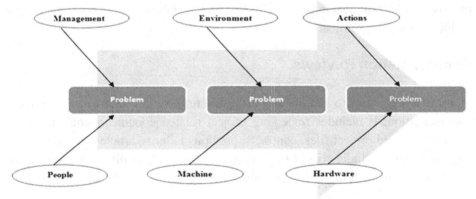

Figure 4. System Flow Chart's example

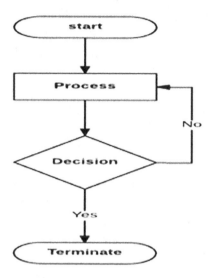

Influence Diagrams

Influence diagrams, as in *Figure 5*, are compact graphical representations of situations which shows various influences, event ordering and decision-making scenarios. Influence diagrams is used to determine that how risks can influence events and decisions?

Checklist Analysis

The checklist of risk categories can be prepared from past information which is collected from previous similar types of projects or from other input sources of the information. This method is used to obtain additional risks for the project.

Figure 5. Influence diagrams

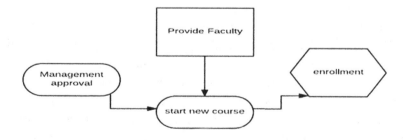

A checklist can be simple and less time consuming. But there is a possibility to prepare an exhaustive one. The team members should ensure to explore items that are not listed on the checklist. This list must be reviewed during the project maturity state to incorporate fresh lessons learned and keep updating it in upcoming future projects' work.

Assumption Analysis

Assumptions analysis is used to determine potential risks in a process. This technique required documentation of identified risks during assessment and required to validate all the assumption made during planning process. It determines risks related to the project regarding result inaccuracy, non-stability, inconsistency or incompleteness. In the beginning, it is required to have accurate, complete and consistent assumptions. Practically, it is not always possible to collect the same. It is advisable for project handling team to review the assumptions and strengthen it. The validity of assumptions support in identifying hidden risks associated with a project.

SWOT Analysis

SWOT is used to determine the Strengths, Weaknesses, Opportunities, and potential Threats to a project. It specifies the goals of the project and determines internal-external factors that can put negative or positive impact on the project to attain targets. The Strengths and weaknesses normally take birth in an organization itself, and the Opportunities and Threats come externally. The SWOT analysis is a crucial part of the project planning task. The attributes of the organization which support the project to meet with goals become Strength of the project. The attributes of the organization those create hurdles on the way of achievement are named as Weaknesses. External conditions which shore-up the project objectives called as Opportunities and the external conditions which could corrupt the project become Threats to the project.

STEP 2: RISK INFLUENCE ASSESSMENT

Typically, in this assessment any action could affect cost, time or technical performance aims. Influences are not only restricted these parameters, it involves political or economic results as well. The chances of each risk actions are also taken into consideration. It includes both subjective and objective assessment methods. Risk assessment, risk dependencies, interdependencies, and the time-frame of certain influence are required to be identified. During assessment, it is necessary to map the assessment influence with decisions records. Generally risks are assessed for cost, time and technical performance targets. Some programs may also include oversight and compliance, or political impacts. It makes available a high set of rating scales for making multi-criteria observations, and ways to combine them into an overall measure of impact or consequence.

To asses impacts project can be divided into few types to make assessment streamlined. As in below in *Table 1* projects are divided into four types- A, B, C, D.

Type A

These category projects required a high ended scrutiny. Three different boards are deployed on the project monitoring. A program board is that board which can monitor the progress and potential involved risks. Besides this, a program board can be observed by another review committee. At the end, there is an involvement of third board for approval of the project. This category involves high risk, high cost and high impact. Level of impacts and probability of Risk, cost and Impact can be seen in Table 1.

Type B

These projects are only observed by the review committee. It doesn't need any other boards.

Type C

These types of projects are observed and approved program board.

Type D

These types of projects are completely approved by the program board, but a management team keeps monitoring and flaws are submitted to the program board.

Table 1. Classification of projects

Probability of Risk, Cost, Impact(P)	Level	Type of project
P > 1	High	A
0.5 <= P< 1	Medium	B
0.25 <= P < 0.5	Low	C
0 <=P <0.25	Very low	D

STEP 3: RISK ANALYSIS

Risk analysis phase comes after identifying and classifying the risks. In this phase level of risks is determined by observing the outputs and every factor associated with risks. The risk analysis process identifies the most influencing factor which has a greatest impact on the objectives of the project. Therefore, this process is required utmost care. Three basics methods are frequently used for underlined process: Subjective Methods, Partial Calculable Methods and Calculable Methods.

Subjective Methods

Experts on the basis of sheer their judgment, experience and intuition make decisions. When risk level is very low that time this method can be a good option, but this method doesn't give warranty and timely availability of resources, which are required to perform analysis. These methods are also suitable when sufficient numerical data is not available. This method involves:

- Interviews
- Brainstorming
- Judgment of the experts
- Questionnaire
- Assessment from multidisciplinary groups.

Partial Calculable Methods

This method involves few scale parameters to weigh the risks and these parameters are categorized into following categories:

- Scale parameter LOW
- Scale parameter Medium
- Scale parameter High

High parameters are interpreted as the probability of risk is highest. Medium parameter considered as average risk occurrence and low parameter indicates the minimal presence of risk. Weighing scale distribution required to be assessed carefully to avoid misinterpretation.

Calculable Methods

Risks are given a concrete range or a value in calculable methods. One of the best ways is to use simulation method. Besides simulation, analysis of impacts and analysis of trends carried out. Results of these methods can be influenced by enormous tools. To get accurate results, a mechanism is prepared which involves few steps as given in *Figure 6*.

STEP 4: RISK MITIGATION PLANNING

After risk analysis, to check the negative impacts of Risk Mitigation is deployed. Risk Mitigation process demands error proof planning before commencing execution of the process. Risk Mitigation is incorporated with project management process to handle potential risks. Once risks are determined, Mitigation is deployed to mitigate either the existing risks or to lower the hovering impacts of the risks. During process, anticipated risks are categorized. Even root causes of identified risks are listed.

Figure 6. Calculable methods require few steps for modeling risks

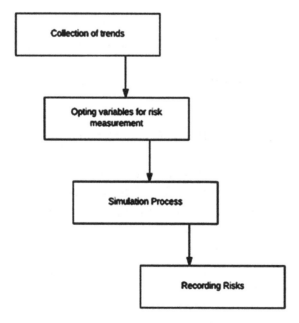

Risk Mitigation Strategies

To apply risk mitigation processes, evaluate the probability of encounter and negative severe outputs of the determined risk. This strategy is suitable for many programs and projects, but it is not necessarily that it will generate fruitful results for all. Risk mitigation process involves:

- **Take:** Accept the existence of risks without curbing it.
- **Ignore:** Ignore risks by restricting program's requirements.
- **Curb:** Deploy mechanism to handle the side effects of the risk.
- **Shifting:** Instead of bearing consequences on oneself, shift accountability and responsibility to some other partner.
- **Supervise:** Supervise the behavior of risks and influences of risks time to time.

Every step listed above desired proper watch for best outcomes. Along with these steps following perspective in engineering can help to achieve mitigation on potential risks.

1. Speedy feedback responses of technical and management experts
2. Motivate parallel development
3. Proper assessment of designs
4. Proper assessment of design tools and techniques
5. Frequently productions of prototypes
6. Frequent prototyping feedback

STEP 5: RISK MITIGATION IMPLEMENTATION

When implementation of a process is talked about then a plan is brought into execution. Implementation involves actions which are taken after preparing designs or suitable plans to make something fruitful. Implementation process involves various activities to start as shown in Figure 7. Risk mitigation implementation has a goal. To achieve that goal this process involves various strategies.

- How to select a risk?
- How to divide risks into different categories?
- How to apply mitigation plan on identified risks?
- How to re-identify new risks?

Figure 7. Risk Mitigation implementation

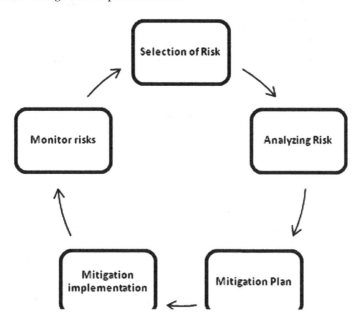

These all the important decisions and required appropriate strategies to carried out all the tasks. All these steps can be iterative or may be different from each other, every time when a process is started. It is possible that in one step one input can be taken into consideration, on the other side second time multiple inputs may be required for further process.

In previous step, planning of the mitigation has been done. Implementation of risk mitigation follows an iterative process:

1. This process requires risk selection,
2. Analysis of selected risk to categorize it,
3. After setting the accurate category of the risk mitigation can be planned,
4. Plan followed by execution,
5. All risks can be monitored carefully to check its existing influences.

Implementation on mitigation planning to ensure mitigation success requires following points to assess:

- Determines what planning, budget, and requirements and contractual changes are needed,
- Identify first what is the plan?
- Identify resources, cost and assess changes that are required.

- Strong communication set up between management and all partners.
- Required right direction to execute plans successfully.
- Record keeping of monitoring.
- Documentation of all the done amendments in the product.

STEP 6: PROGRESS MONITORING

There are enormous types of risks listed as below:

Size of Code Risks

These risks encounter when size of project code becomes too large to handle. Changes can be desired any time in the code. A developer must be ready for amendments. If code size is not anticipated or if code tracking management is missing and a change occurred, there can be risks to the whole project after changes. Developers might be confused which module changes can affect another module. This negligence on the part of developer might lead the project to failure.

Users Risk

These risks occur when customer refuses to be the part of review process with software developer. To ensure consistency of the project regular interviews with end users are required. This refusal can give major setback to the business, as no project can be completed without willingness of the users.

Technology Risks

These risks occur when user is made available with the project which can be outdated soon. This happened when developer team lacks keeping updating about changes in ongoing technology. Technologies keep changing rapidly. This risk is required adequate attention.

Quality Risks

If quality of a project doesn't stand parallel to the needs of end user that can wash all the efforts put to complete a project. This can happened due to miscommunication between end user and developer team, misinterpretation of developers about input from end user and incomplete information provided by the end user.

Development Environment Risks

These risks occur if developers are not provided with requisite resources for development process. It can lead to the failure of the product. Developer must be provided with abundant resources. Besides this, team can be given more time to achieve targets.

Team Members Risks

This risks encounters due to inability of developers to work on given resources. Root causes behind these risks are lack of interest, lack of experience and incapability of the developer. If any of the team members fails to perform the job then it can destroy complete project. This risk is the catastrophic risk and result of this risk is hard to amend.

All the above listed risks can destroy the complete project. Project influences' can be categorized into various categories as shown in *Table 3* and their chances of occurrence, according to the type of risk have been given in *Table 4*.

When risks are highlighted, impacts analyzed, done planning for mitigation, mitigation done then the next process is to continuously monitoring the risks to find whether identified risk is still unfavorable or has been removed completely. This process includes reduction in time, cost, fewer requirements of resources, enhances quality & making circumstances better to reduce the effects of risks on project's target.

Size of Code Risks

To handle this kind of risk, monitoring of different modules of the code is required to be performed. If risks encounter in the future, related to any code, that time code size monitoring can help us to manage the code as well while mitigating risks. In project, modules are interconnected. If one module is undergone through some

Table 2.

Probability of Occurrence	Risk Type	Influence on Project
0.35	Size of code	B
0.3	User	C
0.25	Technology	B
0.45	Team members	A
0.35	Quality	A
0.4	Development environment	B

Table 3. Influences' description

Influence on Project	Description
A	Highest
B	Medium
C	Lowest
D	Nil

amendments the whole code is required to be changed. To avoid chaos, keeping size track is mandatory. Long size of the code might bring anyone into trouble but proper record keeping of modules can make this complex job easy to handle.

User Risks

User of a project might be unsatisfied from the current project's working. During monitoring of such kind of risk it is mandatory to arrange formal meeting with user to show the progress of the product as per user's requirements. If in formal meeting a customer shows disinterest then project can be shown through web chat or other chatting webs. Regular feedback can be collected from the users and same can be incorporated in the product. This process is iterative in nature. Product is demonstrated to the user, feedback is collected, revision is done and then the whole process is repeated until a user gets satisfied.

Technology Risks

This risk emerges due to day to day rapid changes occurrence in the technologies. This risk can be monitored while keeping knowledge stock up to date about emerging technology. It becomes mandatory for a developer to make a product portable. Portable products are those products which can function on any system. If developer makes

Table 4. Chances of occurrences of risks

Probability of Occurrence	Risk Type	Influence on Project
0.35	Size of code	B
0.3	User	C
0.25	Technology	B
0.45	Team members	A
0.35	Quality	A
0.4	Development environment	B

a project according to one machine, it might be possible that once product is ready then previous machine, on which project is supposed to work, has been updated and right now doesn't support the project. Monitoring of technology becomes a vital point to be taken into consideration.

Team Members Risks

Generally, it happens that people working on a project hardly spend quality time with each other which results in giving birth to the team member's risks. For example, a person might have problem to implement or deploy a project module. Due to lack of communication among team members leads to frustration during these kinds of halts. If employees spend quality time with each other they can resolve each other's problem. Moreover, interaction boosts up the confidence among team as members can stay close to extend help whenever required.

Quality Risks

Quality can be achieved when all the underlined requirements meet the objective of the product. Quality risks can be monitored through regular feedback from users and developers. Feedback from users can be received on prototyping. Team members can discuss and show their work to each other on fixed interval of times. Team members can give suggestions to each other for betterment. After compiling all the inputs current product can be changed and final new product can be reviewed by the whole team before launching it to the market or handing over to the customer. Quality is the parameter which cannot be compromised at any cost.

Development Environment Risks

Being proactive and keeping eye on latest launched IDEs can allow a developer to use inexpensive, comparatively less expensive but far better in effectiveness. Monitoring of working comparison of currently being used IDEs and latest launched technology helps in selection for better one. This can result in reduction in time, cost and can generate better quality products with the help of inexpensive resources.

STEP 7: REASSESSING EXISTING RISKS

Reassessing existing risks is performed due to the following reasons:

1. To find New Risks.
2. Deleting record of the no longer existing risks from record file.

3.   To enter New Risks into the record file.

It is required to check influence or chances of the occurrence of the risks time to time. It is remained same as it was earlier or not. Whenever a risk is determined it has to go through the full cycle of risk management process, as time to time it keeps changing its effects the project execution. Few risks with time, lost their impacts on the projects. Even then, it might be possible that in record file their influence factor might be not updated. When a risk is reassessed that time record associated with a risk is updated. As the project starts reaching towards completion phase, all the existing risks start to eliminate or reduce, but influence of existing risks increases.

In this process, risk audit is a powerful tool for risk assessment/re-assessment. Two risk audits cannot be same, as projects are not similar every time. Therefore, risks audits can have various variety. Before starting risks audit process, a developer can primarily outline the type of a project. Here, documentation of the project plays a vital role. Project related information is written in the documentation for future use. Documentation can include future scope of the project, shortcomings about the project and advantages of the project.

Risk Audits

Generally, audits include inspection or cross checking of the project. It is done to ensure the removal of risks. Audit can be done either the development or management team. Sometimes audits are being done by outsider experts to certain the quality of the project. Indeed, there are two ways in which audit can be done:

- **Internal Audit:** Done by internal team or management.
- **External Audit:** Done by experts, who are not the part of the development.

Normally, an audit involves four important steps as follows and shown in *Figure 8*:

1.   Define audit's outline.
2.   Set deadline for completion of the audit.
3.   Information compilation.
4.   Results of the audit.

When outline of the audit is prepared that time, it is decided who will be involved in the audit. To avoid further delays in the project launch, time bound schedule is prepared for the audit for a given project. During information compilation risks are collected, analyzed and information associated with a risk is properly written. At

Figure 8. Risks Audit

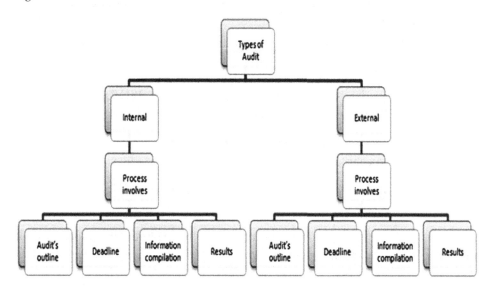

last, all recommendations and suggestions are listed in the final documentation of the audit which is mandatory for project success.

Risks audit generate two main outputs as a result:

- Assessing the influences of Risks after mitigation.
- Assessing the quality risk management process.

In audit, all remaining risks are identified and their existing influences are measured. Besides this, management process is also come under the audit to ensure the quality of reviewing the risks. It is depending upon the management that when they plan to get audited their project. Management decides the auditor team. It also decides the deadline and budget of the audit.

REFERENCES

Antunes, R., & Gonzalez, V. (2015). A Production Model for Construction: A Theoretical Framework. *Buildings.*, *5*(1), 209–228. doi:10.3390/buildings5010209

Crockford, N. (1986). *An Introduction to Risk Management*. Cambridge, UK: Woodhead-Faulkner.

Dorfman, M. S. (2007). *Introduction to Risk Management and Insurance*. Englewood Cliffs, N.J: Prentice Hall.

Hubbard, D. (2009). *The Failure of Risk Management: Why It's Broken and How to Fix It*. John Wiley & Sons.

International Organization for Standardization. (2009). ISO/DIS 31000 Risk management — Principles and guidelines on implementation.

International Organization for Standardization. (2009). ISO/IEC Guide 73 Risk management — Vocabulary.

Kokcharov, I. (n.d.). What Is Risk Management? Retrieved from http://www. slideshare.net/igorkokcharov/what-is-project-risk-management

Parker, D., & Mobey, A. (2004). Action Research to Explore Perceptions of Risk in Project Management. *International Journal of Productivity and Performance Management, 53*(1), 18–32. doi:10.1108/17410400410509932

Risk Communication Primer—Tools and Techniques. Navy and Marine Corps Public Health Center.

Saghee, M., Sandle, T., & Tidswell, E. (Eds.). (2011). *Microbiology and Sterility Assurance in Pharmaceuticals and Medical Devices* (1st ed.). Business Horizons.

Simon, P. & Hillson; D. (2012). *Practical Risk Management: The ATOM Methodology*. Vienna, VA: Management Concepts.

Taylor, C., & VanMarcke, E. (Eds.). (2002). Acceptable Risk Processes: Lifelines and Natural Hazards. Reston, VA: ASCE, TCLEE.

Chapter 2
Risk Management Metrics

Rimsy Dua
Chandigarh University, India

Samiksha Sharma
Chandigarh University, India

Rohit Kumar
Chandigarh University, India

ABSTRACT

This chapter describes how risk management deals with the detection, the evaluation and the precedence of the risks in the process of project management. There is always an uncertainty factor related to the decisions of an investment while managing a project. Risk management is a proactive approach to deal with such future events that can lead to slow performance of the software project management. For successful risk management; there are different metrics that have been used in the past and are being getting used in the present for inspecting the progress of a project at specific points in a timeline that help in reducing the amount of risk. For the adoption of effective metrics for risk management, data is required. All of the metrics can be applied to the different domains of project, process and product. The chapter also covers strategies to advance, distinguish, estimate, and forecast the risk management process. A review of the key point indicators (KPIs) are also integrated along with the project metrics to signify the future and the present renderings.

INTRODUCTION

Risk is a state that involves disclosure to threat. In normal day to day life people face enormous kind of risks that can happen from their personal actions or financial activities. Despite of all the other categories that belong to risk; this chapter covers

DOI: 10.4018/978-1-5225-6029-6.ch002

the marketable and the industry risks that organizations face while executing project management. In today's era organizations suffer from broad collection of risks that can lead to negative outcomes or bogus results. Different categories of risks an organization can face are control risk, opportunity risks and hazard risks (Hopkin, 2017). Hazard risks are those than can hinder an organization from achieving particular set of objectives, developing that objective is opportunity risk and creating a fiction of unpredictability in outcomes is control risk. Risk management deals with supervising, managing and estimating such risks. Risk management is adopted in private as well as public sectors in order to have a proactive approach towards the threats that can occur. While designing software, an organization may suffer from enormous number of risks such that personal risks, technical risks, financial risks and management risks (Westfall, 2004). Personnel risks arise due to lack of preparation and skill of the working employees whereas technical risks can happen because of wrong followed procedures and standards. For financial risks; cash runs, capital and return on savings are the main cause. At last, the management itself sometimes responsible for the project risks because of communication gap, lack of planning, proper training, authority and experience among employees.

Risk management process starts with first recognizing the risks. After identifying the risk, investigation is done on various types of identified risks (Boehm, 1991). When an investigation is performed risks are prioritized according to the extent of threat they can confer to the software. A risk management plan is prepared after prioritizing various risks, that plan will involve actions to be taken against risks. A risk management plan can reduce the probability of risk occurrence to a greater extent. After the completion of plan, a set of pre-defined actions is applied to the project and a constant monitoring or tracing is performed that signifies the degree of risk at each stage of project development (Rasmussen, 1997). Tracing of project at various stages gives insight about diverse count of new risks and old plans can be updated according to the newly identified risks after tracing the development of project at different timestamps. Figure 1 given below exemplifies the risk management process.

- **Risk Identification:** Risk identification deals with recognizing diverse risks that a project can come across during development process. Risk identification is the pre-process as it gives insight about risks that can lead to system failure. The process of identification involves key set of activities like communication between the team members and documentation. In the documentation, risk occurrences are defined along with their relationships.
- **Risk Assessment:** After identifying all the risks, assessment is performed where risk analysis is carried out. An evaluation process is executed that signifies how much threat it can confer to the project. So briefly risk assessment deals with analysis of the identified risks and evaluating them on

Figure 1. Risk Management Process

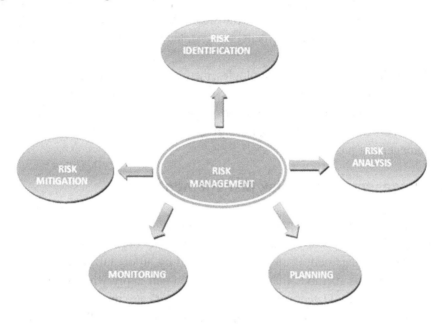

the source of degree of threat that can possess. Risk assessment also helps in prioritizing different identified risks, which helps in reducing their impact.

- **Risk Control:** Subsequent to analysis and risk evaluation, control programs are being developed that holds different set of risk control activities. Controlling a risk is required as it reduces the impact of risk to a greater extent. After prioritizing the risks, control programs are applied that gives an organization a vision of how to diminish the degree of threat.
- **Monitoring:** Monitoring deals with tracing of project development process at various check points. The major advantage an organization can get is identification of new risks at various levels of project progress. Organizations keep on updating their project plans in accordance with the tracing reports and builds up new strategies to cope with the new identified project risks.

RISK MANAGEMENT IMPACT ON PROMISING MARKET DECISIONS

Enterprise risk management deals with identifying, evaluating, controlling and tracing the risks that an organization can face in terms of capital and investments or savings. In Enterprise risk management a wide range of risks including operational, accidental and financial are covered. Enterprise risk management encloses set of actions that involves inception of content, performing risk identification, evaluating and analyzing risk, giving a priority to the identified risk and reducing the impact of risks. So, enterprise risk management can be stated as a controlled and regimented approach for handling risks.

Also, ERM supports plans, technologies, method, processes and information used by the working organization to enhance its work skill to manage uncertain occurring risks. ERM thus enhances the overall performance and value of an organization by reducing the barriers of risks. Figure 2 given below demonstrates the enterprise risk management process.

Risk Assessment and Risk Management

Risk Assessment deals with performing evaluation of the existing security system in which the current security strategies adopted by the organization are estimated whereas risk management is an application used by an organization that consists of set of rules and methods that an organization can apply while evaluating the risk (O. salvi, 2006). Detecting and analyzing the risk are the major operations to be performed under risk assessment but the procedures to be followed for the risk assessment are recited in the risk management process. So both risk management and risk assessment play an important role in identifying and mitigating the discovered risks. Figure 1 represented the risk management process while figure 2 will give the insight to the different states to be followed in the risk assessment process.

Figure 2. Enterprise Risk Management

Let's have a brief look at the various stages of risk assessment taking an example of medical subject.

- **Identification of Threat:** The first step towards risk assessment is identifying the threat; if an example of medical problem is taken then the identification case will comprise of finding the health issues caused due to pollutant.
- **Response Assessment:** After identifying the threat, diverse range of responses is checked for illustration let's have a quick view of the same medical case in which one will examine the health problems that can arise at different stages of exposures.
- **Exposure Assessment:** Evaluation of the degree of exposure where according the recited medical case above the total number of pollutant will be viewed that affected the population of people and the total count of the individuals being exposed to the pollutants in a specific phase of time.
- **Exemplifying Risk:** Risk characterization gives insight about the possibilities of threats that can occur from the discovered risks. With respect to the recited medical case risk characterizing will signify the other health problems that can develop from the exposed population.

All the above-mentioned steps are considered while performing the risk assessment that contributes towards the stable security system making it less prone to errors. So, the existing security system is refined by continuous evaluation using risk assessment process and the chances of failure are reduced to much lower extent.

Above mentioned steps in figure 2 contribute to risk assessment; starting with the identification phase then the response assessment and the exposure assessment. At last, characterizing risk deals with further exposure due to the discovered risk. At last in brief preface to the above explained approach, Risk management covers all the procedures and standards to mitigate the risk whereas risk assessment is to evaluate the existing security structure to make sure that the system at last suffers from fewer errors and could be made highly efficient.

WHAT ARE THE DIFFERENT CATEGORIES OF SOFTWARE RISKS A PROJECT CAN SUFFER FROM?

Software project risk is basically a prospective event that can cause a loss in the development of software project. Most of the software projects are beset with potential risk. Software risk identification is the preeminent task in the effective risk management of the software project management. Constant and efficient software project monitoring is mandatory for the effective recognition of the potential risks

Figure 3. Risk Assessment

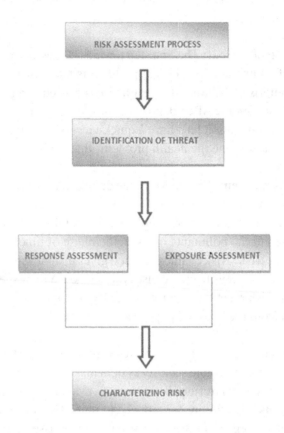

in the software project. Different software project managers may be confronted with different category of risks. There can be variegation in software project risk depending on the cost, schedule and realization of software development goals. Risk assessment is an activity of evaluating the risks that can cause an expected loss in the software development project. It involves risk analysis and risk evaluation. Software project risk assessment will result in efficacious result if it is accomplished from multiple dimensions. Risk identification may involve several approaches varying from ad hoc approach to formal approach. Risk assessment in ad hoc approach depends on some program that appears at the time of software project development. Informal approach of risk identification involves discussion with all the team members who are directly or indirectly associated with the software project. It also necessitates the documentation of risks for the future use. If repetitive procedures are followed for the identification and specification of the risk then that approach is the periodic approach. Formal approach is followed when there is comprehensive assessment of the risk.

Different software projects may confront different types of risks:

- **Schedule Risk:** Individual software projects have an inimitable nature which is one of the problematic issues for the correct schedule of the software project. Continuous monitoring of the project is a prerequisite for the development of the project as per schedule.
- **Budget Risk:** Wrong cost estimation of the software project may lead to budget risks. Expanding the scope of the software project may result in budget risk. It is advisable to use more than one estimation method for the correct cost estimation of the software project. Having a good insight into the challenges of the software project is the main factor that will lead to realistic cost estimation of the software project.
- **Operational Risk:** These types of risks are associated with the day to day operational activities of the software project (Rekha, 2015). Silo approach followed by different software teams may lead to conflicts thereby affecting the operational activities of the software project. Effective team communication can reduce operational risks.
- **Technical Risk:** Sometimes companies have to reduce the functionality of the software keeping in view the budget overruns and schedule overruns. This may result in technical risk. Incessant change in requirements of the software project is one of the major causes of technical risk. Sometimes the software project is complex to implement and there is a difficulty in integrating the modules of the software project. These issues might enhance the technical risks of the software project.
- **Programmatic Risk:** These risks are beyond the operational limits and are outside the control of the program. These types of risk generally involve environmental impacts. These are fundamentally uncertain risks that may be caused due to disruptions in communication or any natural calamity.
- **Resource Risk:** Delays in software project development can occur if the employees are not skilled in designing because in most of the software projects, Employees must be skilled in HTML/CSS so that the frontend development can be completed without any delay. Project development team must not change during the development of the software project otherwise its quite difficult to maintain the same tread with the new employees.
- **Requirement Risk:** Continually changing the requirements of the software project may lead to requirement risks. Sometimes, requirements that are mandatory to be included for the software project development are incorrectly specified or are not cleared to the developer. All the requirements must be correctly specified and understood by the developer.

Risk Management Metrics

Risk is one of the critical factor due to which the development of the software project is affected. Basically, Risk identification, Risk impact analysis and Risk mitigation (Miguel.2015) are the three main stages of risk management. A decisive role is played by risk identification in the successful development of the project. If the risk is identified at a later stage of software project development then it can lead to a variance in the cost, time and budget of the software project. Basically, a Quality Assurance team is responsible for the effective risk identification. If the risk identification is good then its mitigation can be done within time. Risk management metric is basically responsible for the risk analysis, risk monitoring, risk response planning, risk control etc. Metrics can be of two categories: Base and Derived. Base metric is defined in terms of single one attribute is base metric and this is independent of all the other metrics. In view of this, Derived metric is the one that is a function of two or more values of base metric.

Risk Management Process

One of the most important things as a system analyst or project manager is that there can be a management of risk on daily basis. If a systematic risk management process is incorporated, and the core 5 risk management process steps are put into action, then it will result in a smooth working of the project.

Risk involves uncertainty, an event whose consequences on project goals can be positive or negative. An important concept is potential for a risk to have a positive or negative effect. Why? It is inappropriate if we say that risks have inherently negative effects. Your project can be developed streamlined, smarter and more profitable If you are also open to those risks that create positive opportunities, you can make your project smarter, streamlined and more profitable. Project risk may assist in creating better opportunities for the project as there is an adage that "Accept the inevitable and turn it to your advantage."

Uncertainty is at the heart of risk. It is not sure that if an event is likely to occur or not. Also, there is an uncertainty about its consequences if it did occur. Likelihood and consequence are the two components that characterize the extent of the risk. Where likelihood is the probability of an event occurring and consequence is an impact or outcome of an event.

Similar steps are followed by risk management processes, although sometimes different jargon is used to describe these steps. Simple and effective risk management process involves these five risk management process steps.

Risk Finding Techniques

To Identify Risk

- **Brainstorming:** When the participants came to know the objectives then a brainstorming conference is conducted where all the participants can give their suggestions about the various occurring risks. All are divided into teams, from which each member will recite the idea of risk probability. So, brainstorming is a group task.
- **Interviews:** For interviews, a set of questions are prepared by the expert of the field, which is then shared by the team members. Every member has to answer the cited set of questions. In this way a generalized viewpoint of every team member is collected through interviews.
- **Workshops:** After all the information is gathered regarding the risk, workshops can be facilitated in order to have more detailed conclusion about the gathered data with respect to risk threats.
- **SWOT Analysis:** SWOT stands for strength-weakness-opportunities-threats, from these four strength and weakness reside inside the organization that mainly depends upon certain factors such as structure, human source, economy and traditions of the organization; all these factors are essentials of an organization as they hold a strong impact on the success of the organization. The other two factors named as opportunities and threats are external to an organization that can be unpredictable for their occurrence. SWOT analysis deals with the precalculating the threats that can damage the working system as well as monitoring the continuous strengths and weaknesses through which organization can be made to grow successfully.
- **Maintaining Risk Surveys and Questionnaire:** An organization should keep on conducting iteratively the survey for risk identification and keeps on maintaining the questionnaire to have response of each individual regarding the threats that can occur in future.
- **Analyzing the Risk Scenario:** In this analysis is carried out based on certain situations. More emphasis is carried on the "what-if" question rather than the scenario. The consequences are noted down first and are considered for determining the future risk threats. Set of pre-defined questions are prepared for the review of the current risk situation.

Risk Ranking Techniques

A risk matrix is a type of risk assessment tool that helps in identifying the extent of the risk. Risk matrix helps in giving the insight idea about the risks occurrences and enhance the decision-making process. Risk can have variety of risk levels that depends upon the probability product with the risk sternness. So, through a risk matrix an estimate is made about the risk probability and the extent or level of the risk, not the accuracy.

Identify Risk Matrix

A risk matrix is developed while analyzing the threats and during the risk audits. Once a matrix is created, a tolerance or threshold must be maintained that will signify the acceptance level of the risk, also it will reveal about the efficacy of the measures used to mitigate the risk.

Consequence and Likelihood Ranges

A risk matrix is a four by four lattice. On the Y alignment (axis) is the "probability/likelihood" depiction range whereas the X alignment(axis) denoted the "consequence" scale. Given below figure 4 demonstrate the risk matrix with the penalty and probability scale.

Insignificant risks are less rigorous and thus acquire the lowest rank. Inversely, catastrophic risks are ranked first among all the other severe risks. The given below table 1 exhibits the rank related with the different categories of risks along with their

Figure 4. Consequences and Likelihood Ranges

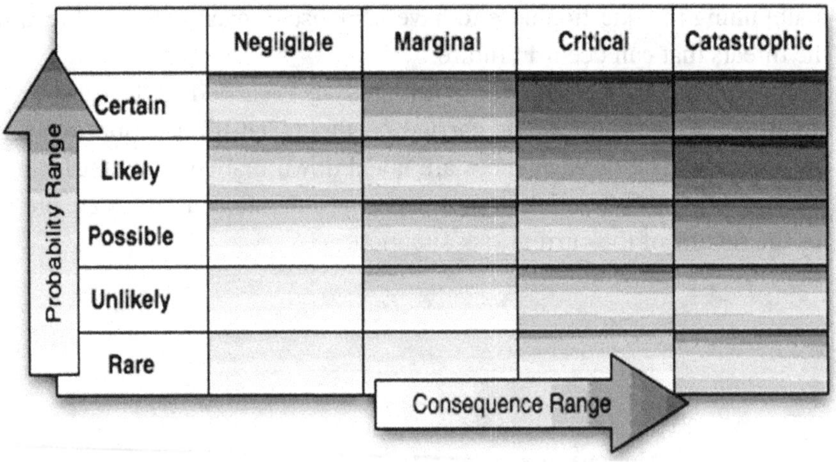

Table 1. Sample Consequence Ranking

S.NO	Risk Consequences	Rank (Numerical Vale)	Impacts
1	Negligible	1	Little or minimal damage
2	Marginal	2	Mitigatable damage where restoration activities can be done
3	Critical	3	Results in partial permanent disability
4	Catastrophic	4	Results in death or permanent disability

consequences which are classified as Negligible, Marginal, Critical and Catastrophic. Let's get into the brief preface of above described categories.

Risk Treatment Approaches

- **Treatment of Risk:** For the Different risk levels, various treatment plans need to be prepared. The risks that are rated high in ranking needs a treatment plan to be preplanned for curing from the large extent of threat, whereas the risks that are ranked as low need less attention and refinement based on the partners review at later stages.
  - Specify what kind of treatment plan will be followed.
  - Documenting the accepted treatment plan.
  - Allocating an owner to treatment plan, that will keep on monitoring the progress.
  - Deciding a declaration date for the target.
- **Anticipate Risk Analysis:** Anticipation involves performing the risk assessment after the treatment plans are designed. Changes in the forecast report can exist if the treatment plans or controls are not adequate for resolving the risk threats and their probability.
  - Checking the Probability of the identified risk.
  - The extent of the identified risk on the work environment.
  - To define the overall ranking related to different risks.
- **Implementing and Monitoring the Risk:** The owner of treatment plan will be responsible for the monitoring and implementation of treatment plan within an organization. The owner will not implement the plans directly but will ensure that all the treatment plans are completed within a given time span. Below mentioned events corresponds to the implementation of risk treatment plan.
  - Whether Structure of Organization is supportive or not to the treatment plan.

- ◦ Economic condition of company to access the plan, availability of resource.
- ◦ Communication, monitoring and continuous evaluation of status of plan.

CONCLUSION

For an organization to achieve specific set of objectives, it's necessary to have risk management as risk is one of the unpredictable events that can occur within the software development process. So, organizations have diverse range of techniques through which they can identify risk and manage it before they make an actual damage to the business. Risk management helps in identifying risk at various development stages of the software product so that necessary action can be taken to protect the product development from any kind of future failures. This chapter introduced the concept of risk management implying the importance of risk, how to identify risk and why risk management is required. Different types of risk are roofed with a brief insight of their effect on the product development. At the end different approaches to treat the risk are covered that have description of how risk can be avoided during the beginning phase. Risk management thus plays an important role in the overall development of the organization as it helps in maintaining the objectives of company by identifying the threats to the future developments which results in strong business decisions without any failures in the present market. An organization can be more financially strong if it suffers from fewer risks.

REFERENCES

Aven, T. (2016). Risk assessment and risk management: Review of recent advances on their foundation. *European Journal of Operational Research*.

Boehm, B. W. (1991). Software risk management: Principles and practices. *IEEE Software*, 8(1), 32–41. doi:10.1109/52.62930

Hopkin, P. (2017). *Fundamentals of risk management: understanding, evaluating and implementing effective risk management*. Kogan Page Publishers.

Rasmussen, J. (1997). Risk management in a dynamic society: A modelling problem. *Safety Science*, 27(2), 183–213. doi:10.1016/S0925-7535(97)00052-0

Rekha, J. H., & Parvathi, R. (2015). Survey on Software Project Risks and Big Data Analytics. *Procedia Computer Science*, 50, 295–300. doi:10.1016/j.procs.2015.04.045

Salvi, O., & Debray, B. (2006). A global view on ARAMIS, a risk assessment methodology for industries in the framework of the SEVESO II directive. *Journal of Hazardous Materials, 130*(3), 187–199. doi:10.1016/j.jhazmat.2005.07.034 PMID:16236437

Sarigiannidis, L., & Chatzoglou, P. D. (2011). Software Development Project Risk Management: A New Conceptual Framework. *Journal of Software Engineering and Applications, 4*(05), 293–305. doi:10.4236/jsea.2011.45032

Sundararajan, S., Bhasi, M., & Pramod, K. V. (2013). An Empirical Study of Industry Practice in Software Development Risk Management. *International Journal of Scientific and Research Publications, 3*(6).

Wanderleya, M., Menezes, J. Jr, Gusmão, C., & Lima, F. (2015). Proposal of risk management metrics for multiple project software development. *Procedia Computer Science, 64*, 1001–1009. doi:10.1016/j.procs.2015.08.619

Westfall, L. (2000, January). Software risk management. In *ASQ World Conference on Quality and Improvement Proceedings* (p. 32). American Society for Quality.

Chapter 3

Software Vulnerability Management:
How Intelligence Helps in Mitigating Software Vulnerabilities

Rimsy Dua
Chandigarh University, India

Samiksha Sharma
Chandigarh University, India

Abhishek Sharma
Chandigarh University, India

ABSTRACT

This chapter describes how with the proliferation of internet users, internet-related security threats are also increasing rapidly because of the software vulnerabilities that arise in software. Basically, there are two terms: bug and vulnerability. No doubt, bug and vulnerability are due to programming errors but vulnerabilities are more dangerous than bugs. Software vulnerability is a kind of flaw that arises in software or is a hole in the security of the software that allows an attacker to exploit that flaw. Unlike bugs, software vulnerability can affect a whole network thereby allowing unauthorised access to the database itself. Integrity and confidentiality of the software product is compromised due to the software vulnerability. These flaws must be patched in order to minimalize the impact of software vulnerability on an organisation. This chapter familiarises the methods of managing software vulnerabilities and discusses mitigation of the risks of different vulnerabilities in a software.

DOI: 10.4018/978-1-5225-6029-6.ch003

INTRODUCTION

A software vulnerability is a flaw in the software due to which the security of the system is compromised. Buffer overflow is one of the vulnerabilities that arises in software systems. This flaw makes the system unresponsive or results in system crash especially when the file is opened by the user and that is too heavy for the program to read. However, these commonly encountered flaws become a major cause of security concern when vulnerability is uncovered and the research is conducted about it. Sometimes a malicious user gets control over the administrator privileges and infects the whole system with malware. All software's or all operating systems comprises of vulnerabilities. A malicious user can easily target the software vulnerabilities even if the software is not showing any sign of attack (DongIlSeo,2013).

Vulnerability management involves the cyclical practice of identification, classification, remediation, and mitigation of vulnerabilities. Repetition of this process helps in mitigating the vulnerabilities in the software effectively. The term vulnerability is often confused with a risk. No doubt, a risk can lead to significant loss as that of a vulnerability but it is not mandatory that all vulnerabilities will involve a risk. There can be vulnerabilities without risk especially when the affected asset has no value. An exploitable vulnerability is basically a vulnerability with one or more instances of fully implemented attacks. An exploit exists for an exploitable vulnerability. An exploit is a code that an attacker creates to target a software vulnerability in applications like multimedia, security programs. There is also a window of vulnerability that decides a time between when a security flaw is introduced in the system that compromises system security and the time when an attacker is disabled. Apart from software vulnerabilities, vulnerabilities can also exist in hardware, site or personnel.

Figure 1 shows the vulnerability management. An attacker can attempt to target a vulnerability in many ways. An exploit is responsible for dropping a malware onto the vulnerable system. This is basically a code that is created in order to target the software vulnerability. After the successful execution of the exploit, a copy of the malware is dropped into the malware system.

Figure 2 shows the impact of software vulnerabilities.

HOW DOES INTELLIGENCE HELP IN REDUCING THE RISK OF SOFTWARE VULNERABILITY?

Many programming languages comprises of vulnerabilities. For instance, an adobe flash player is supported by java programming language. This program sometimes prompts the user to download plug in and that plug in contains within it a malicious code that takes advantage of the vulnerability in the system thereby compromising it.

Figure 1. Vulnerability management

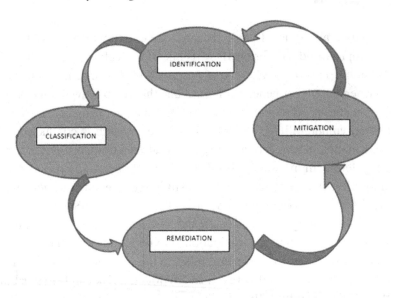

Figure 2. Impact of software vulnerabilities

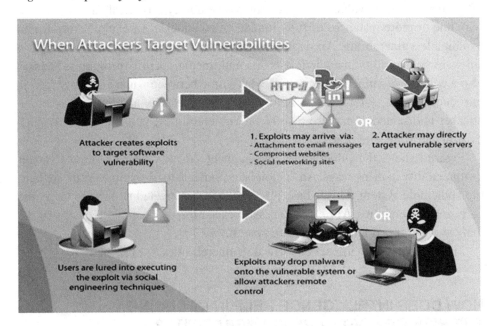

It is not mandatory that all software vulnerabilities will infect the system with malware. Actually, there is a term named "Vulnerability Intelligence" that makes use of intelligence in managing software vulnerabilities. The concept of vulnerability intelligence takes into account only those vulnerabilities that can really affect an organization or compromises with its security. First, there is a need to filter only those vulnerabilities that can really affect the system or an organization. In this way, these focused vulnerabilities will assist in improving an overall performance of the software system and also mitigating its level of risk (Zavarsky, 2011).

Figure 3 shows the role of vulnerability intelligence in risk mitigation.

STRUCTURE OF THE VULNERABILITY MANAGEMENT SYSTEM

The structure of vulnerability management system is composed of various blocks and these blocks are basically responsible for effective management of the vulnerability in the software systems. Following are the blocks that assists in the structuring of the vulnerability management system.

- Database Management
- Vulnerability Selection
- Patch Management
- Security Management
- Vulnerability Assessment Block

Figure 3. Role of vulnerability intelligence in risk mitigation

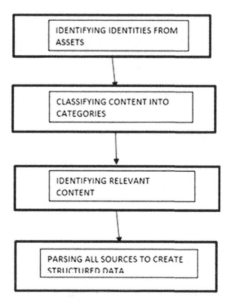

Figure 4 shows the structure of software vulnerability management.

Database Management Block, is basically used for the management (Jin Tae Oh.2013) of vulnerability database. This database keeps track of all the known vulnerabilities that can actually target real computer systems. Vulnerability databases can be categorized in various ways like Open Source Vulnerability Database, National Vulnerability Database U.S. Common vulnerabilities and Exposures(CVE) are published by National Vulnerability Database. CVE is a paramount through which different vulnerability databases are linked so that different security patches can be shared together to inhibit a malicious user from infecting the private systems (Telang, 2011).

Vulnerability Selection Block, executes the function that selects some priority vulnerabilities that truly targets the real computer systems. By doing so, the task of adding security patches for different vulnerabilities becomes easy. If only priority vulnerabilities are selected first then it becomes easy for the system administrator also to respond to these vulnerabilities.

Figure 4. Structure of software vulnerability management

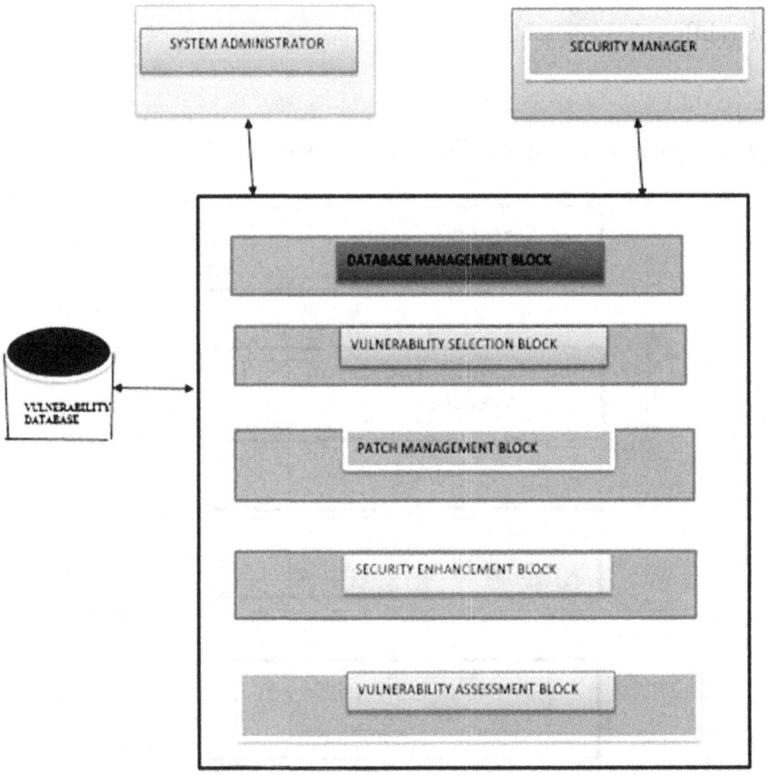

Patch Management Block, executes the function that selects whether the patch information is included in the vulnerability or not. If the patch information is included then the corresponding security patches are added to the software thereby reducing the vulnerability of the system. A connection is maintained with the patch management system to work out the patch of the software (Byers, 2008).

Security Enhancement Block, executes the function that analyze what are the different security solutions that are required to resolve the vulnerabilities. It also analyses the degree to which security of the software system is enhanced when security solutions are deployed for the vulnerabilities.

Vulnerability Assessment Block, executes the function that assesses the severity of the vulnerability by checking whether the patches for that vulnerability are added by the system administrator or not. It also checks what different security solutions are available for the known vulnerabilities.

CVSS (COMMON VULNERABILITY SCORING SYSTEM)

Relative severity of vulnerabilities in the software flaw must be known and same can be calculated in information technology systems through sets of formulas and security metrics. Three metric groups are included in CVSS namely Base metrics, Temporal metrics (Geon L yang Kim,2013) and Environmental Metrics. All these metrics further consists of set of metrics. Figure 5 shows the base metric group.

Figure 6 shows the temporal metric group. Figure 7 shows the environmental metric group. The fundamental characteristics of vulnerabilities are represented by Base metric group. These characteristics are constant over time and user environments. The characteristics that change over time are categorized as Temporal metrics. On the other hand, those characteristics of vulnerabilities that are relevant and unique to a particular user's environmental represents Environmental metric group.

Figure 5. Base metric group

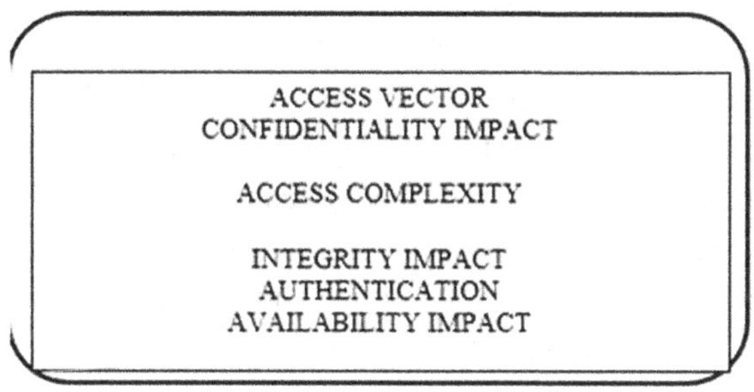

ACCESS VECTOR
CONFIDENTIALITY IMPACT

ACCESS COMPLEXITY

INTEGRITY IMPACT
AUTHENTICATION
AVAILABILITY IMPACT

Figure 6. Temporal metric group

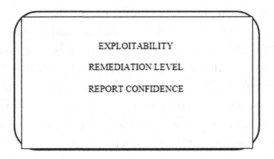

Figure 7. Environmental metric group

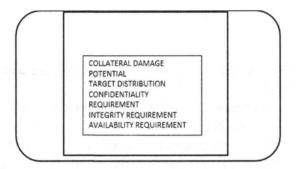

HOW CAN A VULNERABILITY DATABASE BE CONSTRUCTED?

There is an existence of some vulnerabilities that have already been collected and managed through NVD (National Vulnerability Database), OSVDB (Open Source Vulnerability Database). It is a good idea that this vulnerability management system makes full use of established vulnerability databases. Many of the established vulnerabilities have been used by OSVDB. However, the vulnerability management system must construct the private database for the vulnerabilities of the domestic software because they don't exist in the public vulnerability databases.

Private Vulnerability Database needs to be constructed by security expert group. Only the base score pf CVSS is included in NVD, i.e., public vulnerability (Kim, 2013) database of USA. In view of this, temporal and environmental score of CVSS is not included in NVD. The management of data must be done in private by vulnerability management system. This is because, data can be used maliciously.

Figure 8 shows the construction of vulnerability management system. Here, vulnerability databases contain some set of known vulnerabilities that must be selected by vulnerability management system. Also, the collection and analysis of private data is accomplished by security expert group.

Figure 8. Construction of vulnerability database

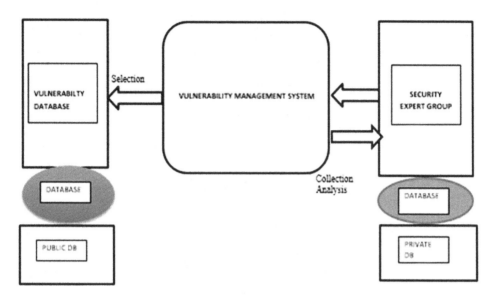

SELECTION PROCEDURE FOR PRIORITY VULNERABILITIES

A software may be prone to number of vulnerabilities (Oh, 2013) but there must be some selection procedure on the basis of which different vulnerabilities of the system are prioritized and also actions must be taken for mitigating the risk of those vulnerabilities. Priority vulnerabilities are selected through the construction of vulnerability database. Public and private databases are the two major categories of vulnerability databases.

An open web based vulnerability data base i.e. OSDVB helps in constructing public database. In view of this to manage private information i.e. known vulnerabilities of the software in an organization or homeland, private database is used.

Figure 9 shows the priority vulnerabilities selection procedure. Priority vulnerabilities are selected by constructing vulnerability database. Vulnerabilities of the software are extracted from vulnerability database by Vulnerability management system in which the type and version of the software is needed.

VULNERABILITY SEVERITY ASSESSMENT PROCEDURE

Asset catalog is the method that is used to select vulnerabilities of the software by vulnerability management system. CVSS (Common Vulnerability Scoring System) score helps in knowing the relative severity of the selected vulnerabilities. Whatever

Figure 9. Priority vulnerabilities selection procedure

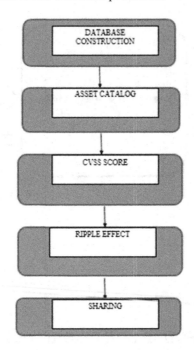

the selected vulnerabilities will be, they all will include CVSS score. Severity of the entire service is known by the system by summing up the CVSS score. Severity of the internet service is higher in case the sum of CVSS score is larger. Severity of the internet service is 0 in case the sum of CVSS score is 0. Severity of the internet service can be reduced by deploying security solutions or by defending that internet service perfectly from attacks (Heymann, 2009).

Figure 10 shows the procedure to assess vulnerability severity.

EQUIFAX: A CASE STUDY IN VULNERABILITY MANAGEMENT

A global information solutions company Equifax was vulnerable to some security attacks. Apache struts is a web application framework for Equifax. Some security breaches were found to occur in this web application framework. Phishing was not an initial entry point into the Equifax network. The vulnerability in Equifax was exploited in its web application framework named Apache Struts. This is because of the vulnerability that attackers managed to take control of the server and the records of 143 million users were filched.

Figure 10. Procedure to assess vulnerability severity

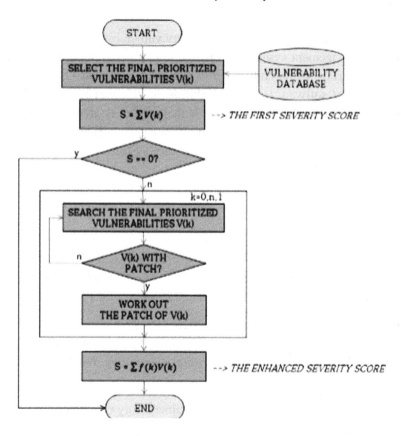

A division of the federal government named US CERT helps Americans to protect their data from security threats. Equifax was notified about serious security threats in its web application framework Apache Struts by U.S CERT. Then the information about serious security breach was passed to IT operations team so that patching can be incorporated in that software timely. On march 9, This security breach notification of US CERT was disseminated internally by email so that software can be upgraded by an applicable personnel. As per the policy of Equifax, the patching of the software required to occur within a time period of 48 hours. However, the vulnerabilities in the web application framework of Equifax were not identified on time. Finally, system was having two breakdowns, One was the failure to identify the vulnerability in an application, Secondly, there was an issue in patching of the software. As a consequence, the discipline of vulnerability management is considered to be much more than the simple scanning and patching of the vulnerabilities.

CONCLUSION

In this chapter, we have studied how the priority vulnerabilities are selected by the vulnerability management system by constructing vulnerability database. Severity of the software flaw vulnerabilities are calculated based on CVSS score. The relative severity of software flaw vulnerabilities is calculated within information technology systems and also the security enhancement degree is assessed. Here the use of intelligence in selecting the vulnerabilities that can have an impact on an organization is the crucial step. In addition to this, system also lets us know about the priority vulnerabilities of different software.

REFERENCES

Bhullar, R. K., Pawar, L., Bajaj, R., & Manocha, A. K. (2017). Intelligent stress calculation and scheduling in segmented processor systems using buddy approach. *Journal of Intelligent & Fuzzy Systems*, *32*(4), 3129-3142. doi:10.3233/JIFS-169256

Bhullar, R. K., Pawar, L., & Kumar, V. (2016, October). A novel prime numbers based hashing technique for minimizing collisions. In *Proceedings of the 2016 2nd International Conference on Next Generation Computing Technologies (NGCT)* (pp. 522-527). IEEE.

Bucko, M. (2008). Short review of modern vulnerability research.

Byers, D., & Shahmehri, N. (2008). A Cause-Based Approach to Preventing Software Vulnerabilities. In *Proceedings of the Third International Conference on Availability, Reliability and Security* (pp. 276-283). 10.1109/ARES.2008.12

Chang, Y. Y., Zavarsky, P., Ruhl, R., & Lindskog, D. (2012). Trend Analysis of the CVE for Software Vulnerability Management.

Frost and Sullivan. (2016). Analysis of the Global Public Vulnerability Research Market.

Gray, A. (2003). An historical perspective of software vulnerability management.

IBM. (2014). Managing security risks and vulnerabilities.

Kim, G., Oh, J., Seo, D., & Kim, J. (2013). The Design of Vulnerability Management System. *International Journal of Computer Science and Network Security*, *13*(4).

Kupsch, J. A., Miller, B. P., Heymann, E., & César, E. (2009). First Principles Vulnerability Assessment.

Taneja, K., Taneja, H., & Bhullar, R. K. (2016, March). Cross-platform application development for smartphones: Approaches and implications. In *Proceedings of the 2016 3rd International Conference on Computing for Sustainable Global Development (INDIACom)* (pp. 1752-1758). IEEE.

Taneja, K., Taneja, H., & Kumar, R. (2017). Multi-channel medium access control protocols: review and comparison. *Journal of Information and Optimization Sciences*.

Telang, R., & Wattal, S. (2007). An Empirical Analysis of the Impact of Software Vulnerability Announcements on Firm Stock Price. IEEE Transactions on software engineering, 33(8).

Wu Qianqian,Liu Xianqjun(2014), Research and design on Web application vulnerability scanning service. In *Proceedings of the Software Engineering and Service Science (ICSESS '14)*.

Chapter 4
Risks Assessment in Designing Phase: Its Impacts and Issues

Ankita Sharma
Chandigarh University, India

Vipin Pal
National Institute of Technology Meghalaya, India

Nitish Ojha
Chandigarh University, India

Rohit Bajaj
Chandigarh University, India

ABSTRACT

This chapter describes how risk analysis is a phenomena or methodology which is considered to be an amalgamation of various contexts to analyze and reach upon a conclusion about the fragility, vulnerability, flaws, defects, possible threats and dangers, which a particular software or system is prone to. It is an organization-level decision support tool which helps in gathering all sorts of data. That data, further, helps in arriving at a conclusion about how fragile or vulnerable a particular system is. Being a risk analyst, possessing deep knowledge, requires that one will analyze all possibilities of any risk, possible in any form, limitations of every risk assessment technique being applied and finally, the practical possibility or possible outcome of a particular risk-calculation strategy applied in a real-time environment.

INTRODUCTION

,

DOI: 10.4018/978-1-5225-6029-6.ch004

Risk analysis is generally considered as a "black art"— part mathematics and part fortune telling. Effective risk analysis, though, is a business-rank conclusion-aid tool. It is, actually, an efficient way of accumulating the required data, so that an effective decision can be generated, totally based on the knowledge of fragility or vulnerability, danger or threats, impacts, influences or effects and equally important, possibility of any particular risk.

All well acknowledged methodologies for risk analysis hold certain pros and cons, but nearly, every methodology, possess a part of brilliant principles and a part of certain limitations or restrictions.

What contributes in differentiating, an exceptional risk analysis technique from an ordinary one is, its capability to apply well-established definitions of risks to a particular software design and obtain absolute mitigating requirements.

For an iterative risk analysis, a high ranking strategy, being used, should be thoroughly amalgamated all around, the Software Development Life Cycle Model (McGraw, 2004). Figure- 1 below, provides a through view of the specific areas, in Software Development Life Cycle Model, which are our target or focus areas i.e. suppose if we are considering risk analysis, the focus will be on the specific parts of the cycles for examining the risk involved.

STANDARD NOMENCLATURE

Various methods for risk analysis split into two major portions or categories:

1. **Commercial Based Risk Analysis**: Prominent examples of Commercial Based Risk Analysis are Insight's CRAMM, Sun's ACSM/SAR, Microsoft's STRIDE, and Cigital's SQM, etc.

Figure 1. Risks in the software development life cycle

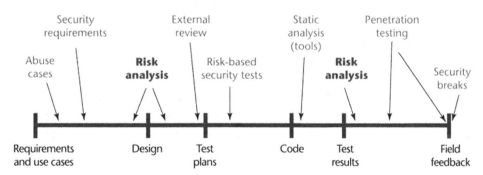

2. **Standards- Based Risk Analysis**: There are many examples such as Software Engineering Institute's OCTAVE, etc.

It would be out of scope to have deep rooted discussion about every prevailing Risk Analysis Methodology. Still, we will be gazing into the fundamental approaches, general feature and characteristics, advantages and limitation and the strength and weaknesses of various Risk calculating techniques.

All existing, well established, Risk assessing Techniques differ from one another and has a unique tactic to calculate the possibility of risk involved. Every approach involves different perspective and instances of different techniques available are:

1. Function loss methodologies tend to make available a loss figure, which balances up for the cost involved for implementation of different controls.
2. Risk Ratings are derived mathematically, equating risks with random classifications of risk or threat, possibility or probability and also impact or the effect.
3. Qualitative assessment Technique calculates risk factor that is based on certain knowledge or information or facts.

Although each basic technique has distinct merits and demerits, but some of the fundamental values or elements are common, which are shared by almost every technique while calculating the risk factor involved during a software design. The common definitions, defining these elements are:

Asset also known as an object can have many forms i.e. it can possibly a system component or a complete system by itself or even any sort of data.

Risk can be defined as the possibility or probability for the asset to suffer a negative impact or unsuitable circumstances. The risk factor or the negative impact can be calculated considering various factors which are

- The ease with which an attack can be executed
- Resources, that are available and the motivational force working for the attacker.
- The present fragile state of the system
- Cost involved and extent of effect of the final result.

Threat is a source of danger or hazards. It can be called as a destructive agent posing a threat on the system. The impact of the threat can be estimated by the motivational force working behind the threat. These threats can result into significant or crucial attacks impacting the system directly.

Vulnerability is known as the system's deficiency or fragility or it weakness to defend itself from the possible risk, threat or any prevailing danger. A system might be vulnerable due many causes, which may be the poor security mechanism adopted by the system, loopholes in designing and implementation or may be a compromised internal control.

It might be a possibility that the entire security setup of the system is at fault, making the system vulnerable to the attack from the outside world. It might also be possible that the security of one or more component can be breached easily, which in return will make the entire system prone to various malicious accesses.

Vulnerabilities can be classified into two main categories:

Flaws are the issues at design level and human expertise have the responsibility to uncover them and get them amended.

Bugs are the issues at implementation level and are corrected using automated scanners.

Countermeasures or safeguards are the controls, authorized for an information system, which can manage, operate and handle the technicality of the system. Altogether, they are responsible for protecting the system's integrity, confidentiality and availability and not the least the data or the information within the system.

They help the designer to fix the possible risks either by detecting the risk or by preventing it, whenever, it is likely to be triggered.

Impact is said to be the magnitude by which a particular risk or threat is going to affect any organization or system. This may also result in breaching of the regulation or law.

Until the magnitude of the impact have been estimated, it would be hard to tackle the technical issues arising due to the malicious attack.

Probability is the possibility, of a particular instance or certain circumstances to occur or take place. It may be expressed in percentile in many cases, although calculating probability is extremely rough.

Even though, most of the techniques use these elements in one or the other way for the possible calculation of risk assessment, but each method diverse from other while arriving at the specific values.

Some methods adopt calculation of nominal value for the assessment of the possible threats, such as calculation of function of loss, while others prefer a checklist method for accessing the vulnerabilities and deficiencies so that the risk impact can be measured (Kumar, 2017).

ILLUSTRATION OF RISK CALCULATION:

An ideal risk estimation technique exhibits risk or threat as financial/economic loss/deprivation, or annualized loss expectancy. The underneath equation can be considered to ponder, in-depth, about the technicality involved in calculation of risk factors.

ALE = SLE * ARO

SLE stands for single loss expectancy

ARO represent annualized rate of occurrence, which can be defined as the possibility of reoccurrence of a disfavored event or possibility of a possible threat or danger.

Let's us take a scenario of an Internet-based equities trading platform, with a possible flaw within the system that could further result in a malicious attempt or unwanted access to the system such as there could be a possibility of an implication, where an unauthorized stock trades can be employed. Let us consider, a particular risk analysis perceives that the mid- and the back-office strategy will detest and nullify any suspicious or nasty operation such that the loss incorporated with a circumstance remain solely, the cost of backing out of the trade.

We are assigning $150 as a cost for any such occurrence, hence SLE = $150. If there exits an ARO with simply 100 such condition per year, the resulting expense/cost, to the company i.e. ALE would be $15,000. The final result in dollars makes available, nothing more than, a rough estimation, although a considerate one, for anyone to determine whether it is wise to invest in mending the fragility or vulnerability. In-case of our imaginary equities trading company, an annual loss of $15,000, might not be of worth getting out of bed for. (Bhullar et al., 2017).

Various other methodologies adopt a more qualitative approach. Let's take a scenario of a Web server making its company's face available to the globe, the vandalization of the Website might be tedious to be specified as a financial loss, although some research have highlighted an association, between security event and un-favored stock-price movements (Cavusoglu, Mishra, & Raghunathan, 2002). When there is an involvement of "intangible assets," such as status, qualitative risk estimation might be a more suitable solution to assess the loss.

Despite the strategy being implied, mostly, the practitioners stress upon a return-on-investment study to get an estimate that weather a particular countermeasure, being used, is cost-effective enough so that a desired security goal can be achieved. Let's consider a scenario where addition of an applied cryptography via native APIs, without any dedicated hardware acceleration applied, to an application server, might result in a cheap setup for a short while, but for example, if it is resulting into a noteworthy reduction in transaction volume throughput, a more suitable ROI may be an investment in crypto-acceleration hardware. Concerned organizations must appoint that particular risk-calculation methodology, which results best in reflecting their demands.

GENERAL THEMES

Majority of the risk-assessment techniques' illustration stresses that recognition or identification, classification or ranking, and equally important, mitigation are all ongoing processes and just not a sole step which is to be fulfilled at any sole level of the software development life cycle. Risk-assessment results and different risk classifications or categories hold together, both, requirements, which are estimated at an early stage in the life cycle and testing, which provides authenticity to the quality of the product.

Being a specialized area or subject, it is not necessary that risk estimation is best accomplished step by step by the design team. Exhaustive risk assessment depends on an in-depth knowledge of business effects or influences, which further needs an in-depth awareness of all the laws, codes, conducts and regulations and in addition to it, it is also needed to be checked that which business model is being supported by the software. Generally, Designers and developers come up with certain presumptions related to their system and the threats or risks it confronts; at the least, the security and risk specialists should be capable to assure that they are able to tackle those assumptions against the generally acknowledged and termed as best practice. They should be in a better situation, where there is nothing to assume.

Grouping the right individuals for a risk assessment is essential: consider the risk estimation group precisely. Knowledge as well as, experience can't be overstressed on the grounds that risk assessment isn't a science, and in-depth idea of vulnerabilities, threats, bugs, defects, also, dangers is a crucial victory factor. A prototypical examination includes number of noteworthy tasks that frequently incorporate many essential sub steps:

- Research as much as could be expected about the assessment target. Sub-steps incorporate going through and getting to know with specifications, architecture documentation, also, other designing substances or materials; debating about, analyzing and conceptualizing with the team; estimating system's or framework's limit plus, information or data delicacy/criticality; investigating the software if it is existing in an practicable state; considering the coding part and other software dimensions; side by side, distinguishing possible threats and risks that might be encountered.

- Talk about security issues encompassing the software or product. Sub-steps incorporate contending about how the software works and deciding territories of contradiction; distinguishing conceivable vulnerabilities, once in a while by utilizing tools or list of regular vulnerabilities; identifying threats and also examining probable fixes; plus acknowledging about of existing and reserved security controls.
- Ponder upon the likelihood of settlement. Sub-steps incorporate identifying threat situations for fragility of system, misuse and adjusting measures against risk or threat volume to decide probability.
- Conduct impact estimation. Sub-steps incorporate deciding the effect on resource or assets and business objectives and taking into view the effect on security.
- Classification or ranking of risks.
- Build up a mitigation procedure or strategy. A sub-step is suggesting countermeasures to mitigate risks.
- Highlight findings. Sub-steps incorporate precisely portraying vital and insignificant risks while giving careful consideration to risk effects, and giving fundamental data about where to spend constrained mitigation assets.

The sidebar on Cigital's solution indicates one commercial case which keeps after the mentioned essential approach.

Figure 2, shows Cigital's ceaseless risk-estimation process, which stays in constant loop at many stages of illustrations through many stages. In Cigital's technique, business objectives decide risks, risks drive techniques, strategies or technique or

Figure 2. Cigital's Risk Management System

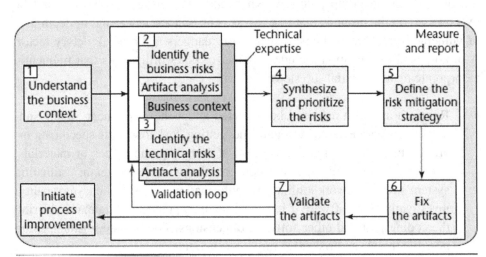

methods yield estimation or measurements, measurements or estimation drives choice or decision support, and choice or decision support drives settle/revamp and application or software quality.

Figure 2 above shows Cigital's risk-management system. Numerous parts of structures can be mechanized—for instance, risk storage or accumulation, mapping of business risk to technical risk, and the show of current status, gradually, after some time.

PRE-REQUISITE KNOWLEDGE

Analysis at Design-phase is in-depth understanding. STRIDE model from Microsoft, for instance, includes the knowledge and application of many risk classification while analyzing (Howard & LaBlane). Similarly, Cigital's SQM approach brings in use, attack paradigm or patterns (Hoglund & McGraw, 2004), and takes advantage of graph/ diagrams to perceive or estimate attack's resilience, deep understanding of design standards for analyzing any ambiguity (Veiga & McGraw, 2001), (Taneja et al., 2017) and information with respect to normally utilized systems or frameworks. (.NET and J2EE being two illustrations) and components of software.

A chief task in design phase risk assessment is developing a persistent sight of the target framework at a sensibly high state. The concept behind is to search the woods, not ending up being lost in the trees. The most justifiable stage for this portrayal is the orthodox or typical view of whiteboard boxes and directing arrows portraying the communication of different critical design parts or components. The essence of software frameworks or systems leads numerous designers as well as analysts to have an impression (erroneously or incorrectly) that a code-level illustration of programming is adequate for identifying designing issues. Despite the fact that this may once in a while be valid, it doesn't, for the most part, hold. Intensive programming's declaration that "the code is the design" speaks about one radical end of this strategy. Lacking a whiteboard level of illustration, architectural threat estimation is probably going to neglect vital risks linked to flaws.

RISK ESTIMATION AND REQUIREMENTS

In all the articles considered previously, definitions about the necessity of security and discussion about abuse cases are being utilized as a soured for generating all the necessary requirements. In a genuine sense, risk assessment starts at this particular point: Basic requirement for design should consider the risks you're attempting to counter. Let's have a sight at the three strategies so that the philosophy about risk can be injected into the requirement accumulating phase. Please keep in mind that the necessities frameworks (requirement system) based on UML tend to be more considerate about the functionality of security over the cases of abuse cases and misuse:

- SecureUML (www.informatik.uni-freiburg.de/~tolo/bars/secuml_uml2002. pdf) is an approach for displaying access-control strategies and their amalgamation into model driven software advancement or development. SecureUML depends on role-depending access control and demonstrates security prerequisites for well-conducting applications in expected conditions.
- UMLsec (www4.in.tum.de/~umlsec/) is an augmentation to UML that makes the displaying of security-related characters, for example, privacy or confidentiality and access control, possible.
- GuttormSindre and Andreas Opdahl (Sindre & Opdhal, 2000) endeavor to show abuse cases as a method for seeing how applications might react to dangers in a less controllable conditions; they inform about the function that the framework or system ought not permit.

A key element in the risk condition is impact. Business impacts by the fact divide into three broad classifications:

- Federal or state laws and regulation (counting the Gramm-Leach- Bliley Act, HIPAA, and the quoted California Senate Bill 1386);
- Monetary or business contemplations (for example, income insurance, control over high-esteem scholarly property, and safeguarding of brand and reputation); and
- Contractual contemplations (counting service-level assertions or agreements also, liability shirking).

The initial footstep to risk assessment at the requirement phase is to separate the requirements among three straightforward classes: must have, important to have, and nice but unnecessary. Until an illegal operation is being run by you, you ought to necessarily class laws and directions or regulations into the principal or first or prime classification—these requirements ought to be right away required and not applicable to further risk evaluation (in spite of the fact that a ROI study can enable you to choose the most affordable mitigations). In the event that the law expects you to ensure private data, for instance, this necessity is mandatory and ought not to be liable to a risk-based choice. Why? Since the administration or the government has the ability to make you go out of business, which is the root of all risks.

You're at that point left with risk impacts—ones that have as factors, potential impact and possibility—that must be overseen in different ways. Instances of mitigations extend from technical safety and controls to business choices for living accompanied with the risk. At the primitive requirement definition level, you may have the capacity to make a few presumptions with respect to which controls are important.

Uniformly adopting these basic ideas will help us keep you in front of most application developers. As you head toward the designing and coding stages, risk estimation should start to test your first suppositions from requirement stage by evaluating the dangers and vulnerabilities, which the design has inherited.

CONSTRAINTS

Conventional risk-analysis result is hard to implement, straightforwardly, to present day software design. Even though possessing a top level of ability in the capacity to foresee the dollar loss for a given occasion and performing Monte Carlo dispersal analysis of earlier occasions to infer a statistically stable probability distribution for future occasions, there's as yet a vast gap between an ALE's crude or raw dollar figure (as already discussed) and a thorough security mitigation definition.

A considerable stressing fact is that conventional risk-analysis methods don't really give a simple guide (including the exhaustive list) of every potential threat or vulnerability and dangers to consider at a segment or component or element / environment or domain level. This is the reason a substantial knowledge or information base and loads of experience is insignificant.

The spiky knowledge issue emerges to some degree because applications now a day, including Web services applications, are intended to traverse various limits of trust. The helplessness of—and danger to—any particular component differs with the level or platform on which that component lies and the conducive atmosphere in which it lives (compare secure DMZ with straight exposed LAN). In any case, couples of conventional strategies decently targetthe relevant fluctuation of danger provided alterations in the core atmosphere. This is a lethal flaw while considering heavily distributed or dispersed applications or Web services.

In present day frameworks, for example, .NET and J2EE, security strategies or technique exist at practically every layer, yet an excessive number of applications today depend on a "reactive" safety or protection setup or infrastructure that solely protects at the network transport layer. This is again and again summed up by stating, "We're secure on the grounds that we utilize SSL and execute bring into implementation firewalls," which opens the way to a wide range of issues, for example, those incited by port 80 attacks, SQL injections, class spoofing, and method overwriting (to give some examples).

One way to deal with conquering these issues is to begin pondering at software risk analysis on a segment by-segment, tier by-tier, and atmosphere by-atmosphere level and after that apply the standards of measuring dangers, vulnerabilities, and impacts or effects at each level.

A REALISTIC OUTLOOK

At the design phase, any risk-assessing process ought to be custom-made to software design. Keep in mind that the goal of this activity is to decide particular vulnerabilities and dangers that prevail for the software and evaluate their impact. A useful disintegration of the application into significant components, forms or processes, information or data stores, and information or data interchange/communication flows, mapped against the atmosphere within which the software will be installed, allows a desktop evaluation for possible dangers and potential vulnerabilities. We can't overstress the significance of utilizing a forest level perspective of a framework while performing analysis for possible risk. Some kind of top stage system prototype makes risk investigation at the architectural level conceivable.

Despite the fact that we could examine by using modeling language, for example, UMLSec to endeavor to display threats or dangers, even the most primary investigation methodologies can yield important outcomes. Consider Figure 3, which demonstrates a basic four-level/tier arrangement configuration design pattern for a standard-issue Web based application. If risk assessment standards are to be applied to this stage of design, we can quickly reach some helpful inferences about the security designs of the application.

Figure 3 represents forest-level representation of a, standard-issue four-level, Web application. In this design, the consumer level tier exists out on the Internet, while the rest of the tires are on internal network, associated with the Internet. Consumers, utilizing the client indirectly, influence information/data in the database, so that the access and control must be managed through all levels/tiers.

During risk-analysis process, top-level designs are considered:

- The risk lying in every level's or tier's environment;
- The sorts of vulnerabilities that might exist in every component including the data-flows;
- The business effect of such technical threats, they are needed to be figured it out;
- The likelihood of such a hazard being acknowledged; and

Figure 3. Forest Level forest representation of web applications

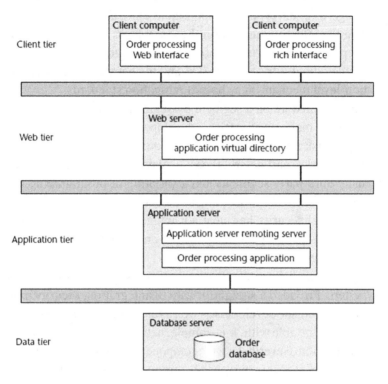

- Any attainable countermeasures which could be applied at every level/tier, considering the entire range of protection measures provided (starting from base OS-level security, passing through virtual machine security instruments, for example, the utilization of Java cryptography augmentations/extensions in J2EE).

In the basic illustration appeared in Figure 3, every level exists in an alternate security domain or assured zone. This specification quickly gives us the aspect of the risk every level deals with. If we consider superimpose data types, (for example, client logon qualifications, records, and requests or orders), their flow such as logon requests, record inquiries, and request/order entries, and most essential, their security categorization, we can reach inferences about the protection for these information/ data components/elements and their transmission given the present design.

Assume that SSL secures client logon flows between the customer and the Web server. Our arrangement design demonstrates that even if the encrypted passage ends at this level/tier (due to the inheriting danger in the zones acquired by the Web and application levels), we should, absolutely, counter intrusion inside and within these two levels/tiers too. This may demonstrate the need to build up yet another encrypted passage or to think about an alternate way to deal with securing this information (perhaps message-level encryption as opposed to tunneling).

Considering the intercommunication threats, it turns out to be quite clear why a particular deployment pattern is profitable, on the grounds that it allows us a chance to consider about infrastructure (OS and the network) security instruments and application-level mechanism as hazard mitigation standards.

Breaking down software on a segment by-segment basis to set up trust areas is an agreeable way for majority of software developers and also considering auditors to start applying a risk management strategy to deal with software security issues. Since most frameworks, particularly those displaying the n-level/tier architecture, depend on many third party segments and a variation of programming languages, characterizing area of interest and adopting an outside/in context like the one regularly found in conventional security has clear advantages. Regardless, cooperation and interaction of various product and languages is an architectural component liable to be a fragility hotbed.

To its true nature, disintegration is a characteristic approach to distribute a framework/system. Provided a straightforward disintegration, security experts will have the capacity to educate developers as well as architects about angles concerning security they're comfortable with, for example, network based segment/component limits and authentication. Nevertheless, the component issue is unsolved and extremely dubious—even the most secure parts can be grouped together and arranged into an uncertain/threat prone clutter.

As associations becomes quite noticeably proficient at distinguishing fragility and its effect on business, the risk estimation group ought to develop the essential way to incorporate extra evaluation of the threats found inside—or enveloping all—levels/tiers. This advancement can reveal technology related vulnerabilities in view of failings other than the trust issues crosswise tier limits/boundaries. Cases of more unobtrusive dangers that must be thrown out with a more refined approach incorporate exchange administration hazards and baiting assaults.

Risk analysis is, efficiently, a great universally useful reference by which we can compare and judge our security design's viability. Since approximately 50 percent of security issues are the consequence of design imperfections, conducting risk estimation at the designing phase is a vital phenomenon of a strong software security program. Handling inconvenience, while applying risk analysis strategies at the designing stage for any application, usually yields profitable, business-pertinent outcomes. The risk estimation process is consistent and applies to a wide range of levels, without a moment's delay distinguishing framework level vulnerabilities, allotting and affect, and deciding sensible mitigation techniques. By keeping in view the subsequent ranked threats, business partners can decide how to manage specific risks and what the savviest controls may be.

CONCLUSION

There are so many risk assessment methodologies prevailing, which are quite diverse from one another in many ways. Yet all of them possess certain edge over the other in some field and are restricted in some field, by some factors too.

Some, risk analysis technologies out their become exceptionally good over other strategies only because they are capable to employ all critical risk definitions to a particular software design so that accurate corrective measures can be drawn which are quite cost effective as well and the entire process results into an exceptionally successful software development having quite rare chance of any sort of vulnerability.

The conventional terminology, that most of the risk analysis techniques bring to use, while drawing an estimate of the amount of risk involved in a particular scenario, is quite common in most of the techniques. Some of the basic parameters considered are: Object to be protected, Risk involved, Threats surrounding the object, how vulnerable the system can be, prescribed countermeasure to curb possible threats, Impact that a persisting risk would lay on the system and Probable chances of a particular threat or danger etc. Further, an example would be considered to illustrate how risk is calculated in a particular scenario and different terminology and values that are considered while calculating risk factor. Further common themes would be discussed, which are a helping hand and provides an in-depth understanding so that risk calculation can be done on a grand scale and no corner is left untouched, while accessing the risk for a particular system. It involves, rigorous learning, intense discussions about every aspect, probability of compromise, impact analysis, ranking of a particular risk, developing strong countermeasures and last but not the least reporting in an absolute manner, providing a crisp situation.

One should be really good with his/her in-depth understanding and knowledge while performing a risk analysis. The analyst must be aware of the functioning of each and every component and also the interaction among the various components in different scenarios. Most importantly he/ she should be able to analyze the data flow and must be able to access the risk and conflicts involved in each and every stage. Further limitations that will be occurring while we will be applying traditional risk assessments to the present-day software designs will be discussed thoroughly.

A practical approach is, finally, needed to be applied taking into consideration every aspect and possibility that has been discussed so far. Here the application of risk assessment methodologies would be applied on every tier of the system and it will then be analyzed separately to get into every probable possibility of risk to be involved.

REFERENCES

Bhullar, R. K., Pawar, L., Bajaj, R., & Manocha, A. K. (2017). Intelligent stress calculation and scheduling in segmented processor systems using buddy approach. *Journal of Intelligent & Fuzzy Systems, 32*(4), 3129–3142. doi:10.3233/JIFS-169256

Cavusoglu, H., Mishra, B., & Raghunathan, S. (2002). *The Effect of Internet Security Breach Announcements on Market Value of Breached Firms and Internet Security Developers* (tech. report). Univ. of Texas at Dallas, School of Management. Retrieved from www.utdallas.edu/~huseyin/breach.pdf

Hoglund, G., & McGraw, G. (2004). *Exploiting Software*. Addison-Wesley.

Howard, M., & LaBlanc, D. (2003). Writing Secure Code (2nd ed.). Microsoft Press.

McGraw, G. (2004). Software Security. *IEEE Security and Privacy, 2*(2), 80–83. doi:10.1109/MSECP.2004.1281254

Sindre, G. & Opdahl, A.L. (2005). Eliciting Security Requirements by Misuse Cases. In Proc. 37th Technology of Object-Oriented Languages and Systems(TOOLS-37). IEEE CS Press.

Taneja, K., Taneja, H., & Bhullar, R. K. (2016, March). Cross-platform application development for smartphones: Approaches and implications. In *Proceedings of the 2016 3rd International Conference on Computing for Sustainable Global Development (INDIACom)* (pp. 1752-1758). IEEE.

Taneja, K., Taneja, H., & Kumar, R. (2017). Multi-channel medium access control protocols: review and comparison. *Journal of Information and Optimization Sciences*.

Verdon, D., & McGraw, G. (2004). Risk analysis in software design. *IEEE Security & Privacy, 2*(4), 79-84.

Viega, J., & McGraw, G. (2000). *Building Secure Software: How to Avoid Security Problems the Right Way*. Addison Wesley.

Chapter 5
Problems, Threats in Software Development Life Cycle and Their Analysis

Deepika Rana
Chandigarh University, India

Manisha Malhotra
Chandigarh University, India

This content has been removed at the discretion of the publisher and the editors.

DOI: 10.4018/978-1-5225-6029-6.chrmm

*This content has been removed at the
discretion of the publisher and the editors.*

This content has been removed at the discretion of the publisher and the editors.

This content has been removed at the discretion of the publisher and the editors.

This content has been removed at the discretion of the publisher and the editors.

This content has been removed at the discretion of the publisher and the editors.

This content has been removed at the discretion of the publisher and the editors.

This content has been removed at the discretion of the publisher and the editors.

This content has been removed at the discretion of the publisher and the editors.

This content has been removed at the discretion of the publisher and the editors.

This content has been removed at the discretion of the publisher and the editors.

This content has been removed at the discretion of the publisher and the editors.

This content has been removed at the discretion of the publisher and the editors.

This content has been removed at the discretion of the publisher and the editors.

This content has been removed at the discretion of the publisher and the editors.

This content has been removed at the discretion of the publisher and the editors.

This content has been removed at the discretion of the publisher and the editors.

This content has been removed at the discretion of the publisher and the editors.

This content has been removed at the discretion of the publisher and the editors.

This content has been removed at the discretion of the publisher and the editors.

This content has been removed at the discretion of the publisher and the editors.

This content has been removed at the discretion of the publisher and the editors.

Chapter 6
An Analysis on Risk Management and Risk in the Software Projects

Rajshree Srivastava
Chandigarh University, India

ABSTRACT

Controlling risk in software project is considered to be a major contributor for a project success. This chapter reconsiders the status of risk and its management in the science and literature. The survey is supported by the recent study of risk practices in government agencies in India, thereby contributing to a gap in research in the public sector. After the study, it is found that the risk is barely been conceived in research. The findings which were found are considered to be a challenging situation for risk management and to project management. Further, it was noticed that software projects do not follow a uniform structure which introduces variations in the risk and projects. Risk management research is not efficient in terms of practice. Directions and implication for the research and practice are discussed in this chapter.

INTRODUCTION

Software projects are considered to be one of the high-risk activities which generates different outcomes of different performance (Charette et al., 2005) According to the survey, it was found from the report of the industry that only quarter of the software projects are successful and rest around billions of dollars are lost annually some due to the project failure or result failure. The commitment of the risk management to the commercial software industry is that it will make the quality of the software

DOI: 10.4018/978-1-5225-6029-6.ch006

product best and delivery on time. Risk management can give benefits to wide range of projects and organization by:

1. Identification of favorable alternative course of action
2. Higher success rate
3. Cost efficient
4. Higher efficiency rate

This chapter makes two contributions, first is on review, analysis on software project risk, risk management and second on the experimental study of risk management practices which is being assessed against the prescriptions in literature. After the thorough analysis, result and conclusion can be drawn for the future research work.

The chapter consists of the following contents: literature; findings; comparison on the practices which are prescribed; limitations; future research work and conclusion.

LITERATURE REVIEW

In this section there is a study of the importance of risk and risk management, limitations in the risk, concept of risk in the project and finally the limitation are being discussed in comparison based on the practice.

Risk

In software projects the term risk is being defined as exposure to specific factors that present a threat in achieving the expected outcomes of any project (Grady et al., 1987). Risk is an uncertain event that occurs if measures are not taken. The result of improper management of risk will lead to failure of the product, loss of the efficiency in the result and so on. One of the limitations of risk is that it is considered very difficult to estimate the impact of probability of risk factors on the software projects which are designed (Fairbanks et al., 2010). The problem to this limitation can be solved by having different variation of probable outcomes rather than depending on one particular probability result.

Why are risk and risk management are considered to be important?

Risk plays an important role for developing any software. Risk management is the steps taken while developing software so that the risk is minimized. Project risk management is a formal notation to manage identifiable risk factors which identifies and respond to the risk of the project throughout (Juarez et al., 2012). It has three four phases namely risk identification, risk assessment, and prioritization, risk response planning i.e. management and documentation and learning.

- **Risk Identification:** This is the first step of risk management whose aim is to identify risk that can create problem, disturbance to the project success. The risks which are being identified are recorded in the form of list with its nature and consequences of each and every risk. This helps us to mitigate the risks which are being identified (Marcu et al., 2010). The records of risk are known as "generic" template which are considered to be one of the powerful way of storing risk occurred and thus will be helpful for the researchers. The steps for the risk management of the project are presented in Figure 1.

- **Risk Assessment and Prioritization:** This step identifies which risk has how much impact on the event of the project. RISK prioritization is being classified according to the impact. The one with high loss will be "1" and so on.

- **Risk Response Planning:** The risk is being categorized into two groups namely risk which are under control and the other one which is under non-controllable. If the cause is under control the team member of the project attempt to prevent the occurrence of the risk, if it is not then the team has to deal with the effects of the risk if they occur (Hong et al., 2009). Here the project risk management will suggest by identifying an alternative course of action in the planning phase so that the risk can be avoided.

A generic table is being recorded in Table 1.

Software Risk Management

It is defined as a set of principles and practices which aim to identify, analyze and handle risk factors to improve the chances of achieving a successful project and failure of any project or software (Boehm et al., 1978). There are four inter-related approaches which are in common practice these include checklists, analytical frameworks, process models and risk response strategies.

Figure 1. Risk management steps of project

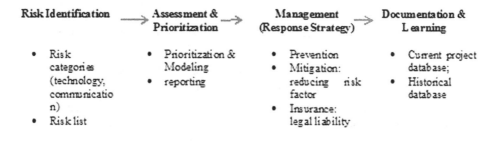

Table 1. A generic table

Categories of Risk	Subcategories
Substance and Production	
Ingredients	Risk from suppliers (i.e. dependency), stability (shell life)
Final product	Formulation change, risk from suppliers, stability
Analytical method	License problem
Regulatory issues	Mixtures, impurity limits
Phase I	Pharmacokinetics
Phase II	Exposure duration
Phase III	Study delay, regulatory requirements
Common regulatory risks	Process time
General Risk	
License	dependency
Trademarks	Visibility/ acceptance of trademark
Cost	currencies

- **Checklist**: It list the top risks, success factor of the projects and the remedial steps. It is being maintained as a record having previous and present details and being updated after each and every new product launched in the market (Fairbanks et al., 2010). The main advantage of the checklist is that it provides low cost way of identifying and assessing the exposure of the risk of any project against major factors.
- **Analytical Frameworks**: It gives the environment for the processes to work efficiently. Each project has its framework where it is first being designed and then further the work is processed.
- **Process Models:** There role is to specify each to individual about the activities which are necessary to manage risk in the software projects these include risk identification, analysis and so on (Duffy et al., 2012). They also manage the activities how it should be sequenced so that it can effectively manage risk and suggest tools, techniques to avoid risk in project.
- **Risk Response Strategies**: It aims is to reduce or eliminate threats which occur frequently. There are four common risk response strategies which are mostly considered:
- **Avoidance**: Its aim is to prevent negative effect which occur in the project and thus impact the project. For example, there might occur a chance to change or design a fresh new project design under un-avoidable circumstances so that risk can be reduced.

- **Transference**: It involves passing the responsibility to a third party. This cannot be concluded that the threat is eliminated; it simply passes the responsibility to a higher management for the further best result. Some of strategies include insurance, warranties, etc.
- **Mitigation**: Sometimes there is requirement of the project to design in such a way that they work independently and function properly. So, designing of the project must be done effectively.

STUDY

The survey is conducted in one of the government agencies in India on software project and risk management practices. The reason for choosing state government was to notice the success and failure rate in software projects in recent years. Government's CIO office gives access to the project agency. Agencies are responsible for their own system work that's why they are considered to be semi-autonomous. The work of the central CIO office is to provide agencies with a policy framework for their project fund for special work which they have taken (Wasserman et al., 2010). They are also invited to participate in the study by nominating one of the best projects among recent completed software projects.

As soon as access and availability of information problem was solved, the study comprised 23 informative perspectives on 17 projects from 17 agencies. One project is being contributed by 10 agencies and three agencies contribute two projects each.

Interviews are being conducted based on the information gathered and case study was introduced based on the project which is designed. The interview contains 150 questions in 9 domain topic areas: development, organization, and project, risk management, information, governance, involvement of third parties and so on (Wasserman et al., 2010). These questions are being raised to know about the status of their project, how they have worked on project management and risk management. For the easy collection of records, participants were asked question to give answer in range from (1 to 10). These were ranked as 1 with the lowest value recorded and 10 with the highest value recorded. For example, if question is being asked: whether the project was completed on time? If the response is true and efficient it was ranked as 10 and so on for the further question asked regarding project. The interview with the participants was around 3 hours and every response was recorded for the analysis of the project. The researchers ordered new antique theme into 10 categories which are related to software project risk factors. Table 2, follows summary of the profile of State government agencies and projects which were included in the study.

Profile of the Agency

Some of the agencies were having small group of employees around 32 employees and some were having large group having 1000 or more. The average size was 650. Table 2 shows a list of agencies which have < 5000 employees.

- **Project Management Experience:** The experience of the manager was around 5-10 years list is shown in Table 2.

Project Profile

For the study, two types of software project were defined as project involving software development and custom-build application system.

- **Project Scope:** Majority of the projects was involved in development or implementation phase of the software or may be both.
- **Applications:** Applications which were taken into consideration were transaction-based system development, packaged implemented dominated project and web application development as shown in the Table 2.
- **Size of the Project:** Most of the projects were completed within 1 year. Some of the projects were very long based for these questions were based on their implementation phase and on the completion phase.
- **Third Parties Involvement:** Around 13 projects were having involvement of third party vendor and most of them were vendor and developer.
- **Executive Involvement:** In the survey it was found that one third of projects had direct involvement of CEO or its equivalent, 50 percent of the project has involvement of senior executive. While most of the senior employed person was involved in the project as a business unit manager.

FINDINGS

In this part there were three findings. First one is related to key practice areas, second with risk factors which were found and last with unexpected findings of multiple different projects based on risk and project management.

Table 2. Study Profile

STUDY	Percentage
Members in Agency	
< 999	50
1000 - 4999	38
5000 - 9999	6
10,000 - 99,999	0
> 100,000	6
CIO Reporting Level	
CEO	38
Director Division	56
Business Unit Manager	6
Study Informants	
Project Manager	70
IT Manager	22
Business Manager	8
Experience of Project Management	
<two years	12
Two-five years	18
Five- ten years	35
> ten years	35
Scope of Project	
Development and Implementation	53
Implementation phase only	32
Development phase only	10
Others	5
Application Part of the Project	
Web-based	35
Transaction-based	29
Package implementation	24
Data publishing	6
Duration to Complete Project	
< six months	22
Six-twelve months	34
One-two years	22
> two years	22
Executive Involvement in the Project	
CEO	33
Division Director	50
Business Unit Manager	17

Key Practice Areas

Practice area is being conducted and summarized in Table 3.

In the table 3, the column responses recorded were the actual response gained from the participants and range is the spread of scores from all the participants.

- **Outcome of the Project:** In this response the average marks given was 8 if the project is successful. Any further increment is based on the successful rate and on the objective of the problem. Further, for any initial startup of the project a budget is being decided for the project so according to that if the project is completed within the budget average response recoded is 8. Duration of the project plays a vital role, any project must be completed within the duration assigned, if it takes longer time than the assigned duration it should be with the valid reason, so average response recorded for this is 8 if its duration is within the assigned duration. Scope and objective of the project should be clear to team members and as well as to the project head. Average response recorded for this task is 8 if the vision is clear and is implemented in the project.

- **Governance of the Project:** In this category three person were involved to govern the project namely steering committee, project sponsor and top management involvement. The role of project sponsor help in the project completion and supports financially to the team members and also helps in launching project successfully in the market. Steering committee also helps in the completion of the project assigned. Top management helps in the guidance of the project and provides necessary raw materials required for the project. They all were being ranked according to their work and average response recorded is 7.

- **Project Management:** The response for the project management was found to be lower than those for project outcome. Responses recorded for these were on the questions related to the management strategy, methodology being adopted, plan adopted for the project to make it successful. The lowest score being recorded was 6.5 having range of scores from 1-10.

- **Risk Management:** While designing any project both pros and cons should be taken into consideration. Designing of any software project should be in such a manner that the risk is minimum (Spriestersbach et al., 2004). Risk should be recorded and mitigation steps should be taken. A record is supposed to be maintained so that all the risks occurred so far is noted down, and whatever steps being taken for that particular risk should be kept in view of the designer and as well as to the team member. This will help to achieve efficiency in the project. In the study it was found that small amount of risk

Table 3. Responses in key practices involved

Questions	Response Recorded	Range
Outcome of the Project		
Was the project objective is solved?	8	5-9
Do business objective is successfully achieved?	8.9	7-10
Do the project is completed within cost decided?	9	6-10
Does the project is completed in the schedule duration?	8.4	7-10
Does scope of the project is taken into consideration?	8.8	6-10
Governance of the Project		
Does the steering committee was effective?	7.9	3-10
Does the project sponsor was effective?	8	1-10
Do top management support was there throughout the duration of project?	9.2	4-10
How was the top-management involved in the project throughout the journey?	7.7	3-10
Did his/her commitment or involvement was benefit for the project?	7.9	1-10
Project Management		
Do the project managed well?	7.8	6-9
Does the aim of the project was clear to the project manager?	7	4-10
Was the methodology applied correct?	7.4	1-10
Do project can handle any new change in future?	8.2	2-10
Do any pre-project review held?	6.5	1-10
Risk Management		
Did there is any specific methodology adopted by risk management?	4.6	1-10
Does the risks being identified in the start of the project?	6.9	1-10
Does risk is being managed throughout the project?	6.6	1-10
Does risk is being prioritized according to its nature?	5.3	1-10
Does the project follow any mitigation plan?	7.6	1-10
Is there any person involved to look after the monitoring risks?	6.4	1-10
Does any unanticipated problems were raised during the project?	7.7	1-10
Implementation		
Do the implementation phase was easy?	6.5	2-10
Do the implementation phase was successful?	8.4	4-10
What was the impact on the organization of your project?	7.1	2-10
Does the strategic objective was having any significant role?	7.9	2-10
How well the organization changes were managed?	6.9	4-9
Third Party Involvement		
Does the third party is having any role in the project?	7.5	2-10
Does the third party manage properly with the management?	8.1	5-10
Does third party contribution play any role for the project?	7	6-9

was practiced in five projects, no risk management was practiced in other five projects and rest have adopted a semi-formal practice (Zibula et al., 2013). The result of the responses is recorded in Table 3. A conclusion from this study is that the project manager did not consider risk management as an important factor, it should be considered as important key component while designing any software project else the result of the successful project will be very less.

- **Implementation:** The success rate of the system which was implemented was high (response recorded 8.4), consistent with the perceptions for the above and it was also noted that the implementation for the project was not a very difficult part on their hand (average response recoded 6.5). In most of the cases around (69%), change in the organization management was governed by individual either proactively or reactively as the system was introduced.
- **Involvement of Third Parties:** Most of project was having involvement of third party. After the study it was found that the result was effective with some variations which can be ignored under some circumstances. Response can be seen in Table 3.

Major Risk Factors

There were around 10 risk factors which were found 4 during the analysis of project; it is summarized in Table 4. The table shows risk factors of 17 projects which were involved. They all were found to be one of factor to reduce software risk while developing new software. Each category is being introduced briefly below.

Table 4. Major risk factors occurred

Categories of Risk Factor	Occurrences in the Project
Governance of project	12
Setup of project	9
Engagement of partners	8
Proprietorship of business	11
Management of project	9
Change management	10
Management of projects	11
Recognition of red flags	15
Risk management	14
Benefits of realization	8

- **Governance of Project:** Project and as well as project members face a lot of problem if the governance bodies are not efficient and does not provide proper guide in the complete duration of project (Spielberg et al., 2009). If the governance is efficient project will have clarity, vision will be clear and the output received (i.e., the project) will be best.

- **Project SETUP:** Many projects face problem when the setup of the project is poor. So, the setup of the project should be clear.

- **Partner Engagement:** Many project members try to engage third party member to work with them. They can be considered as one of the project asset depending upon how they work (Robertson et al., 2006). Some agencies try to divide work by involving third party member and have result. Sometimes it may be risk or may be productive.

- **Business Proprietorship:** Ownership of the business, sponsorship and participation were found to be critical risk factor for the project. Many project managers believe that the success of the project, depends upon committed and capable business sponsorship plays a vital role.

- **Project Management:** Performance and outcome of the software projects are found to be critical by project management experience and its capability.

- **Change Management:** Due to the improper management of organization, many projects face implementation and user related issues. Projects have less chance of implementation problems if organization changed is managed concurrently from the starting of the project to the end of the project.

- **Management of Projects:** Project management is defined as a formal methodology or practices involved in making the project successful. After the study it was found that formula methods should be used only where there is requirement.

- **Management of Risks:** The aim should not be just identifying the risk but it should also be able to place mitigation and contingency strategies. Whenever any threat is raised it should quickly respond. It might be possible that these threats may or may not harm the project but has the ability to affect the project completely.

Types of Project

There are four different project types which are found in the study namely 'pure' project form, operational activity, breakthrough activity and hybrid form (Fernandes et al., 2015). The characteristics of these project types are having different challenges and issues with respect to risk management and project. These four different types of projects are being summarized in table 5.

Table 5. Types of project

Types	Features			
	'Pure' Project Form	**Hybrid Form**	**Operational Activity**	**Break-Through Activity**
Characteristics	Discrete, structured, operated, temporary activity, managed under conventional project management disciplines.	Having features of both 'pure' project form and operational activity, work independently.	Executed by functional units.	Short- time frame is used, focused mainly to small designated team.
Count of projects	Five	Six	Five	one
Time horizon	Variable	Short-medium	Short-medium	short
Control of locus	Governance framework and project manager.	Functional management and project.	Line management	executive
Risk management	Normal	Within control	Within control	intuitive
Project management	Normal	Within control	Un controllable	none
Advantage	Objective of the project is achieved.	They use specialist resources.	Mainly focuses on operational effort further avoids artificial overheads	Give its full effort to give quick result.
Weakness	Depended on third party.	Difficult to enforce accountability	Project and risk management risk	Project and risk management risk
Challenges	Risk management skills, achieving/ maintaining project.	Resource demands.	Quality control	Risk management.

- **'Pure' Project Form:** It is one of the type of project which is based on traditional approach i.e. well-structured and managed under risk management disciplines and practices. In the study there were 5 types of project which were acknowledged (Wasserman et al., 2010). Pure project form has one advantage that is it enables attention and gives more attention and effort towards the objective of the project so that it can have normal distortion. Dis-advantage of this project is that it involves participation of stakeholders from outside of the project team assigned.

- **Hybrid Form:** It is a combination of both 'pure' project form and as well as operational activity. In this core project exist, but the project parts are been delivered one by one and operate independently (Spiliotopoulos et al., 2010). Total six projects were found in the study out of which 5 projects were formal or informal risk management and one with practiced no risk management. The main challenges which hybrid form face was to balance objective, practices and resource demands. Longer the duration of project, greater will be the challenges to fulfill the demands on the specialist resource; this becomes a challenge for the risk management.

- **Operational Activity:** In this activity the project is being executed by functional units with their organizational structure. Five projects of this type were found in the survey, three where with no risk management and two was having informal risk management. The main challenge for this type of project was regarding balancing of operational practices with the accountability for project delivery and as well as with the project delivery. Sometimes practices, objective and structures do not meet with the requirement as they were not directly linked with the functional unit this leads to failure of the project.

- **Breakthrough Event:** This is the last project type. In this project there is a small group of members which are dedicated towards their work and aims to achieve specific and high priority objective based on practices and methods. There was only one project in the survey. One of the biggest advantages about this project is that it focuses on quick result. Their aim is to achieve high with successful result in a short duration of time.

DISCUSSIONS

In this chapter for the literature risk, risk management is examined and for the study, software projects government agencies of India were taken for the complete study. There are three conclusions which are drawn after the study: firstly, the risk management plays an important role in any software development phase or in project. Secondly, the risk and risk management theory studied is not sufficient to handle threats associated with the uncertainties faced by software projects. Third, the understanding and assumptions of risk and risk management is not sufficient in the literature of research.

Limitations of the Study

The findings of the experimental results need to be understand carefully as it has some limitations. Firstly, the result is based on the public sector which may be false. Secondly, the sampled data is very small, is not randomized and is dominant by the cases that were interpreted by the participants to make it successful (Heitkotter et al., 2013). This may further result in biased result after the study. Third, the study is totally focused on software project only. They have not given any importance to infrastructure, outsourcing projects, process redesign as these are also considered important factor for the development of project.

RESEARCH SIGNIFICANCE

After the complete survey the chapter provides some relevant research areas to the researcher in the domain.

- In the chapter it was found that the project managers were more concerned about the magnitude of probable impacts, further the risk practices which were there in software projects does not focus on the current view, they adopt more quantitative assessment of risk.
- From the literature review and from the response recorded it was noted that the scope of risk management is being precisely compared with the threats that can impact the software projects. So, there is opportunity for the researcher to further extend the scope of threat management with the support of software projects.
- The chapter suggests that there is a requirement for further research on the project management and integration of the risk.
- The chapter suggests that agencies expectation is very high from the engineering solutions to the management problems. For the managers the engineering based tools and techniques are easy to work upon it but it is not useful for the one who is unskilled. It will take more time, tools and techniques should be used which are useable to all the team members.
- The young professional would gain benefit from the further research which will focus on end to end execution and also front-end risk evaluation and monitoring processes.

Practice Implications

- In the chapter it was found that the organizations were not able to handle full application knowledge in practice which leads to increase in the risk management. For example, in the initial ground risk was identified but later that risk was further not studied throughout the project.
- One of the ways to reduce the risk can be to have pre-evaluation of the project in between so that if there is any further requirement to adopt some methodology it will be implemented successfully.
- One of the challenge which the organization face about the business executive and managers is that they only focus and care about the outcome. At any cost they want outcome from any means that did not consider the risk which they will face later on. So if the project is launched successfully that could be said as a luck for the organization.

- Pre-evaluation of the project is a kind of opportunity for re-evaluating and improving the risk management processes, its strategies, tools and techniques which can be beneficial for the project outcome.
- The manager should develop such a strategy that the risk which are not been identified should be identified and work should be taken on spot to reduce that risk.
- Project handlers and manager of risk should not wait for the researcher to meet out there needs.
- Project handlers should themselves work upon it, gain experience and face the challenges and lays their own mitigation plans for the success of software project.

CONCLUSION

This chapter survey and reassessed the present status of research in risk management in the literature on some software projects of Indian center agencies. It can be said that the software projects are complex, multi-dimensional that is susceptible to failure. The risk of the threat found in the projects should take seriously and mitigation should be followed to achieve beneficial outcomes of the project. In the development of risk and management of risk it is found that was not successful result when it comes in terms of practice.The members of the software project development must learn from each other to reduce the failure rate of the project and practice on the project to make them successful by adopting better risk management.

REFRENCES

Bhullar, R. K., Pawar, L., Bajaj, R., & Manocha, A. K. (2017). Intelligent stress calculation and scheduling in segmented processor systems using buddy approach. *Journal of Intelligent & Fuzzy Systems*, *32*(4), 3129–3142. doi:10.3233/JIFS-169256

Boehm, B. W. (1978). *Characteristics of software quality*. North Holland.

Charland, A., & Leroux, B. (2011). Mobile application development: Web vs. native. *Communications of the ACM*, *54*(5), 49–53. doi:10.1145/1941487.1941504

Duffy, T. (2012). *Programming with mobile applications: Android, iOS, and Windows Phone 7. Boston*, MA: CengageLearning.

Fairbanks, G. (2010). *Just-enough software architecture: A risk-driven approach*. Boulder, CO: Marshall &Brainerd.

Fernandes, J. M., & Machado, R. J. (2015). *Requirements in engineering projects.* Springer; doi:10.1007/978-3-319-18597-2

Gabbard, J. L., Fitch, G. M., & Hyungil, K. (2014). Behind the glass: Driver challenges and opportunities for AR automotive applications. *Proceedings of the IEEE, 102*(2), 124–136. doi:10.1109/ JPROC.2013.2294642

Grady, R., & Caswell, D. (1987). *Software metrics: Establishing a company-wide program.* Upper Saddle River, NJ: Prentice Hall.

Heitkötter, H., Hanschke, S., & Majchrzak, T. A. (2013). Evaluating cross-platform developmentap-proachesfor mobile applications. In *Proceedings of the 8th International Conference on Web Information Systems and Technologies, LNBIP* (*Vol. 140*, pp. 120–138).Springer.10.1007/978-3-642-36608-6_8

Hong, J., Suh, E., & Kim, S. J. (2009). Context-aware systems: A literature review and classification. *Expert Systems with Applications, 36*(4), 8509–8522. doi:10.1016/j. eswa.2008.10.071

Juárez-Ramírez, R., Licea, G., Barriba, I., Izquierdo, V., & Angeles, A. (2012). Orchestrating mobile applications: A software engineering view. In R. Aquino-Santos & A.E. Block (Eds.), Embedded systems and wireless technology: Theory and practical applications (pp. 41–72). Boca Raton, FL: CRC Press. doi:10.1201/ b12298-3

Koren, I., & Krishna, C. M. (2010). *Fault-tolerant systems.* San Francisco, CA: Morgan Kaufmann.

Marcu, M., Tudor, D., & Fuicu, S. (2010). A view on power efficiency of multimedia mobile applications. In K. Elleithy (Ed.), Advanced Techniques in Computing Sciences and Software Engineering (pp. 407–412). Springer. doi:10.1007/978-90-481-3660-5_70

Meyer, B. (2019). *Touch of class: Learning to program well with objects and contracts.* Berlin: Springer.

Robertson, S., & Robertson, J. C. (2006). *Mastering the requirements process* (2nd ed.). Boston, MA: Addison-Wesley.

Roman, G. (1985). A taxonomy of current issues in requirements engineering. *IEEE Computer, 18*(4), 14–23. doi:10.1109/MC.1985.1662861

Spielberg, R. F. (2009). *Handbook of reliability, availability, maintainability and safety in engineering design.* London: Springer.

Spiliotopoulos, T., Papadopoulou, P., Martakos, D., & Kouroupetroglou, G. (2010). *Integrating usability engineering for designing the Web experience: Methodologies and principles*. Hershey, PA: IGI Global. doi:10.4018/978-1-60566-896-3

Spriestersbach, A., & Springer, T. (2004). Quality attributes in mobile web application development. In Product Focused Software Process Improvement, *LNCS* (Vol. *3009*, pp. 120-130). doi:10.1007/978-3-540-24659-6_9

Taivalsaari, A., & Systä, K. (2012). Cloudberry: An HTML 5 cloud phone platform for mobile devices. *IEEE Software*, *29*(4), 40–45. doi:10.1109/MS.2012.51

Wasserman, A. I. (2010). Software engineering issues for mobile application development. *FSE/SDP Workshop on Future of Software Engineering Research* (pp. 397-400). doi:10.1145/1882362.1882443

Zibula, A., & Majchrzak, T. (2013). Cross-platform development using HTML5, jQuery Mobile, and Phone Gap: Realizing a smart meter application. In Web Information Systems and Technologies, *LNBIP* (Vol. *140*, pp. 16-33). doi:10.1007/978-3-642-36608-6_2

KEY TERMS AND DEFINATIONS

Risk: Any exposure to some specific factor which will create hindrance while achieving the expected outcomes of a project.

Risk Management: It is defined as set of principles and practices whose aim is to identify, analyze and handle risk factors so as to deliver a best software project.

Chapter 7
New Classification of Security Requirements for Quantitative Risk Assessment

Neila Rjaibi
ISG, Tunisia

Latifa Ben Arfa Rabai
ISG, Tunisia

ABSTRACT

Objective assessment metrics are continuously recommended and a financial analysis of the risk is required in order to justify the security improvements. It is, thus, critically important to validate the security applications as trustworthy and to generalize this research work to other systems. The chapter addresses firstly the problem of quantifying the security of large scale systems, originally the level of e-learning systems. The risk analysis model considers the variability between the system's stakeholders, the requirements, the components and the security attacks. But, in case of large systems, other security challenges are crucially important to be considered. Indeed, our risk analysis model is strengthened to include the development of new requirements classification.

INTRODUCTION

We focus on measuring (quantify, assess) the system's security economically. It refers to the development of security metrics for cost benefit analysis in order to determine the level of risk involved. We offer a quantitative and objective basis for security assurance and report it in practice (Rjaibi and Rabai, 2015a, 2015b).

DOI: 10.4018/978-1-5225-6029-6.ch007

An economic dynamic model for information security risk analysis and management is developed. It helps in defining the assets, measuring economically the risk, managing the risk toward decisions making. It is illustrated originally to the level of e-Learning systems, more precisely to the popular and current LMS architectures, because it lacks a measurable value and evidence of cyber security. Our model is simple and relies on a few number of inputs which form the system's security specifications and provide one output which is the average loss per unit of time ($/H) incurred by a stakeholder as a result of security threats. We create an original version of the model using as a basis the Mean Failure Cost metric. Our risk management model serves as an explanation tool of the structural relation between security specifications and cost. It serves as a decision support tool which expands security investments (Rjaibi and Rabai, 2015 a, b).

But being a large-scale system other security measures and challenges are considered. Our model is enhanced and enriched to incorporate the development of important security metrics. Cost effectiveness metrics are enriched with a new hierarchical security requirements classification.

Objective assessment metrics are continuously recommended and a financial analysis of the risk is required in order to justify the security improvements. It is, thus, critically important to validate the security of their applications as trustworthy and to generalize this research work to other systems.

This chapter underscores:

- The security requirements models
- The developing of a holistic security requirements taxonomy
- The illustration of a quantitative risk analysis model using the novel taxonomy
- The impact of the taxonomy in leading precise evaluation and more efficient decisions

SECURITY REQUIREMENTS MODELS

We intend to present a summary of security requirements' models. They form constraints on the system's functions into multi levels classification.

The ISO 7498, 1989

This standard model provides a description of security services (ISO 7498-2,1989; Firesmith, 2003; Sekaran, 2007):

- Authentication (Identification)

- Authorization: ability to access particular resource
- Confidentiality (Privacy)
- Integrity: (Modification of data)
- Non-Repudiation: (Deny sending)
- Availability
- Security auditing

The CIA Triad Model

The confidentiality, integrity and availability model forms a basis in information security. It contains trio requirements and may cover other like: Accountability and Non-Repudiation (Stoneburner et al., 2001).

The Parkerian Hexad, Donn Parker, 2002

In 2002, Donn Parker proposed an alternative model for the classic CIA triad that he called the six atomic elements of information or the Parkerian hexad, it is a set of six elements of information security. The Parkerian hexad adds three additional attributes to the three classic security attributes of the CIA triad (confidentiality, integrity, availability) (Jule et al., 2010).

The list of security requirements:

- Confidentiality
- Possession
- Integrity
- Authenticity
- Availability
- Utility

New security requirements are explained as follow:

Possession or Control: "…suppose a thief were to steal a sealed envelope containing a bank debit card and its personal identification number. Even if the thief did not open that envelope, it's reasonable for the foolish victim to be concerned that the thief could do so at any time. That situation illustrates a loss of control or possession of information but does not involve the breach of confidentiality…" (Jule et al., 2010).

Utility means usefulness. "…for example, suppose someone encrypted data on disk to prevent unauthorized access or undetected modifications and then lost the decryption key: that would be a breach of utility. The data would be confidential, controlled, integral, authentic, and available they just wouldn't be useful in that form…"

Software Requirements

This model is proposed by Alam (2010) and forms 9 requirements as presented in Table 1:

- To explain the fair exchange by an example, "…the buyer or supplier should be able to prove that the payment is made or not, good is supplied or not, and to reclaim the money if the payment or good is not delivered…"
- Freshness means fresh information (Alam, 2010).
- Secure Information Flow: High data may influence low data, but it is not possible for the opposite case (Alam, 2010).
- Guarded Access is a fundamental requirement is information security. It refers to the ability to access a system

Taxonomy of Security Quality (Firesmith, 2004)

Firesmith also defined a detailed quality model for security and survivability. The model describes relation between concepts that contribute to systemic qualities (Christian, 2010). According to Firesmith indicates that his classification in terms of quality factors forms significant requirements (Firesmith, 2004). It is very useful during the requirement elicitation phase.

1. **Access Control:** Possibility in reducing access to resource only for permitted users:
   a. Identification is "the degree to which the system identifies (i.e., recognizes) its externals before interacting with them."
   b. Authentication is "the degree to which the system verifies the identities of its externals before interacting with them."
   c. Authorization is "the degree to which access and usage privileges of authenticated externals are properly granted and enforced."
2. Attack Detection
3. Integrity means defense from intentional and unauthorized corruption:
   a. Data Integrity
   b. Hardware Integrity
   c. Personnel Integrity
   d. Software Integrity
4. **Non-Repudiation:** Refuse the transaction
5. Privacy
   a. Anonymity
   b. Confidentiality

6. Security Auditing is the degree to which security personnel are enabled to audit the status and use of security mechanisms by analysing security-related events.

7. Physical Protection is the degree to which the system protects itself and its components from physical attack

The Accelerated Requirements

Mead and Hough, 2005 (ARM) list the groups and the requirements contained in each:

- **Group A:** Confidentiality
- **Group B:** Access control
- **Group C:** Data integrity
- **Group D:** Manageability
- **Group E:** Usability
- **Group F:** Authentication

Software Security Requirement's Taxonomy (Caldern and Marta, 2007)

This taxonomy incorporates four items which are refined in the second level (Caldern and Marta, 2007)

1. **Non-Repudiation:** "Non-repudiation refers to the situation in which a person cannot claim to have not performed some action."
2. **Integrity:** "Are required to restrict actions threatening integrity"
   a. **Modification Requirements:** For example, the application should not allow customers to modify the sale price.
   b. **Deletion:** Example, "The system shall not allow users delete historic accounting records generated during the last five years"
   c. **Datum Validation Requirements:** Example: "The system shall not allow users input strings longer than required length."
   d. **Exception Handling Requirements:** Verifying the values of '0' in inputs
   e. **Prerequisite Requirements:** For example, "A user request must be authorized before being processed." Example: The system shall not allow users to withdraw money from their account before the system checks funds availability
   f. **Separation of Duty Requirements:** Example: "Application shall not allow a Purchase Department member to use account payable system options"

    g.   **Temporal Requirements:** Example: "System shall not allow stock exchange transactions outside normal stock exchange hours"

3.   **Availability:** It guarantees the continuity of the service and covers three criteria which are: (Response time requirements, Expiration requirements and Resource allocation requirements)

4.   **Confidentiality**

    a.   **Encryption Requirements:** Application should guarantee the encryption of sensitive data

    b.   **Authentication Requirements:** Authentication is "concerned with ensuring that users are who they say they are, and remain so during the session"

    c.   **Aggregation Requirements:** The system cannot provide a large number of records

    d.   **Attribution Requirements:** Checking the access to the log files

    e.   **Cardinality Requirements:** Application need verifies the number of simultaneous connections for a user

Ontology Framework of Security Requirements (Lasheras, 2009)

Modeling security requirements is improved by semantic web technologies. Lasheras (2009) describes an ontology-based framework for representing and reusing security requirements based on risk analysis.

Lasheras, presents an ontological representation for security requirements, this facilitate the determination of inconsistency in requirements and also the semantic processing in requirements analysis. This contribution leads to rigorous NLP (Natural Language Processing). The implementation of the ontology is based on the OWL language standard, IEEE and ISO27002 standard (Lasheras, 2009). It forms basic presentation that could be refined in later time and will be useful for other refinements in the system or in the quantification of threats.

Security Requirements Reusability and the SQUARE Methodology, Travis Christian, 2010

The elements are (Christian, 2010):

- Confidentiality
- Integrity
- Availability

- Accountability
- Conformance

DEVELOPING A HOLISTIC SECURITY REQUIREMENTS TAXONOMY

Discussing Security Requirements Models and Taxonomy

We intend to enrich security metrics with a new hierarchical security requirements classification.

- Privacy
- Integrity
- Non-repudiation refers to the situation in which a person cannot claim to have not per-formed some action
- Availability: System content must be available, for example when a user takes a course, obtains data or a service through an online e-learning system, this service needs to be available in reasonable time
- Resource allocation, expiration and Response time (Caldern and Marta, 2007)
- Manageability:
  - ◦ Auditing (ISO 7498-2, 1989; Firesmith, 2004)
  - ◦ Accountability (Travis, 2010)
- Access control:
  - ◦ Authorization
  - ◦ Identification
  - ◦ Authentication (Identification)
- Physical Protection:
- Attack Detection:
- Usability (usefulness, utility)
- Manageable security, Available security, Consistent APTs and Reduce risks
- Fair Exchange
- Freshness (Alam, 2010).
- Secure Information Flow (Alam, 2010).
- Conformance (Alam, 2010).

Security Requirements Factors and Sub-Factors: A Survey

Table 1, presents security requirements factors and sub-factors.

Table 1. The construction of the holistic taxonomy of security requirements

Security Requirement Factors	References	Security Requirement Sub-factors	References	References Relation between (Factor-Sub factor)
Privacy	ISO 7498 -2:1989 CIA triad Donn Parker Firesmith Mead and Hough Travis Christian	Anonymity	Firesmith	
		Confidentiality	Firesmith Mead and Hough	
		Encryption		Caldern and Marta
		Aggregation		Caldern and Marta
		Attribution		Caldern and Marta
		Consent and notification		Caldern and Marta
		Cardinality		Caldern and Marta
		Traces		Caldern and Marta
				Caldern and Marta
Integrity	ISO 7498 -2:1989 CIA triad Donn Parker J. Jurjens Firesmith Mead and Hough Caldern and Marta Travis Christian ISO 7498 -2:1989	Data		Firesmith Caldern and Marta
		Hardware		Firesmith
		Personal		Firesmith
		Software		Firesmith
Non-repudiation	J. Jurjens Firesmith Caldern and Marta ISO 7498 -2:1989			
Availability	ISO 7498 -2:1989	Response time		Caldern and Marta
	CIA triad	Expiration		Caldern and Marta
	Donn Parker	Resource allocation		Caldern and Marta
Manageability	Travis Christian Mead and Hough	Security Auditing	ISO 7498 -2:1989 Firesmith	Mead and Hough
		Accountability	Travis Christian	Mead and Hough

continued on following page

Table 1. Continued

Security Requirement Factors	References	Security Requirement Sub-factors	References	References Relation between (Factor-Sub factor)
Access control)	Donn Parker J. Jurjens Firesmith Mead and Hough	Authentication (Identification)	ISO 7498 -2:1989 Donn Parker J. Jurjens Mead and Hough	Firesmith
		Identification	Firesmith	
		Authorization	ISO 7498 -2:1989	Firesmith
Physical Protection	Firesmith			
Attack/Harm Detection	Firesmith			
Usability (usefulness, utility)	Donn Parker	Manageable security		Mead and Hough
		Security is available		Mead and Hough
		Consistent Application Programming Interfaces		Mead and Hough
		Reduce risk		Mead and Hough
Fair Exchange	J. Jurjens			
Freshness	J. Jurjens			
Secure Information Flow	J. Jurjens			
Conformance	Travis Christian			

Proposed Holistic Security Requirements Taxonomy

Table 2 proposes a classification of security requirements in two levels (level one includes 13 criteria or requirements, level 2 forms thirty-one requirement, the model serves as a standard one.

Comparative Study and Contribution

We compare our proposed model and contribution versus the literature (Table 2).

Table 2. The proposed holistic model

Conformance	Conformance		
Secure Information Flow	Secure Information Flow		
Freshness	Freshness		
Faire Exchange	Faire Exchange		
Usability	Reduce Risk		
	Application Programming Interfaces		
	Available Security		
	Manageable Security		
Attack finding	Attack/Harm Detection		
Physical defend	Physical Protection		
Access Control	Authorization		
	Identification		
	Authentication		
Manageability	Auditing		
	Accountability		
Availability	Response in Time		
	Expiration		
	Resource Allocation		
Non-repudiation	Non-repudiation		
Integrity	Software		
	Personal		
	Hardware		
	Data		
Privacy	Trace		
	Cardinality		
	Content		
	Attribution		
	Aggregation		
	Encryption		
	Confidentiality		
	Anonymity		

Table 3. Software requirements

- Fair Exchange

- Role base access control

- Authenticity

- Secrecy and Integrity

- Non-repudiation

- Freshness

- Secure Information Flow

- Guarded Access

- Fair Exchange

ILLUSTRATING A QUANTITATIVE RISK ANALYSIS MODEL USING THE NOVEL TAXONOMY

Improvement in the ST' and DP' Matrices

We already define and refine holistic security requirement taxonomy; then we intend to ameliorate the security risk analysis model based MFC metric. Changes are made on the ST' and DP' matrices.

The stake matrix (ST', Table 5), it is a matrix filled by the users of the system, it breaks down the list of intervenes and the list of security requirements, each cell represents the loss generated in dollars for example. Data is collected through an investigation for UVT.

The dependency matrix (DP', Table 6) is filled by the system architect (i.e., cyber security operations and system administrators) according to how each component contributes to meet each requirement; each cell represents probability of failure with respect to a requirement given that a component has failed

Table 4. Comparing our model versus the literature

Literature Model / Reference of the Model	ISO	The Parkerian hexad	The Taxonomy of security quality	The ARM	The SQUARE Methodology	Software Security	Software SR
Our model / factor/Sub factor	ISO	Jule et al., 2010 / Donn Parker, 2002	Firesmith, 2004	Mead and Hough, 2005	Travis Christian, 2010	Caldern and Marta, 2007	Alam, 2010 / J. Jurjens, 2005
Conformance					•		
Secure Information Flow							•
Freshness							•
Fair Exchange							•
Usability		•		•			
Reduce risks				•			
Consistent APTs				•			
Available security				•			
Manageable security				•			
Attack Detection			•				
Physical Protection			•				
Access control		•	•	•			•
Authorization	•		•				
Identification			•				
Authentication	•	•	•	•			•
Manageability			•				
Accountability			•		•		
Security Auditing	•		•	•			
Availability	•	•			•		
Resource allocation						•	
Expiration						•	
Response time						•	
Non-repudiation	•		•			•	•
Integrity	•	•	•	•	•	•	•
Software Integrity			•				
Personal Integrity			•				
Hardware Integrity			•				
Data Integrity			•			•	
Privacy	•	•	•	•	•		
Traces						•	
Cardinality						•	
Consent and notification						•	
Attribution						•	
Aggregation						•	
Encryption						•	
Confidentiality		•		•			
Anonymity		•					

The impact matrix (IM) is filled by analysts according to how each component is affected by each threat; each cell represents probability of compromising a component given that a threat has materialized, it depends on the target of each threat, likelihood of success of the threat as presented in Table 5.

The threat vector (PT) the threat vector represents the probability of occurrence of a particular threat this is done by simulating the operation of the system for a particular period as presented in Table 6.

Table 5. New Extended Stake Matrix (ST')

Conformance	Conformance	40	30	10	20
Secure Information Flow	Secure Information Flow	10	10	0	5
Freshness	Freshness	5	2	1	1
Fair Exchange	Fair Exchange	10	2	0	2
	Reduce risks	20	20	5	5
	Consistent APTs	20	20	10	10
Usability	Available security	20	20	1	7
	Manageable security	30	0	0	10
Attack Detection	Attack/Harm Detection	30	20	0	10
	Physical Protection	20	10	0	10
Physical Protection	Authorization	10	30	5	5
	Identification	10	30	5	5
Access control	Authentication	10	30	5	5
	Accountability	20	10	2	7
	Security Auditing	5	0	0	3
Manageability	Resource allocation	22.5	22.5	1.5	7.5
	Expiration	22.5	22.5	1.5	3.75
Availability	Response time	15	15	0.75	3.75
	Non-repudiation	10	20	0	5
Non-repudiation	Software Integrity	7.5	4.44	0.38	1.47
	Personal Integrity	10	6.6	1.66	2.1
	Hardware Integrity	5	4.44	1.66	2.1
	Data Integrity	7.5	4.44	0.83	1.05
Integrity	Traces	3	0	0	1.65
	Cardinality	6	0	0	3.3
	Consent and notification	1.5	0	0	1
	Attribution	12	0	0	0
	Aggregation	6	0	0	3.3
	Encryption	9	17.1	5	2.31
Privacy	Confidentiality	40	20	0	10
	Anonymity	12	22.8	0	3.3
		Admi	Teach	Studt	Tech
SR *(level 1)*	**Security Requirements** *(level 2)*	Stakeholders			

Referring to the variety of literature's models, our proposed classification of security requirements into two levels is used to improve the assessment accuracy of the risk analysis model (Tables 9, 10).

Table 6. Modified Dependency Matrix (DP')

Security requirements	Security Requirements Sub factor	Components						
		Browser	Web server	Application Server	DB server	Firewall server	Mail server	No failure
Conformance	Conformance	0	1.66 10-3	1.66 10-3	1.66 10-3	0	1.66 10-3	9.93 10-1
Secure Information Flow	Secure Information Flow	4.2 10-2	4.2 10-2	4.2 10-2	4.2 10-2	0	4.2 10-2	7.9 10-1
Freshness	Freshness	0	1 10-3	1 10-3	1 10-3	0	1 10-3	9.97 10-1
	Fair Exchange	0	1 10-3	1 10-3	1 10-3	0	1 10-3	9.97 10-1
Fair Exchange	Reduce risks	0	0	0	0	3 10-3	0	9.97 10-1
Usability	Consistent APIs	5 10-4	5 10-4	5 10-4	5 10-4	0	5 10-4	9.97 10-1
	Available security	3 10-3	3 10-3	3 10-3	3 10-3	3 10-3	3 10-3	9.82 10-1
	Manageable security	0	3 10-3	3 10-3	3 10-3	3 10-3	3 10-3	9.85 10-1
Attack /Harm Detection	Attack/ Harm Detection	0	24.4 10-3	24.4 10-3	24.4 10-3	0	24.4 10-3	9.024 10-1
Physical Protection	Physical Protection	0	0.7 10-3	0.7 10-3	0.7 10-3	0.7 10-3	0.7 10-3	9.965 10-1
	Authorization	0	4.2 10-3	4.2 10-3	4.2 10-3	4.2 10-3	4.2 10-3	9.79 10-1
	Identification	0	4.2 10-3	4.2 10-3	4.2 10-3	4.2 10-3	4.2 10-3	9.79 10-1
Access control	Authentication	0	4.2 10-3	4.2 10-3	4.2 10-3	4.2 10-3	4.2 10-3	9.79 10-1
	Accountability	3 10-3	3 10-3	3 10-3	3 10-3	3 10-3	3 10-3	9.82 10-1
Manageability	Security Auditing	3 10-3	3 10-3	3 10-3	3 10-3	3 10-3	3 10-3	9.82 10-1
	Resource allocation	0	3.3 10-3	3.3 10-3	3.3 10-3	0	3.3 10-3	9.868 10-1
Availability	Expiration	3.3 10-3	3.3 10-3	3.3 10-3	3.3 10-3	3.3 10-3	3.3 10-3	9.802 10-1
	Response time	3.3 10-3	3.3 10-3	3.3 10-3	3.3 10-3	3.3 10-3	3.3 10-3	9.802 10-1
Non-repudiation	Non-repudiation	2 10-2	3.3 10-2	3.3 10-2	0	1 10-2	3.3 10-2	8.71 10-1
	Software Integrity	7 10-3	7 10-3	7 10-3	7 10-3	7 10-3	7 10-3	9.58 10-1
	Personal Integrity	0	0	0	0	0	0	1
	Hardware Integrity	0	7 10-3	7 10-3	7 10-3	7 10-3	7 10-3	9.65 10-1
	Data Integrity	0	7 10-3	7 10-3	7 10-3	0	7 10-3	9.72 10-1
Integrity	Traces	0	0	0	0	3.33 10-2	0	9.667 10-1
	Cardinality	0	0	0	0	0	0	1
	Consent and notification	0	0	0	0	0	0	1
	Attribution	0	0	0	0	0	0	1
	Aggregation	0	0	0	0	0	0	1
Privacy	Encryption	0	0	0	0	0	0	1
	Confidentiality	2 10-2	3.33 10-2	3.33 10-2	5 10-2	1 10-1	3.33 10-2	7.3 10-1
	Anonymity	0	0	0	0	0	0	1

Table 7. The Impact matrix

Threat Component	BroA	ImC	DoS	CryptS	DOR	InfL	Bu	CSRF	CSS	FURL	InjecF	MFile	No Threats
Browser	0,477	0,119	0,006	0,000	0,000	0,000	0,000	0,000	0,000	0,397	0,000	0,000	0,000
Web server	0,273	0,137	0,001	0,000	0,000	0,000	0,342	0,007	0,014	0,227	0,000	0,000	0,000
Application server	0,271	0,135	0,007	0,000	0,000	0,000	0,338	0,007	0,000	0,225	0,014	0,003	0,000
DB server	0,187	0,094	0,005	0,155	0,155	0,155	0,234	0,005	0,000	0,000	0,009	0,002	0,000
Firewall server	0,143	0,143	0,714	0,000	0,000	0,000	0,000	0,000	0,000	0,000	0,000	0,000	0,000
Mail server	0,375	0,187	0,009	0,028	0,028	0,028	0,000	0,009	0,000	0,312	0,019	0,005	0,000
No Failure	0,523	0,813	0,286	0,845	0,845	0,845	0,658	0,991	0,986	0,603	0,981	0,995	1,000

Table 8. The PT Vector (PT)

Threats	Probability
Broken authentication and session management (BroA)	4.20 10-3
Insecure communication (InsC)	3.00 10-3
Denial of service (Dos)	3.08 10-3
Insecure cryptographic storage (CrypS)	7.00 10-4
Insecure direct object reference (DOR)	7.00 10-4
Information leakage and improper error handling (InfL)	7.00 10-4
Bu er overflow (Bu)	1.00 10-4
Cross Site Request Forgery (CSRF)	4.20 10-4
Cross Site Scripting (CSS)	1.80 10-4
Failure to restrict URL access (FURL)	9.80 10-3
Injection flaws (InjecF)	2.17 10-3
Malicious file execution (MFile)	5.04 10-4
No Threats	974.44 10-3

Table 9. New Measurements

Stakeholders	Mean Failure Cost $ /hour
Administrator	643,457
lecture	455,374
Student	81,768
Technical staff	208,878

Table 10. Measurements for e-learning Systems with 6 requirements

Stakeholders	Mean Failure Cost $ /hour
Administrator	0.617
lecture	0.59
Student	0.047
Technical staff Administrator	0.173

IMPACT OF THE TAXONOMY IN LEADING PRECISE EVALUATION AND MORE EFFICIENT DECISIONS

The risk analysis model allows deep analyses and computations providing quantitative assessments of different security requirements which will be translated into security recommendations facilitating the selection of the best solution:

Our risk analysis model incorporates 31 security requirements instead of 6 primaries security requirements. The model incorporates more details of matrices features, data and precise assessments such as the risk in financial terms, the Probability of failing requirement Ri once component Ck has failed.

We consider confidentiality as a primary security requirement or a secondary requirement of privacy according to the new taxonomy, probabilities in matrices and the stake are more significant.

The new taxonomy helps in getting more efficient decisions:

- The combination between the new risk analysis model incorporating all the possible security requirements and the MFCR metric, leads to identify which requirement is more critical than the other, and which threats and architectural component are critical than the other. Using taxonomy of 31 security requirements is more significant than using six basic security requirements. This leads to identifies critical assets and possible associates appropriate countermeasures.
- The new risk analysis model based on the taxonomy of security requirements will be extended to a security risk management model. We will illustrate how the taxonomy leads to precise decisions. Using 31 security requirements is more significant to draw suitable security measures.
- Our approach also enables enterprises to gain predictive insight according to assessments presented in the 3 matrices and the vector as well as improves decision making thus establishing a proactive cyber defense strategy which is highly personalized.

A full taxonomy of security requirements may answer the question: How likely is it that we will meet these requirements? And leads to provide a product design based on the specified requirements taxonomy.

CONCLUSION

Security risk measurements are strengthening by a new taxonomy of security requirements. We develop novel and holistic security requirements taxonomy to cope with the orthogonal classification problem. We build a functional, unified and hierarchical taxonomy of security requirements. It incorporates 13 security requirements and then refined in layer into 31 sub-factors. Then this taxonomy is used in security risk assessment.

Our future investigation is to present a cyber security risk management model via highlighting the three remaining steps of the security risk management process. Then, we exploit its characteristics in decision making through a rigorous and quantifiable analysis of financial income.

REFERENCES

Alam, M. (2010). Software Security Requirements Checklist. *Int. J. of Software Engineering*, 3(1), 53-62.

Baars, H., Hintzbergen, J., Hintzbergen, K., & Smulders, A. (2010). Foundations of Information Security Based on Iso27001 and Iso27002. Van Haren Publishing.

Caldern, C., & Marta, E. (2007). A Taxonomy of Software Security Requirements. *Avances en Sistemas e Informtica*, 4(3), 47–56.

Christian, T. (2010). Security Requirements Reusability and the SQUARE Methodology (no. cmu/sei- 2010-tn-027). Carnegie-Mellon Univ.

Firesmith, D. (2003). Engineering security requirements. *Journal of Object Technology*, 2(1), 53–68. doi:10.5381/jot.2003.2.1.c6

Firesmith, D. (2004). Specifying Reusable Security Requirements. *Journal of Object Technology*, 3(1). Retrieved from http://www.jot.fm

International Organization for Standardization (ISO). (1989). ISO 7498-2 Information Processing Systems - Open Systems Interconnection – Basic Reference Model, Part 2: Security Architecture.

Kumar, R. (2017). DOS Attacks on Cloud Platform: Their Solutions and Implications. *Critical Research on Scalability and Security Issues in Virtual Cloud Environments, 167*.

Lasheras, J., Valencia-Garca, R., Fernndez-Breis, J. T., & Toval, A. (2009). Modelling Reusable Security Requirements based on an Ontology Framework. *Journal of Research and Practice in Information Technology*, 41(2).

Mead, N. R., & Hough, E. D. (2005). *Security Quality Requirements Engineering (SQUARE)*. Carnegie-Mellon Univ. doi:10.21236/ADA443493

Rjaibi, N., & Rabai, L. B. A. (2015a). Developing a Novel Holistic Taxonomy of Security Requirements, In *Proceedings of the 2015 International Conference on Soft Computing and Software Engineering*. Elsevier.

Rjaibi, N., & Rabai, L. B. A. (2015b). Expansion and practical implementation of the MFC cybersecurity model via a novel security requirements taxonomy. *International Journal of Secure Software Engineering*, 6(4), 32–51. doi:10.4018/IJSSE.2015100102

Sekaran, K. C. (2007). Requirements Driven Multiple View Paradigm for Developing Security Architecture. In *Proceedings of World Academy of Science* (pp. 156–159). Engineering and Technology PWASET.

Stoneburner, G., Hayden, C., & Feringa, A. (2001). *Engineering principles for information technology security (a baseline for achieving security)*. Mclean VA: Booz-Allen and Hamilton Inc . doi:10.6028/NIST.SP.800-27

KEY TERMS AND DEFINITIONS

Estimation of Threats: Risks calculation by understanding the main threats and particular situation in the related environment. The framework for information security management can be easily designed.

Identification of Assets: We need to examine security characteristics in compliance with the supported infrastructure application and mention some related security incidents and problems. A survey methodology of expert users is recommended.

Large Scale System: Is a software-intensive system of ultra-large size with large amounts of hardware

Security Assets: Covers stakeholders, security requirements, architectural components and security threats

Security Risk Analysis Process: Used to assess security threats and their potential impact in order to anticipate attacks, to weaken their impact and to propose some countermeasures.

The ISO/IEC 27001:2005: Is a process of security risk management, to carry out risk assessment and risk treatment: It proposes an iterative generic approach of risk management which is the Deming's "plan-do-check-act" approach to manage risk. The ISO norm was applicable to all types of organizations such as commercial enterprises, government agencies and others.

Chapter 8
Estimating Risks Related to Extended Enterprise Systems (EES)

Jasleen Kaur
Chandigarh University, India

Rajinder Kaur
Chandigarh University, India

ABSTRACT

This chapter describes how risks are inherent in all systems. Risk is the ability of losing or gaining something of value. Values, like social status, financial wealth, or physical health, may be won or lost while taking threat as a result of a given movement. Risks also can be termed as the intentional interaction with ambiguity or uncertainty. Uncertainty is a capability, unpredictable, and uncontrollable final results; risk is an effect of action taken regardless of uncertainty. Extended Enterprise Systems (EESs) are defined as a complex structure of unique but interdependent and distributed organizational systems which are related in an autonomic manner to acquire goals beyond the reaching capacities of each. The purpose of this chapter is to estimate a set of critical risks that come across in proper logistics and the functioning of EESs. Identifying, analyzing and managing the risk in the EESs will result in an increase in the overall effectiveness and efficiency of the system. So, estimating risk could serve as the most important and powerful weapon in the hands of a decision maker of an EES.

DOI: 10.4018/978-1-5225-6029-6.ch008

INTRODUCTION

The term system is described as a collection or set of elements and method. Element includes products like software, hardware and peoples where processes include equipment, procedures, facilities and materials which might be associated and whose behavior satisfies functional and customer desires. Similarly, enterprise is defined as a goal-oriented complex system of resources like human, statistics, monetary, physical and activities, commonly trouble, risk, and time period (Rouse, 2005).

However, the necessities of trendy marketplace governed by means of excessive opposition, battles and globalizations amongst supply chains, have modified the focal point on how an agency conducts its commercial enterprise. Enterprises are steadily transferring on from working as a stand-on my own entity to producing goods and offerings via network of semi-independent or independent groups (Huang et al., 2008).

As an end result, enterprises have become prolonged organisms based on network capable of working in extraordinarily complicated environments (Mansouri et al., 2009). In order to seize the dynamic nature of such entities, present procedures may be combined to introduce an Extended Enterprise System. EES is defined as a complex structure of unique but interdependent and distributed organizational systems which are related in an autonomic manner to acquire goals beyond reaching capacities of each (Mansouri & Mostashari, 2010).

The form of relationship and interactions among constituent systems of any such community is probably defined primarily based on coordination, collaboration, hierarchy, or a combinatorial form. Regardless of the interconnectivity forms and policies that effects in a multiplied adaptability and flexibility without being vulnerable to sudden, unexpected vulnerability that could place it in a great threat through astronomical financial losses and a gradient fall in its normal market share, thereby result to the loss in its competitive advantage. Since introducing a "riskfree" method that enables the "best" functioning of an EES is nearly impossible inside the presently triumphing business environment, having a clear information about the crucial risks related to the functioning of an EES is genuinely important for its sustenance and growth inside the enterprise environment.

Furthermore, the bounds for evaluation and control of risks related to an EES are inherited from an abundance of inter- as well as intra-organizational relationships (Sutton et al., 2007; Sutton, 2006) that stretches properly beyond those related to its enterprise-centric counterparts, and therefore warrants a first-rate deal of interest from decision-makers as a part of designing a well-established risk mitigation approach. However, regardless of the rapidly developing reputation of EES amongst practitioners, there is nevertheless an enormous void within the open literature on comparing the critical risks related to an EES, something that the current studies is attempting to shed a few light on.

The objective of this is to assess a set of crucial risks that would stand in the manner of proper functioning and logistics of an EES. Starting with a review of the literatures on risk management and EES, this is going directly to identify a set of critical risks that could make an EES susceptible in nature, thereby leading to losses, both market share as well as financial.

The risks that are identified are then accordingly prioritized with a view to verify their relative criticality. This enables decision-makers of any EES to determine the relative criticality of the established and identified risks and in turn develop suitable risk mitigation techniques, thereby minimizing its economic losses and growing its competitive favor. Conclusions have been drawn and suggestions provided based totally on the findings of the research in conjunction with suggesting possible guidelines of future research. The contributions inside the domain of EES and systems engineering is two-fold. First, this identifies and explores the essential risks, which, if not addressed, can doubtlessly amplify the exposure of an EES in the industry. Secondly on the base of proposed model, policy-makers can use the estimated and identified risks along with their subsequent ranking to decide their associated criticality for making risk mitigation techniques for EEs.

EXTENDED ENTERPRISE SYSTEMS

In contemporary business environment it is necessary for businesses to make strategies that permit them to evaluate the key external and internal impacts, which authorize their competitiveness or makes them prone to foreseen or unforeseen situations. Therefore, it's far very vital for firms to attain the capacity of gratifying rising enterprise needs through the reconfiguration of system's structure. This has delivered approximately a brand-new kind of organizational structures based on relationship with other companies via sharing of statistics and sources inside and toward their limitations. As a result, there has been a shift from centralized and disintegrated corporation systems to more united, collaborative and open organization systems (Tan et al., 2006).

These kinds of business enterprise systems are regularly known as Extended Enterprises (EE). Extended enterprise is called "a broad system of companies or enterprises (Boardman & Sauser, 2008) that represents the holistic idea of enterprises along its internal additives and external connectors along with commercial enterprise companions, providers, and customers (Slade & Bokma, 2002). From the identical holistic perspective, an extended organisation combines all its processes, applications, human beings, and expertise in pursuit of better performance and effectiveness (Markus, 2000; Kosanke et al., 1999).

The structure of an EES offers opportunities to increment the degree of interactions which complements the ability for constituent structures to reply unexpectedly to changing enterprise possibilities. However, the complexities as a result of the multiplied degree of interrelationships and interdependencies also can introduce new risks to the system (Fiksel, 2006). As an end result, it's most important to evaluate a set of feasible risks that might show to be causal for the failure of an EES.

RISK MANAGEMENT

Risk is a pervading part of all the actions. It can be defined in a different meaning and different words like hazard and uncertainty. Risk is classified by the following parts

- **The Risk Event:** What might happen in favor of the project.
- **Event's Uncertainty:** The uncertainty of the occasion, how likely the occasion is to arise, i.e., the risk of the occasion occurring. A positive or sure occasion does now not create hazard, even though it may additionally create benefit or loss.
- **Potential Loss /Gain:** It is necessary that there be some amount of loss or benefit involved in taking place of the event, i.e., a result of the event taking place. We will use "loss" as a well-known term to encompass in line with physical damage and personal injury, and "benefit" to encompass earnings and advantage.

Risk control or management can be termed as the procedure which targets to help organizations recognize, examine, and take action on all their dangers in order to growing the tendency of their achievement and reducing the probability of failure (Ganguly & Mansouri, 2011). Enterprise Risk Management has come to be a vital subject matter in current complex, interrelated commercial enterprise surroundings (Wu & Olson, 2010) and corporations have begun devoting big financial and human assets to create risk management techniques that might offer them with an aggressive side over their market competitors and decrease their economic or financial losses (Ganguly et al., 2010).

A successful risk management approach for any enterprise begins with risk identification. Risk identification may be described as defining, documenting, describing, discovering, and communicating risks earlier than they emerge as problems and adversely affect a system (Barati & Mohammadi, 2008). A risk identification process ensures the identity of the widest variety of risk related to the venture (Barati & Mohammadi, 2008; Kasap & Kaymak, 2007) and output a listing of possible risks related to the diverse method stages of a project (Cooper, 2005).

Once the risks are diagnosed, they are properly treated depending on the project's nature. Furthermore, type of risks (schedule risk, cost risk, financial risk and so on.) allows reduce redundancy and provides for less complicated control of risks in later levels of the risk analysis system. It also aids a company to facilitate the procedure of analyzing and evaluating the risks for determining its relative criticality (Ganguly et al., 2011).

RISK MONITORING

It is a process which examine and tracks the degrees of risk in an organisation. As well as monitoring the threat itself, the discipline examines and tracks the potential of risk management techniques. The findings that are produced via threat tracking strategies may be used to assist to create new techniques and replace older strategies which may additionally have proved to be useless. (Wang, Mylopoulos & Liao, 2002).

The motive of risk monitoring is to keep track of the risks that occur and the effectiveness of the responses which can be carried out by corporation. Monitoring can help to envision whether or not proper rules were observed, whether new risks can now be identified or whether or not preceding assumptions to do with those dangers are still legitimate. Monitoring is important because threat is not static. The purpose of risk monitoring is:

The reason is to decide if:

- Risk responses should be implemented according to the plans.
- Action of risk responses are as powerful as expected.
- Assumptions of the project are still valid.
- Risk vulnerability has changed from its previous state, with analysis of trend.
- Proper regulations and methods are followed.
- New risks have happened that were not previously recognized.

Various Types of Risk Monitoring

- **Discretionary:** These risk monitoring techniques are not required via law, but are completed by using groups to assist them to research from activities which have happens in the past.
- **Obligatory:** These risk monitoring strategies are required via law for a few businesses, to make certain that proper threat management and monitoring processes are used.

- **Reevaluation:** Secondary or tertiary evaluation of risk and risk control techniques.
- **Continuously:** Monitoring that's usually ongoing.

In order to execute risk monitoring, risk have to be recognized and examined. Once a risk action plan has been created, a timeline should also be created to make sure that checkups are accomplished in a well-timed style. In order to display the implementation of moves, check boxes can be used, to reveal that each step of the method has been followed. Notes ought to be saved at each stage of the implementation and movement system, in order that those can be analyzed and stated throughout the monitoring section of the technique.

The tracking method generally takes place as soon as the risk action plan has been carried out. As soon as the plan is in place, the tracking segment can also start, to assess the outcomes that the plan has on the dangers in question. However, monitoring may additionally take place even though no formal plan has been put into place but, as an instance monitoring the threat of a weather concern might also occur at the same time as the risk management group discusses what their preferred course of movement could be (Modarres, 2006).

Risk tracking is essential because it enables to spotlight whether or not techniques are effective or not. Risk monitoring can significant upon the organization's management of risk because it is able to cause the identity of latest risks. Strategies can also want to be modified or updated depending at the findings of threats tracking techniques.

RISK MITIGATION

It is a process of establishing various action and option to increase opportunities and decrease risks or threats to project mission or objective.

The steps involved in risk mitigation are making of mitigation plans which are designed to handle, terminate, or reduce threats upto an acceptable level. Once the planning is done, the next step is continuous monitoring to determine the efficiency and effectiveness of the project (Webster, 2016).

It includes following handling options:

- **Suppose/Admit:** Cooperate with the functional users to design a collective knowledge about risks and their consequences. Risks may be classified as schedule, performance parameters and impacting traditional value. Design an understanding of all these consequences. User can be brought into a goal impact classification is vital to select which suppose/admit option is finally chosen. Users will make decision whether accepting the implication of a threat is acceptable. Provide the users with the exposure affecting a threat, countermeasures that can be executed, and residual threat that may occur. Help the users to find out costs in terms of time and finance (Stewart, M. G. (2008)).

- **Shun or Avoid:** Again, deal with users to accomplish a collective knowledge of the consequences of risks. Users are provided with projection of scheduled modification that is needed to overcome risks related to technology and improvement to enhance overall performance. Evaluating abilities that will be delayed and any affects as a result of dependencies on other efforts. These statistics better permits customers to interpret the functional consequences of a "shun or avoid" option.

- **Manage:** It helps in managing risks by evaluating various mitigation options. For instance, one choice is to use commercially valid abilities in preference to a contractor developed one. In growing options for managing risk for your application, searching for our capability answers from similar risk conditions of different clients, enterprise, and academia. When considering an answer from every other company, take unique care in determining any architectural modifications needed and their consequences.

- **Transfer:** Reassigning responsibility, duty, or authority to another organisation for handling a risk is one of the difficult tasks. It may make sense only when risk required expertise in a specific area that is not usually available in office. But, moving a risk to some other enterprise can bring about dependencies and lack of manage that could have their own headaches. Position yourself and your purchaser to keep in mind a transfer alternative by using obtaining and retaining recognition of corporations within your purchaser area that target specialized needs and their solutions. Obtaining this consciousness as early within the software acquisition cycle as possible, whilst transfer alternatives are greater effortlessly applied.

- **Monitor:** Once a threat has been recognized and a plan put in area to control it, there can be a probability to adopt a "heads down" mindset, in particular if the performance of the mitigation appears to be working on "cruise manage." Oppose that slop. Intermittently revisit the fundamental premises and adoption of the risk. Examine the environment to see whether or not the condition has changed in a manner that impacts the nature or effect of the risk. The risk may modify sufficiently in order that the modern mitigation is ineffective and wishes to be scrapped in favor of a distinctive one. On the other hand, the threat can also be reduced in a manner that permits assets vowed to it to be redirected (Menoni, S., et.al. (2012)).

Mitigation Plan Can Be Determined by:

- **Comprehension of the Users and Their Desires:** The customers/functional choice makers could be the choice authority for approval and fending off risks. Support the close connection with the customer community in every part of the system engineering life cycle. Realize that challenge achievement is very important to the consumer community.
- **Track Down the Specialists and Make use of Them:** Find out the experts outside and within MITRE. MITRE's technology centers exist to offer guide of their distinctiveness areas. They apprehend what's viable, what is labored and been carried out, what's easy, and what's difficult. They have the understanding and experience crucial to risk evaluation in their field of expertise. Understand inner facilities of excellence, domesticate relationships with them, and understand how and when to use them.
- **Identify Threats that Recur**: Recognize and maintain understanding of the risks that are "constantly there", dependencies, modifications in needs, interfaces, environment and necessity, information safety, and gaps or holes in program and contractor office talent set. Help create a reputation via the authorities that these dangers will arise and recur and that plans for mitigation are needed up front. Recommend diverse mitigation procedures which include adoption of a prototyping, evolution strategy, engagement, experimentation, with large stakeholder network.
- **Motivate Threat Taking:** The consequences of not taking risks, some of which can be terrible. Help the client and users remember the fact that truth and the capacity outcomes of being overly timid and not taking positive risks for your software. An instance of a negative result for not taking a threat when turning in a complete capability is that an adversary might comprehend a gain in opposition to our functional users. Risks are not contest, but absolutely bump in the street that needs to be expected and handled.
- **Identify Opportunities:** Help the government to see possibilities and understand that could arise from a threat. When thinking about options for handling a selected risk, make sure to evaluate whether or not they provide an opportunistic benefit through improving performance, potential, flexibility, or perfect attributes in other regions no longer immediately related to the threats.
- **Support Planned Consideration of Mitigation Alternatives**: This piece of advice is right every time, however mainly whilst helping a fast-paced, short response government program that is reshuffling various competing priorities. Carefully evaluation of mitigation options and motivate by using

discussion with team members. This is the form of the prudence "go slow to go rapid."

- **Not Every Risk Need Mitigation Plans**: Risk events evaluated as medium or high criticality have to move into risk mitigation implementation and planning. On the alternative hand, consider whether or not a few low criticality risks might simply be tracked and monitored on an eye fixed listing (Grabowski, M., & Roberts, K. H. (1998)).

MODEL AND MISSION OF THE RESEARCH

The mission of the research tests on examining a set of crucial risks that an EES may come across as part of its functioning. Figure 1 affords the reader with a flowchart of the proposed framework.

As shown in Figure 1, the proposed model for evaluation is consisting of 3 stages.

The first stage is to enlist the diverse part or components of an EES. As assessment of the available open literature on EES indicated, not like a single organization, an EES is created from a combination of components and sub-additives that capability in conjunction to each other so one can obtain the general goal. Therefore, it is of utmost significance to enlist the viable additives or components (at least those which can be critical) that any EES might be consisting of, earlier than transferring onto the risk evaluation phases, and therefore, this forms the primary stage of the research process.

Once the components were recognized and indexed, a set of important risks that could function a roar block towards the right functioning of an EES was assessed based on tools and strategies of risk identification (the second level or stage of the research procedure).

Figure 1. The Proposed Model

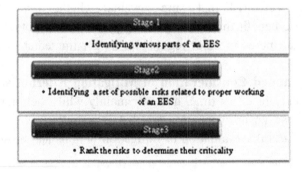

The third and final level of the assessment framework devoted its interest to prioritizing and studying identified risks to discover their relative importance. This framework can prove to be a critical tool in determining and designing a risk mitigation approach for any EES.

Following the improvement of a conceptual version representing the main ideas of interest (Figure 1), the next level become to decide the research method. (Ganguly et al., 2010), as part of a preceding study on risk evaluation proposed a set of procedures that can be used as a part of any risk identification model. Table 1 display the research levels supplied in Figure 1 and the corresponding procedures used in each and every level.

Table 1. Levels and procedure to be used

Levels	Description	Procedure Used
I	Identifying various parts of an EES	Surveys, review literature, interviews and discussion with expertise in the area of enterprise systems, software engineering and management of projects
II	Identifying a set of possible risks related to proper working of an EES	Review literature, modeling, meta analysis, interviews and discussion with expertise in the field of software engineering, risk management and enterprise management.
III	Rank the risks to determine their criticality	Survey of industry experts

Figure 2. Risk Mitigation

RESEARCH FINDINGS

Identifying Various Parts of an EES

As cited previously relating the dialogue on models and research objectives, the primary stage of the research procedure is to become aware of the diverse components of an EES. An EES is a community of "useful resource interdependencies" that consist of providers, buyers, supplier, clients, authority's corporations, and different outside businesses which can be critical to the success and right functioning of the employer (Tillquist, 2002).

From the definition, it is therefore obvious that an EES, unlike stand-alone and single organisation is made from a set of interdependent additives that desires to function in harmony to gain the needed objective. As a result, it becomes notion that having right information of the numerous additives or components of an EES might permit a smoother transition to understanding and identifying the viable risks related to an EES. Table 2 provides the reader with the essential components of an EES together with an operational definition of the same.

Identifying a set of Possible Risks Related to Proper Working of an Extended Enterprise System (EES)

The procedure or risk evaluation commenced with evaluating a set of feasible risks/ threats related to an EES. The set of threats listed in Table 3 are the most usual set of risks that may be related to the proper and powerful functioning of an EES. In this

Table 2. Main components of an EES

S.no	Main Components of EES	Functional Definition
1	Connectivity	The mandated-based emerging forces or legal guidelines that joins a variety of actors with every other in a same network
2	Sharing of knowledge	The procedure through which network collects, manages and stores its actor's knowledge and then set policies for its distribution among its receivers
3	Valve chain	Development of value via network which is generally converted into financial measures
4	Delivery of services	The final goal of the network, which is a deliverance of products and services generated by the network; this component is determined by metrics related to time and finance
5	Governance	The authority that distribute network recourses i.e., information, knowledge, financial capital, channels and procedure as well as policy making rights among the actors of the network.

Table 3. Types of risks and their functional definition

S.no	Types of risks	Functional Definition
1	Risk of disconnection	Exposure of the actors of the network in losing connectivity with their environment because of incompetent communication
2	Risk of incompetent knowledge dispersion	Exposure in making right decisions by the network because of unavailability of proper knowledge or incompetence in knowledge sharing and management
3	Risk of financial fall down	Exposure against common failure of financial stability of the network resulting from systemic problems
4	Risk of delay in performance	Exposure of the network in well-timed reply to its desires and demands caused by systemic delays of interaction between the actors of network
5	Risk of incompetent Governance	Exposure of the network to productivity as well as to carrying out struggle decision arguments and activities due to useless structure of the governance, law and management of assets for the whole network

context, a set of five main categories of possible risks have been evaluated. These are listed in Table 3 in conjunction with their operational definitions.

Based at the available literatures in addition to discussion with SME's on enterprise, management and system engineering the set of risks described in Table 3 became concept to be the most usual and important ones. Nevertheless, having stated this, the diagnosed set of risks in Table 3 also can be modified and altered according to the functioning and nature of the EES.

Rank the Risks to Determine Their Criticality

The final level of the research consisted of prioritization of the risks that allows you to examine their relative criticality. This becomes achieved via a survey analysis on the set of the evaluated risks exhibited in Table 3. In the context of this study, a pattern of 50 enterprise specialists spanning various commercial strata had been surveyed for their feedback.

The surveyed professionals had been nicely-versed with the idea of enterprise structures and systems engineering. The survey carried out made out of a established questionnaire asking for the respondents to evaluate the probability of the diagnosed risks, on a scale of ranging from "Very Low" (indicated by 1) to "Very High" (indicated by means of 5). Furthermore, they have been asked to evaluate the capability effect of the respective risk to an EES at the same five-factor scale as cited. The survey comments from the receiver changed into analyzed to determine the general value of the risk. The cost of the risk was then calculated totally based on Equation (1) following.

$$\alpha_j = \frac{\sum_{i=1}^{n}\left(\beta_i * C_i\right)}{N} \tag{1}$$

Where,

α_j = Value of the j_{th} risk;

β_i = Occurrence and the tendency off the j_{th} risk as provided by the i_{th} receiver;

C_i = Consequence of the j_{th} risk as provided by the i_{th} receiver;

N = Total number of receivers.

As seen from Equation (1), the cost of a particular risk is the average of the product of its possibility / likelihood and outcome. Since the value of the tendency lies between 0 and 1, the responses of the surveys related to the tendency turned into a scale ranging from 0 to 1. A response of "very low" was taken into consideration as having possibility 0.1 (as assigning 0 might have represented no significance of the risk) and a reaction of "very high" became connected a possibility value of 0.9 (as assigning 1 might have represented a complete importance of the risk). Following this reason, the survey responses at the possibility of the threats/ risks were mapped to the possibility using the scale as shown in Table 4.

Once the receiver of the surveys has been assigned their corresponding Risk tendency values, the next level was to arrive on the final cost of all of the evaluated risks (α_j, where j - 1 - 5) the usage of (1). The mean values of the recognized risk are given in Table 5 along with their standard deviation. Furthermore, a reasonable appropriate and acceptable value of standard deviation shows that the receivers had

Table 4. Mapping of Risk Tendency with Survey Response data

Survey Response data	Risk Tendency
1	0.1
2	0.3
3	0.5
4	0.7
5	0.9

Table 5. Mean and Standard Deviations of the evaluated Risks

Identified risks	Mean	Standard deviation	Rank
Risk of incompetent Governance	3.296	0.764	1
Risk of financial fall down	3.184	0.888	2
Risk of delay in performance	2.663	1.011	3
Risk of incompetent knowledge dispersion	2.441	0.927	4
Risk of disconnection	1.871	1.156	5

been fairly in agreement with every other, instead of separately surveyed, concerning the relative significance of the evaluated set of risks related to an EES.

Based on the evaluation of the collected data, the most vital type of risks related to enterprise is risk due to incompetent governance. Since an EES is consist of a combination of intra and inter dependent components that needs to operate harmoniously, an incompetent governance of the enterprise may lead to a breakdown of the whole structure of an EES, therefore results in a huge economical and financial losses.

Furthermore, it was verified by discussion with the expertise in this field that most of the financial risks suffered by an EES was caused due to ineffective and incompetent governance therefore again validating the importance of risk related to incompetent governance. Financial risk comes in a close second behind the risk related to incompetent governance. This was then followed by the risk of delay in performance, the risk incompetent knowledge dispersion and the risk of disconnection as shown in table 5.

At the end, it ought to be repeated that the set of the diagnosed and enlisted risks within the studies are under no potential a holistic set of threats attached with an EES. Rather, they may be said as a set of critical threats that have to be considered even as comparing an EES as component of threat mitigation techniques. Furthermore, the set of risks provided may be expanded, modified or reduced relying upon the behavior of the project, the era, and most significantly, the commercial enterprise process logistics of the business enterprise in query. Finally, it must additionally be stated that the relative importance of the risks as exhibited in Table 4, could also range relying on the prevailing enterprise surroundings and the situations facing the EES.

CONCLUSION

The research presented in this chapter dealt with analyzing a set of critical risks related to an EES. With the development importance of EES as an organizational shape, addressing and evaluating the risks could serve as a vital weapon inside the hands of the decision-makers of an EES - specially, while creating their risk mitigation techniques. This, in turn, will result in an increment in the ordinary efficiency of the EES. Although the studies evaluate and discusses the 5 important risks related to the functioning of an EES, this set can then be similarly changed or narrowed to in shape the particular necessities of the EES. It is anticipated that this will serve as a guide for any business enterprise planning to make risk mitigation techniques to ensure an effective functioning of an EES.

Moreover, this research also focusing on examine the relative significance of the possible risks related to an EES. This, at the side of the set of evaluated risks, carries critical managerial implications for a business enterprise. it is the responsibility of the manager to maintain a possible set of risk related to an EES and understand, evaluated, monitor and address the risk. By using relative criticality, the managers and the selection-makers could then be able to decide the risk that they need to cope with more forcefully. Therefore, those are the two benefaction of this research in the field of systems engineering, organization control, risk mitigation and risk management.

Future research would be focusing toward more exploration in classification and evaluating the risks related to an EES. Dividing the diagnosed risks into further sub-categories will allow the policy-makers to formulate a much better and targeted risk mitigation techniques. Furthermore, determining the correlation between the recognized risks as might serve in better understanding of the risks along with their intra and inter-dependence, and therefore, developing an improved risk mitigation method. This consequently can serve as a very vital factor of future research work in this place. Moreover, the usage of other methodologies of risk identification and evaluating them with the methodologies used within the proposed studies can be considered as topics for other research work in future.

At the last, the software of comparable frameworks for risk evaluation in actual-lifestyles instances of EES may be a very useful expense to the prevailing studies. Such case research will result in improvement of an extra distinct and applicable list of risk factors at each unique enterprise and/or business, which have an EES structure.

REFERENCE

Barati, S., & Mohammadi, S. (2008, September). Enhancing risk management with an efficient risk identification approach. In *Proceedings of the 4th IEEE International Conference on Management of Innovation and Technology ICMIT '08* (pp. 1181-1186). IEEE. 10.1109/ICMIT.2008.4654537

Boardman, J., & Sauser, B. (2008). *Systems thinking: Coping with 21st century problems.* CRC Press. doi:10.1201/9781420054927

Cooper, D. F. (2005). *Project risk management guidelines: Managing risk in large projects and complex procurements.* John Wiley & Sons, Inc.

Fiksel, J. (2006). Sustainability and resilience: toward a systems approach. *Sustainability: Science, Practice, & Policy, 2*(2).

Ganguly, A., & Mansouri, M. (2011, April). Evaluating risks associated with extended enterprise systems (EES). In *Proceedings of the 2011 IEEE International Systems Conference (SysCon)* (pp. 422-427). IEEE. 10.1109/SYSCON.2011.5929075

Ganguly, A., Mansouri, M., & Nilchiani, R. (2010, April). A risk assessment framework for analyzing risks associated with a systems engineering process. In *Proceedings of the 2010 4th Annual IEEE Systems Conference* (pp. 484-489). IEEE. 10.1109/SYSTEMS.2010.5482460

Ganguly, A., Nilchiani, R., & Farr, J. V. (2011). Identification, classification, and prioritization of risks associated with a disruptive technology process. *International Journal of Innovation and Technology Management, 8*(02), 273–293. doi:10.1142/S0219877011002313

Grabowski, M., & Roberts, K. H. (1998). Risk mitigation in virtual organizations. *Journal of Computer-Mediated Communication, 3*(4).

Huang, C. D., Behara, R. S., & Hu, Q. (2008). Managing risk propagation in extended enterprise networks. *IT Professional, 10*(4), 14–19. doi:10.1109/MITP.2008.90

Kasap, D., & Kaymak, M. (2007, August). Risk identification step of the project risk management. Portland International Center for Management of Engineering and Technology. doi:10.1109/PICMET.2007.4349543

Kosanke, K., Vernadat, F., & Zelm, M. (1999). CIMOSA: Enterprise engineering and integration. *Computers in Industry, 40*(2), 83–97. doi:10.1016/S0166-3615(99)00016-0

Mansouri, M., & Mostashari, A. (2010, April). A systemic approach to governance in extended enterprise systems. In *Proceedings of the 2010 4th Annual IEEE Systems Conference* (pp. 311-316). IEEE. 10.1109/SYSTEMS.2010.5482432

Mansouri, M., Mostashari, A., & Ganguly, A. (2009). Evaluating Agility for an Extended Enterprise Systems: The New York City Transportation Network Case. In *Proceedings of the 1st Annual Global Conference on Systems and Enterprises*.

Markus, M. L. (2000). Paradigm shifts-E-business and business/systems integration. *Communications of the Association for Information Systems, 4*(1), 10.

Menoni, S., Molinari, D., Parker, D., Ballio, F., & Tapsell, S. (2012). Assessing multifaceted vulnerability and resilience in order to design risk-mitigation strategies. *Natural Hazards, 64*(3), 2057–2082. doi:10.100711069-012-0134-4

Modarres, M. (2006). *Risk analysis in engineering: techniques, tools, and trends.* CRC press.

Rouse, W. B. (2005). Enterprises as systems: Essential challenges and approaches to transformation. *Systems Engineering, 8*(2), 138–150. doi:10.1002ys.20029

Slade, A. J., & Bokma, A. F. (2002, January). Ontologies within extended enterprises. In *Proceedings of the 35th Annual Hawaii International Conference on System Sciences HICSS '02* (pp. 541-550). IEEE.

Stewart, M. G. (2008). Cost effectiveness of risk mitigation strategies for protection of buildings against terrorist attack. *Journal of Performance of Constructed Facilities, 22*(2), 115–120. doi:10.1061/(ASCE)0887-3828(2008)22:2(115)

Sutton, S. G. (2006). Extended-enterprise systems' impact on enterprise risk management. *Journal of Enterprise Information Management, 19*(1), 97–114. doi:10.1108/17410390610636904

Sutton, S. G., Khazanchi, D., Hampton, C., & Arnold, V. (2007). Risk analysis in extended enterprise environments: Identification of critical risk factors in B2B e-commerce relationships.

Tan, W., Xue, J., & Wang, J. (2006, October). A service-oriented virtual enterprise architecture and its applications in Chinese tobacco industrial sector. In *Proceedings of the IEEE International Conference on e-Business Engineering ICEBE'06* (pp. 95-101). IEEE. 10.1109/ICEBE.2006.13

Tillquist, J. (2002). Strategic Connectivity in Extended Enterprise Networks. *Journal of Electronic Commerce Research*, *3*(2), 77–85.

Wang, H., Mylopoulos, J., & Liao, S. (2002). Intelligent agents and financial risk monitoring systems. *Communications of the ACM*, *45*(3), 83–88. doi:10.1145/504729.504733

Webster, L. R. (2016). Risk Mitigation Strategies. In *Controlled Substance Management in Chronic Pain* (pp. 163–180). Springer International Publishing.

Wu, D. D., & Olson, D. (2010). Enterprise risk management: A DEA VaR approach in vendor selection. *International Journal of Production Research*, *48*(16), 4919–4932. doi:10.1080/00207540903051684

Chapter 9
Meta–Heuristic Approach for Software Project Risk Schedule Analysis

Isha Sharma
Chandigarh University, India

Deepshikha Chhabra
Chandigarh University, India

ABSTRACT

This chapter illustrates a technique to shorten the time duration using structured method. This is done by considering multiple resource constraints apart from time for the software project. The resource constraints are due to limited availability of resources (hardware, software, people, etc.). The difficulty is to locate minimal duration schedule. This is done by assigning the start time for each activity with the clear representation of precedence among them and resources available. There are various optimization approaches available but authors have selected a genetic algorithm. This method emulates the concept of biological evolution that is based on natural selection. This chapter concludes that additional research is needed in this area to provide better outcomes.

INTRODUCTION

Software business is a high-speed growing industry with deadline constraints and resource constraints issues. Resources available are not in abundance and for the success of software project the resources need to be allocated to reduce the probability

DOI: 10.4018/978-1-5225-6029-6.ch009

of not meeting the deadline as per the total duration estimated for the completion (Singh, 2008).

Project management is a multifaceted choice making process that takes into consideration two domains i.e. time and cost. While managing the project decisions are to undertake related to planning and scheduling. While planning a project, planning for the requirements of several resources is to be carried out. Planning is a bit strategic process that usually makes use of Gantt Charts for generation of resource profile and allocation of the resources. It also helps in leveling the resources.

Scheduling on the other hand is the process of assigning resources to project. This helps in determining the begin and end times of the detailed activities. The process however becomes complex when a large number of process are competing for limited projects. The major goal is the assignment of limited resources to solve the problem optimally. A large number of tools exits that will help in project scheduling the only prerequisite is the knowledge about the duration for activities, their precedence order and number of resources required (Buriol, 2005). The two important techniques however are Critical Path Method (CPM) and Program Evaluation and review Technique (PERT) (Singh, 2008).

The problem with these two methods is that they do not consider the resource constraints during scheduling. For these two methods there are unlimited resources available for the project i.e. not a valid assumption for practical situations (Charette, 2005; Deepti, 2004). Moreover, they are applicable to only one project at one time. But the reality is that we have less of resources in number and multiple projects are running at one time in practical.

Both of these methods do not consider the constraints related to resources and hence are not enough for scheduling projects in software industry. There is a need of such an algorithm that would be resolving recourse related constraints that will balance between time and cost tradeoffs. For that purpose, Genetic Algorithm is to be used that will help in solving optimization problems based on natural selection. The main aim of this chapter is to develop such an algorithm using the concept of GA that helps in minimizing the total duration of the projects and in solving the Resource Constrained Multi-Project Scheduling Problem (RCMPSP) (Hartmann, 2008).

PROJECT SCHEDULING UNDER RESOURCE CONSTRAINTS

In practical the development of projects is done by dividing the work into number of activities. Each activity is assigned a time frame in which the task is to be completed. In order to complete one or more activities a large number of resources are required. Each resource has limited capacity and an activity can't be started until and unless all its predecessors has yet not completed (Hulett, 2004). This problem is known as Resource Constrained Problem. In such problems resources from the pool of given resources with limited capacity are allocated to activities of the project for their completion. Under this situation there is need of such a project scheduler that helps in minimizing the total completion time of the project subject to the fact that precedence order and resource constraints are respected (DeMarco, 1997).

Project Management and Resource management go hand in hand and are crucial areas in the overall success of the software projects. It is the responsibility of the software planner to exploit time and precedence based schedule as source for the management of resources for the project (Simmons, 2002).

A plan of action should be there to deliver the project within the frame of limited funding and time effective project management is difficult and complex. Different jobs are allocated different resources (including human resources) exhibiting different characteristics, intriguing composite dependencies, constraints and uncertainties into consideration with an aim to meet goals related to costs and time. Designing a Software Project Management structure involves simulating or imitating the project plan to see how uncertainties about task duration, cost, resource constraints impinge on the outcome (Mendes, 2006; Deepti, 2004; David, 2004).

One question that always comes in mind while managing the software projects is the similarity of the management of the software project with the management of any engineering project. The answer is sometimes YES and sometimes NO. The basic tool used for managing the projects involves constructing the network of activities for the project. The following steps are to be followed:

- All project activities are to be identified
- Precedence among the project activities are recognized
- Concurrencies and Resource requirements between project activities are established
- Generation of random duration for each activity is to be done
- Risky areas are identified (Buriol, 2005)

The intention of risk analysis is to curtail time delivery. A missed opportunity leads to reduction in market impact, makes the customer dissatisfied and can increase internal costs also. Following questions are important while analyzing software project:

- Distribution of Resources over the software projects?
- Availability of risk management tools and methods? (Charette, 2005)

Varieties of tools are available to address the concern issues of planner and project. Depending on the financial statement available, it is possible to choose a tool with the superiority and functionality to suit your needs. Schedule risk model need not be unjustifiably multipart or time consuming. Probabilistic illustrations allow for much more pragmatic predictions than are possible by conservative methods, so they make it possible for plans to be reasonable without a large amount of detail. Risk modeling enables planners to give an absolute observation of a project, from the top down, to whatever level of detail is apposite. (David, 2004)

META –HEURISTICS ALGORITHM

Resource constrained software projects are scheduled using several methods in past to have optimal solution. In mathematical optimization and computer science, a Meta heuristic is a higher-level modus operandi or heuristic premeditated to find, engender, or decide on a heuristic (partial search algorithm) that may provide a adequately good solution to an optimization problem, especially with unfinished or faulty information or limited working out capacity. Meta heuristics mock-up a set of solutions which is too large to be completely sampled. Meta heuristics may make few assumptions about the optimization problem being solved, and so they may be usable for a variety of problems. A number of meta heuristics methods are available like Ant Colony, Memetic Algorithms, Simulated Annealing, Greedy Search, Scatter Search, Immune Systems, Genetic Algorithms (Franco, 2006; Haupt, 2004; Leonidas, 2006).

Out of these methods, Genetic algorithm is chosen to optimize the schedule for resource constraints software projects because of two reasons. Firstly, GA has capability to deal with complex problems involving parallelism. Secondly GA deals with varieties of optimizations. Genetic Algorithm is an optimization problem that is more connected to evolutionary computation. It helps in finding out optimal solution(s) for a given computational problem (Deb, 2012). They imitate biological process of reproduction and natural selection. The algorithms are more efficient than random and exhaustive search. Genetic algorithm is such an optimization technique that enables one in setting the level of randomization and level of control. Due to this feature, problem such as lack of continuity, derivatives, linearity are overcome. (Matthew, 1996; Mendes, 2006).

In genetic algorithm approach of risk analysis, the problem is represented in terms of chromosomes based on the random keys. The schedules are determined using heuristics. The main operations of Genetic Algorithms are: Selection, Crossover and Mutation

Selection is the process in which during each successive generation, a portion of existing is selected to reproduce a new generation. The selection is done according to their fitness. The more fit the chromosome is, the more is the chance of its selection (Okada, 2008)

Crossover is the process of taking two solutions and generating a new solution from it

Mutation is the process of changing randomly the genes of individual solution to avoid the problem of local minima (Liu, 2005; Guo, 2008; Hartmann, 2008).

The new approach for risk analysis is based on the utilizing the power of genetic algorithm.

PROBLEM DESCRIPTION AND CONCEPTUAL MODEL

The problem and the conceptual model are described using Figure 1.

The following notations are used here

P: no. Of projects where p€P

T: no. Of Activities where t €T, t = {Tp + 1 + 1 ... Tp}

Q: set of limited resource types where q€Q

The Resource constrained scheduling problem involves finding the schedule of activities by considering the resources available, precedence constraints.

Let FTi represents the end time of an activity for a software project i

The conceptual model of Resource Constrained software project is defined by the following objective function.

Figure 1. Network of Project

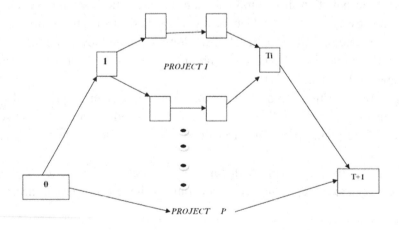

$$MINIMIZE\ Performance\ Metric\ (FTi,\ i = 1\ ...P) \tag{1}$$

SUBJECT TO:

$$FTm <= FTi\text{-}di\ i = 1...\ P + 1 \tag{2}$$

$$\sum Si,\ k<=Sk\ k\epsilon K \tag{3}$$

$$FTi >= 0\ i = 1...\ P+1 \tag{4}$$

Equation (1) minimizes the performance measure
Equation (2) represents the precedence constraints between activities
Equation (3) represents the limited resource constraints
Equation (4) imposes the end time for each activity is non-negative

For any resource constrained software project, the main aim is to shorten the total lifespan of the software project hereby optimally utilizing the limited resources. A number of approaches are suggested to solve the problems. In the coming section a new approach to solve the project scheduling is presented.

THE NEW APPROACH

The new approach uses the power of a genetic algorithm coupled with a new schedule generation procedure. The standard genetic algorithm is used to solve optimization problems. genetic algorithm imitates the genetic biological process of reproduction. Before applying the genetic algorithm, the first step is the representation of the problem to be solved in terms of fitness function (Peter, 1999; Beasl, 1993). This process is termed as encoding for problem to be solved. The possible solution to the problem is represented in terms of set of parameters termed as genes. The genes are joined together to form chromosome. When genetic algorithm is applied the selection of parents are done for reproduction and are recombined to generate children that are more optimize then the parents' chromosomes. The children are the possible solutions. The Genetic algorithm approach is described in figure 2.

In Genetic algorithm the chromosome is representing the time duration for each activity. For each chromosome two operations are applied

- Decoder
- Schedule Generator

Figure 2. Genetic Algorithm

GENETIC ALGORITHM
{

    Produce the initial population Ai

    Evaluate the fitness function of population Ai

    Repeat until the criteria is met

    {

        SELECTION

        CROSSOVER

        MUTATION

        EVALUTAION

        New Offspring is generated with more optimal fitness than the parent

    }

}

Decoder phase transforms the chromosome in Genetic algorithm into precedence of activities, start time and delay times.

Schedule Generator phase uses the precedence and delay time defined in first phase to generate parameterized schedule

Figure 3 represents the phases according to new approach applying Meta heuristic approach.

Figure 3. Phases according to New Approach

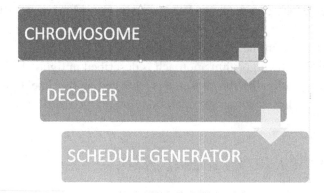

Decoder

A chromosome represents a solution to the given problem and is encoded in terms of vector of random numbers.

Each chromosome is made of N genes where N=2v+k
v represents the number of activities in software project
k represents the number of projects executed in parallel in company

CHROMOSOME ch=

(GENE$_1$ ...GENE$_v$,

GENE$_{v+1}$...GENE$_{2v}$,

$GENE_{2v+1}... GENE_{2v+k})$ (5)

Where first v genes determine the priority of each activity. The genes between v+1 and 2v determine delay time in practical scheduling of activities. The last k activities are helping in finding out the completion date of each of the k projects

The chromosome when fed to decoder helps in determining schedule generation parameters. The decoder in this approach is responsible for converting the chromosome into priorities, delay time and completion dates. Figure 4 shows the concept of decoder in new approach

The decoding of the project is done using the following equations

Figure 4. The concept of decoder in new approach

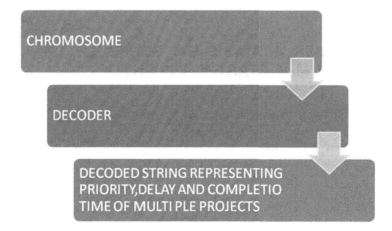

$$PRIOR_v = (SLACKv \,/\, MAXIMUMSLACK) * (0.6 + 0.4 * GENE_v) \qquad (6)$$

$$DELAY_v = GENE_v * 1.5 * MaximumDur \qquad (7)$$

$$COMP\_DATE_k = EARLY\_REL\_DATE_k + GENE_{2v+k} * (START\_DATE_k - EARLY\_REL\_DATE_{k)} \qquad (8)$$

Where

PRIOR is the priority for each activity v.

SLACK is the difference between the due date of project k to which activity v belongs to and longest path from beginning of activity v to end of project k.

MAXIMUMSLACK is the maximum value of slack for all the projects

DELAY represents the decoded value for the delay schedule for each activity v

MaximumDur is the maximum duration among all the given activities durations.

COMP_DATE represents the completion date for the project k

EARLY_REL_DATE is the early release date for the project k

START_DATE is the starting date for the project k

Schedule Generator

The schedule generator phase of the new approach uses the following algorithm to generate parameterized schedule. The basic idea behind this optimized schedule generator is to control the delay time for each activity that will subsequently have effect on the overall completion time for the given project. The process starts with calculation of Earliest Start Time and Earliest End tine for each activity according to the priority calculated using decoding process

ALGORITHM: RISK_ANALYSIS_GA_ SCHEDULE_ GENERATOR (V, M, K, START (T), FINISH (T))

```
Step 1: Read input data.
[Read V, M, K, START (T), FINISH (T)   T =1, 2...N]
Where V= number of activities, M= number of nodes in the
Project network, K=number of
Project undertaken parallel
Step 2: For each Project P Repeat step 3 to 11
Step 3: Initialize critical index counter and frequency counter
```

to zero.

[Critical (V) = 0 $\forall'$ V = 1, 2 ... N

Freq (V) = 0 $\forall'$ V= 1, 2 ... N]

Step 4: Generate decoded activity duration samples using Equation 6, 7, 8 as discussed in **Step 5:** Initialize run counter [Set RUN = 1, Where RUN is simple integer variable]

Step 6: Traverse the network for forward pass and calculate Earliest finish time EF (V) in terms of precedence only

[EF(v) = ES(v) + TIME(v) $\forall'$ V = 1, 2... where TIME(v) is set of values (PRIOR(v), Delay(v)

EN(v) = max{EF[all activities terminating in v]} $\forall'$ v = 1, 2 ... M

ES(V) = EN(Start(V)) $\forall'$ V = 1, 2 ... N]

Step 7: Traverse the network for backward pass

[LS(V) = LF(V)- TIME(V) $\forall'$ V = 1,2...N

LN(v) = min{LS[all activities originating in v]} $\forall'$ v = 1, 2...M

LF[every activity terminating in node v] = LN(v) $\forall'$ v = 1, 2...M]

Step 8: Declare activity i as critical and the Freq(i) for the activity.

[IF LS(K)- ES(K)<= ERROR Then mark K as critical activity and Update Freq[K] = Freq[K] +1]

Step 9: IF (RUN <= NRUNS) then go to step 4.

Step 10: Compute the criticality index counter, Critical (V), for each activity.

[Critical (V) = Freq (V)/ NRUNS $\forall'$ V = 1, 2...N]

Step 11: Print criticality indices of each activity.

RESOURCE CONSTRAINTED PROBLEM EXAMPLES

A. Example 1 (8 Activities)

An 8-activity project problem is described here where the table 1 showing the precedence relations and durations

Table 1. Precedence relations and durations of problem [8 activities]

Activity	Precedence	Duration	Resource
Act1	-	15	Res1
Act2	Act1	20	Res2
Act3	-	10	Res1
Act4	Act3	30	Res2
Act5	-	27	Res1
Act6	Act5	30	Res2
Act7	Act2, Act4	24	Res3
Act8	Act4, Act6	18	Res3

B. Example 2 (13 Activities)

A project with 13 activities is considered here. The details of activities and the precedence, duration and resource requirements for each activity are given in Table 2.

Table 2. Thirteen Activity Problems

Activity	Precedence	Duration	Resource
A1	-	12	R1
A2	-	15	R1, R4
A3	-	16	R1
A4	A1	11	R2
A5	A1	11	R2
A6	A2, A3	15	R2
A7	A4	12	R4
A8	A5	13	R3
A9	A5	8	R3
A10	A7	9	R4
A11	A8	9	R4
A12	A9, A6	6	2R1, R3
A13	A10, A11, A12	5	2 R2, R4, 3R5

RESULTS

The results for the above given problems in Table 1, Table 2 is given in Table 3. The problems given in Table 1, 2 is analysed using CPM/PERT and Genetic Algorithm. The results using Genetic algorithm is found to be more feasible as compared to the one observed using CPM/PERT. The graph representation for the comparison between two methods is shown in figure 5.

CPM/PERT is step by step process that aids in project management by defining the critical and non-critical activities for the given project. Genetic algorithm on the other hand uses the process of natural selection that generate optimized solutions for the given software project. The optimization is achieved by changing the activity duration for each software project. The new approach presented in this chapter compliments the traditional project scheduling and risk analysis process by optimizing the project schedule

Table 3. Comparison between CPM/PERT and Genetic Algorithm Approach for Project Scheduling and Risk Analysis

S.NO	EXAMPLE	DURATION	
		CPM/PERT	GA
1	EXAMPLE 1 (EIGHT ACTIVITY PROJECT NETWORK)	80	104
2	EXAMPLE 2 (THIRTEEN ACTIVITY PROJECT NETWORK)	50	55

Figure 5. Graph Representation for the comparison between two methods

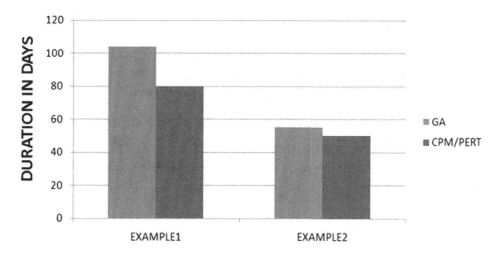

CONCLUSION

The resource constraints project scheduling problem is one of the most difficult problems in Operations Research. There is increase in the importance of project scheduling under resource constraints problems in future due to tighten resource limitations. In future there would be better project scheduling literature under resource constraints problems. The given new approaches in this chapter match the traditional CPM /PERT approach for scheduling by optimizing project schedule. The above results state that new approach is able to find the best known solutions from the given example set.

REFERENCES

Beasley, D., Bull, D. R., & Martin, R. R. (1993). An overview of genetic algorithms: Part 1, Fundamentals. University Computing. Department of Computing Mathematics.

Buriol, R., Resende, M. G. C., Ribeiro, C. C., & Thorup, M. (2005). A hybrid genetic algorithm for the weight setting problem in OSPF/IS-IS routing. *Networks*, *46*(1), 36–56. doi:10.1002/net.20070

Charette, R. N. (2005). Why software fails? *IEEE Spectrum*, *42*(9), 42–49. doi:10.1109/MSPEC.2005.1502528

Cooper, D. F. (2005). *Project risk management guidelines: managing risk in large projects and complex procurements. John Wiley & Sons, Inc.*

David, T. H. (2004). *Integrated Cost / Schedule Risk Analysis*. PMI Paper.

Deb, K. (2012). Optimization for engineering design-Algorithms and examples. New Delhi: PHI learning Private Limited.

Deepti, V., Ramanamurthy, N., & Balasubramanian, K. U. (2004). Effective Risk Management: Risk Analysis Using an Enhanced FMEA Technique. In *Proceedings of Annual Project Management Leadership Conference, India.*

DeMarco, T., & Lister, T. (2003, October). Risk Management during Requirements. *IEEE Software, 20*(5).

DeMarco, T. (1997). *The Deadline – A novel about project management.* Dorset House Publishing.

Franco, E. G., Zurita, F. L., & Delgadillo, G. M. (2006). A genetic algorithm for the resource constrained project scheduling problem. School of Industrial Engineering, University dad de La Sabena.

George, S. (2008). *Schedule risk analysis - part 2: The six-step process*. Finance Week.

Guo, Z. X., Wong, W. K., Leung, S. Y., Fan, J. T., & Chan, S. F. (2008). Genetic optimization of order scheduling with multiple uncertainties. *Expert Systems with Applications, 35*(4), 1788–1801. doi:10.1016/j.eswa.2007.08.058

Hartmann, S. (2008). A competitive genetic algorithm for resource-constrained project scheduling. *Naval Research Logistics*.

Haupt, R. L., & Haupt, S. E. (2004). Practical genetic algorithms (2nd ed.). New Jersey: John Wiley and Sons, Inc.

Leonidas, S. G. F. (2006). Optimization of Resource Constrained Project Schedules by Genetic Algorithm Based on the Job Priority List. *Information Technology and Control, 35*(4).

Liu, Y., Zhao, S. L., Du, X. K., & Li, S. Q. (2005, August). Optimization of resource allocation using genetic algorithms. In *Proceedings of the Fourth International Conference on Machine Learning and Cybernetics*, Guangzhou.

Mendes, J. J. M., Goncalves, J. F., Resende, M. G. C. (2006, November). A random key based genetic algorithm for the resource-constrained project scheduling problem (Technical Report: TD-6DUK2C, Revised). *AT&T Labs Research.*

Okada, I., Zhang, F., Yang, H. Y., & Fujimura, S. (2008). A random key-based Genetic algorithm approach for resource-constrained project scheduling problem with multiple modes. In *Proceedings of the international multi-conference of engineers and computer scientists*.

Brucker, P., Drexl, A., Möhring, R., Neumann, K., & Pesch, E. (1999). Resource-constrained project scheduling: notation, classification, models and methods. *European Journal of Operational Research, 112*(3-4).

Simmons, L. F. (2002). Project Management-Critical Path Method (CPM) and PERT Simulated with Process Model. In *Proceedings of the 2002 Winter Simulation Conference*. 10.1109/WSC.2002.1166468

Singh, V. (2008, January). A simulation-based approach to software project risk management. *Asia Pacific Business Review*.

Wall, M.B. (1996). A Genetic Algorithm for Resource-Constrained Scheduling.

Chapter 10
Development and Enhancing of Software and Programming Products by Client Information Administration in Market

Abhishek Sharma
Chandigarh University, India

Lokesh Pawar
Chandigarh University, India

Manjot Kaur
Chandigarh University, India

ABSTRACT

This chapter describes how client information administration (CIA) assumes a vital part in the creation of high-quality programming items or software products. As CIA in enterprise software (ES) advancement is relatively new, this raises inquiries on how CIA empowering agents can be utilized to help ES advancement organizations enhance their product quality. In this study, human, authoritative and mechanical CIA empowering influences were recognized from prior literature. The weights of these elements were dictated by specialists from the ES advancement organizations. In view of the essential factors, a hypothetical model was created. The proposed display was assessed by circulating an overview survey to chiefs in ES advancement organizations. The outcomes demonstrated that "client inclusion" together with "trust" were the most powerful factors, followed by the "CRA innovation framework" and the "cross-useful participation." The proposed processes demonstrated in this investigation can be utilized as a rule for the use of CIA in ES advancement organizations to enhance product quality.

DOI: 10.4018/978-1-5225-6029-6.ch010

INTRODUCTION

Client information (CI) is progressively critical for organization aggressiveness. Subsequently, look into on customer knowledge management (CIA) is quickly expanding. CIA enables organizations to use their extraordinary CK to enhance the new item execution, upgrade product\service quality, and cut costs. In any case, organizations craving to build up a well-working CIA confront challenges. Specifically, there is an absence of research on how firms ought to send Human, Hierarchical and Innovative conditions to oversee CK and turn out to be more receptive to client needs (Sande, 2016; Salojärvi et al., 2013; Garrido-Moreno & Padilla-Meléndez, 2011). Numerous past examinations in programming quality upgrade have just centred around the specialized parts of programming quality, for example, dependability, viability, and usefulness. Be that as it may, due to the idea of Undertaking Programming (ES), the exchange and reconciliation of CK for customization, improvements, upkeep and preparing is required. Clients are a standout amongst the most vital partners in any venture (Relationship for Undertaking Administration, 2006). There is almost certainly that fitting correspondence and coordinated effort with clients in various periods of the ES advancement venture can help in expanding the general fulfillment of clients and the general achievement of a whole task (Schaarschmidt et al., 2015). CIA could be utilized to encourage the gathering of client input and the accumulation and use of client data (Zhang, 2011). As the mix of CI in ES advancement is as yet youthful, there is an absence of hypothetical system to completely catch the utilization of CIA to enhance programming quality in ES. Likewise, there is a essential need to additionally investigate how hierarchical factors, for example, CIA can upgrade the ES quality. There are critical difficulties with respect to the exchange and reconciliation of CI inside programming organizations. Attafar et al. (2013) revealed that an absence of senior administration sense of duty regarding CIA, poor correspondence, an absence of social preparation, and an absence of client administration abilities are hindrances to the CIA. The significant issues confronting the successful use of CIA in any organization are authoritative, not specialized (Smith and McKeen, 2005). As indicated by Al-Shammari and Worldwide (2009), fruitful CIA requires the change of organizations from product–centric operations to 2 customer centric operations. Attafar et al. (2013) noted that an important barrier to CIA is interdepartmental conflict. When internal departments operate autonomously, cooperation between such departments is limited. Thus, several likely benefits of CIA are not exploited (Garrido-Moreno et al., 2014; Khodakarami and Chan, 2014). Moreover, Skotis et al. (2013) reported that one of the most important challenges of CIA is a lack of CI absorptive capacity in organizations. Salojärvi et al. (2010) noted that the most companies lacked systematic processes for CIA. According to Davenport et al. (2001), the utilization of CI is a 'stumbling block' for several firms. However, the rate of absorption and application of CIA in ES is low, for example, only 27% of the ES development companies that proposed products in ELECOMP 2014 (Big annual ICT exhibition in Tehran) had a CIA strategy to increase production efficiency and provide better service to customers. Many studies in the field of Information Systems (IS) have investigated the significant factors that influence CIA. Research on the factors that enhance CIA in the ES development to improve software quality improvement is one of the less explored and examined topics in IS (Kannabiran and Sankaran, 2011). Particularly for developing countries, according to an investigation of 22 software development companies that proposed products in ELECOMP 2014, 63% of the ES development companies used Customer Relationship Management (CRM) systems, 36% of them had a solution or guidelines for the use of CI to increase the quality of products and services. 61% of them mentioned that the software production process in their companies is product-centric rather than customer centric (Khosravi et al., 2017). An inadequate theoretical framework for antecedent factors of CIA in general, and a lack of comprehensive theoretical framework for the effect of CIA on software quality in ES development, reflect a fundamental need to further explore the solutions for this issue (Aho and Uden, 2013; Kannabiran and Sankaran, 2011). Accordingly, the major question of the current study that reflects the gap in the literature was emerged as: "What are the antecedent factors that influence CIA for ES quality improvement in the ES development companies?" This paper is divided into the following sections. In Section 2, the theoretical foundation is reviewed. In Section 3, a research design framework was developed. In Section 4, the research hypotheses are formulated. In Section 5, the result of data collection and analysis was reported and compared with previous studies. In Section 6, the implications and suggestions for future studies were described. Section 7 presents the conclusion.

LITERATURE REVIEW

Client Information Administration

According to Campbell (2003), CI refers to the ordered and structured information pertaining to the customer driven by methodical processing. Gebert et al. (2002) offered a commonly acknowledged definition of customer knowledge: "the vigorous blend of value, experience, and perceptive information that is required, generated and imbibed during the process of transaction and interchange between the organization and customers". Gebert et al. (2002) classified CI into three main categories. The first type called "knowledge for customers" refers to knowledge about products, markets and suppliers applied to satisfy customers' knowledge needs. The second type is referred as "knowledge about customers," which is created based on the analysis of historical customers' data and information. The third type, which is known as "knowledge from customers", refers to the customers' feedbacks. Another type of CI stated by Smith and McKeen (2005) is co-created knowledge. This knowledge can be captured during the cooperation between an organization and its customers. As per Sofianti et al. (2010), CIA is the strategic practice based on which forward-looking organizations unshackle their customers from being submissive recipients of products and services to authorization as the knowledge partners. The CIA pertains to obtaining, sharing, and using the knowledge within customers for the benefit of those customers as well as the organization. It is termed as an on-going practice of creating, distributing and utilizing CI within a business entity and between a business entity and its customers.

The Generic CIA Framework

According to the Knowledge-Based View (KBV), knowledge is a distinctive resource and organizational performance relies on how well its members can improve the organization's knowledge base, assimilate various knowledge areas, and deploy the knowledge for the development of high quality and pioneering products (Eisenhardt and Santos, 2002; Grant, 1996). Lin (2007) proposed a general framework of Knowledge Management (KM) processes which is supported by KBV (see Fig. 1). This framework involves three main aspects: Enablers, Processes and Outcomes. Lin (2007) arranged Enablers into three categories which are: Human, Organizational and Technology. In this framework, Enablers are the mechanism for developing individual, organizational and technological capabilities to facilitate knowledge management in the organization (Lin,2007). The Processes refers to the process of collecting, sharing and applying the experience, expertise, know-how, and contextual information in the organization. The Outcomes exposes the consequences of the degree of knowledge management effectively achieved in a company's performance, innovation capability and product and service quality (Lin, 2007). Salojärvi et al. (2013) follow this general framework for proposing the model for CIA. Other scholars recognize the existence of different influences on CIA activities, such as Human, Organizational, and Technological factors (Ghobadi, 2015; Salojärvi et al., 2013; Lin, 2007; Feher and Gabor, 2006).

The Generic CIA Framework (see Fig. 2) incorporates CIA enables (Human, Organizational and Innovative precursor factors), the CIA forms (Acquisition, Storage, Sharing and Application) what's more, the CKM results. Late examinations have featured diverse results for CIA, for example, business execution, operational execution, upper hands, advancement, benefit quality and item quality (Tseng, 2016; Fidel et al., 2015a; Fidel et al., 2015b; Salojärvi and Sainio, 2015; Choi and Ryu,

Figure 1. The General Framework of Knowledge Management Processes (Lin, 2007)

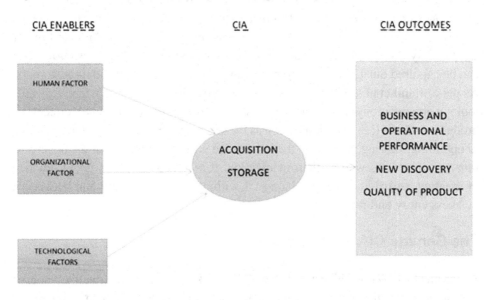

2013). In the accompanying segments, three imperative parts of the Generic CIA Framework (CIA enables, CIA procedures and CIA results) are clarified

- **CIA Enablers**: CIA enablers are instruments to actuate CIA, break the snags of CIA, and give Organizational, Human and Technological condition to encourage CIA (Khosravi et al., 2014; Liao and Wu, 2010; Gebert et al., 2002). As indicated by Gibbert et al. (2002), KM empowering influences are the pivotal perspectives which set the CKM thoughts in motion for accomplishing CIA results. CIA empowering influences and CIA rehearses are basic requirements for efficacious CIA (Garrido-Moreno et al., 2014). The KBV empowers us to expect that the utilization of human, hierarchical and innovative capacity would enhance the learning administration process which can prompt item and administration viability (Durmuşoğlu and Barczak, 2011). Concerning the Human measurement, most researchers concur that CIA relies upon the human qualities, including abilities, encounter, inspiration, qualities, and convictions (Attafar et al., 2013; Nagati and Rebolledo, 2012; Al-Shammari and Global, 2009). Furthermore, in regard to the Organizational measurement, the climate of the association is by and large made to catch effectively the advantages of advancement steady culture. With regards to CIA, the diverse parts of the authoritative atmosphere are basic drivers of CIA, for example, cross-practical participation (Khodakarami and Chan, 2014), remunerate frameworks (Garrido-Moreno et al., 2014),

Figure 2. Generic CIA Framework

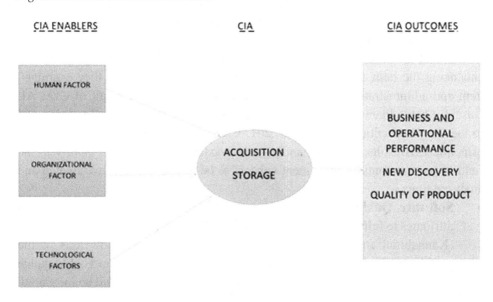

and top administration bolster (Salojärvi et al., 2010). At long last, alluding the Technology measurement, ICT can be viably utilized to encourage the codification, incorporation, and scattering of CIA (Khodakarami and Chan, 2014; Rollins and Halinen, 2005).

- **CIA Processes**: There are four principle forms associated with the CIA, with which the information is utilized in the association (Salojärvi et al., 2010). The procedure starts with the periods of procuring and putting away the information into the CIA+ framework, and is trailed by the periods of scattering and utilizing of the learning among the groups (Al-Busaidi, 2013; Salojärvi et al., 2010). A large portion of the analysts in the CIA range specified that CIA has four measurements (Khodakarami and Chan, 2014; Yang et al., 2014; Skotis et al., 2013; Mukherji, 2012; Talet, 2012; Buchnowska, 2011; Ranjan and Bhatnagar, 2011; Gibbert et al., 2002). Likewise, Yang et al. (2014) measures CKM idle variable with four perspectives (Securing, Storage, Dissemination and Utilization).

- **CIA OUTCOMES:** Researchers have talked about various results of CIA, for example, enhancing the proficiency of the company's operation (Hammami and Triki, 2011), upgrading the nature of items (software and products) and administration or services (Alamgir and Quaddus, 2012). This relates to improving the business substance's capacity to distinguish client prerequisites and additionally, the business and operational execution (Aho and Uden, 2013; Alamgir and Quaddus, 2012). The KBV hypothesizes that

CIA may create a long haul, reasonable upper hand for the business element as CI-based assets are socially complicated and extreme to emulate (Hammami and Triki, 2011).

Dous et al. (2005) led an overview in the diverse ventures and found that enhancing the item quality is one of the critical results of CIA, they examined item and administration quality is the piece of the execution result of CIA. Al-Busaidi (2013) likewise found that the securing of CI is emphatically connected to the items' execution (Al-Busaidi, 2013). Therefore, item quality is one of the principle CIAresults. Notwithstanding, the impact of CIA on item quality in the field of programming improvement appears to be one of the less investigated and analyzed topic.

- **Software Quality:** Quality is the capacity of an arrangement of natural attributes to fulfill necessities. The express "fulfilment of client prerequisites" (Kannabiran and Sankaran, 2011) envelops a few right now tons of the product quality. In this investigation, keeping in mind the end goal to gauge the product quality build, programming quality ascribes should be measured. The survey was led to remove more iterative characteristics of programming quality in the writing and utilize them to gauge programming quality in the model. As indicated by the consequence of this survey, Reliability, Efficiency, Usability, Maintainability and Usefulness were observed to be more iterative than different characteristics in the writing. Kannabiran and Sankaran (2011) utilized similar characteristics in their examination for measuring the product quality build.

Research Methodology

As indicated by Kumar (2012), disclosing how to answer the exploration questions is the fundamental capacity of look into outline, which drives the specialists from wide suppositions to nitty gritty techniques for information accumulation and investigation. The accompanying subsections altogether clarify each stage and their stages.

- With a specific end goal to recognize the current research hole and difficulties with regards to ES quality writing, a survey was directed. To this end, the absence of far reaching research on improving ES quality by utilizing the CIA was found. In like manner, the real issue of the present examination that mirrors the hole in the writing was risen as "What are the forerunner factors that impact the CIA for the ES quality change in the ES advancement organizations?" Therefore, to address the primary inquiry of this investigation from the focal point of the Generic CIA Framework, three different inquiries were asked: (1) what are the Human, Organizational and

Figure 3. Research Design Framework

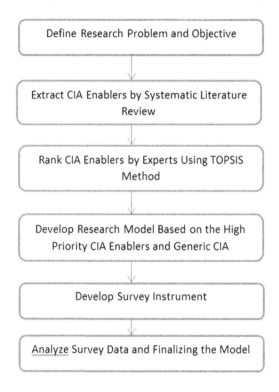

Technological predecessor factors that affect CIA in the association? (2) what are the predecessor factors that impact CIA for the ES quality change in the ES advancement organizations? (3) what is the reasonable research display that goes for cultivating the ES quality by utilizing CIA factors inside the ES improvement organizations?

- The primary target of this investigation was to distinguish the Human, Organizational and Technological predecessor factors that affect CIA in the association. To this end, a thorough precise writing survey was led. Keeping in mind the end goal to choose the suitable investigations for removing the CIA forerunner factors, seven databases (AISeL, Emerald Insight, IEE Explore, Science Direct, Scopus, Springer link, Taylor and Francis Online) were investigated. Additionally, the articles were chosen by separating the outcomes in light of title, catchphrases and by perusing the theoretical and utilizing consideration and rejection criteria. The after effect of our inquiries demonstrated that since 2011, the quantity of articles concerning has developed significantly. The majority of the new CIA articles have explored CIA results. Thusly, new patterns in CIA showed the investigations about the connection between CIA also, hierarchical execution, the CIA and authoritative learning and development, CIA and the item and administration quality. Notwithstanding, considers with respect to the CIA empowering influences are less investigated. Along these lines, 72 articles from 2002 until the point that 2016 were chosen. In the wake of inspecting these articles, 22 CIA predecessor factors were separated. Precursor factors were ordered to Human, Organizational and Mechanical elements. These variables were separated from the articles that explored CIA in the diverse setting and nations. They chose thinks about investigated CIA factors in the 14 unique settings. They chose contemplates were performed in the 19 distinct nations, of which the greater part of them are produced nations. At that point, the exploration techniques for chose articles were reviewed. The most articles have utilized review technique. The after effect of extricating the CIA predecessor factors demonstrated that "Client Centric Culture", "Joint effort System" and "CRA Technology Infrastructure" have the most recurrence in the writing, while "Protected innovation", "Program Champion" and" Trust" are less iterative components (see Table 1).

- The second target of this investigation was centred around the positioning of potential factors that impact CIA for the ES quality change with regards to the ES improvement organizations. The Hypothetical CIA Model was created in view of 22 predecessor CIA factors that have been separated from the writing. The specialists in the field of ES improvement in Iran assessed the proposed display. The Theoretical CIA Model is produced by removing the precursor factors from the writing. At that point, Technique for request of Preference by Similarity to Ideal Solution (TOPSIS) as a Multi-Criteria Decision Making (MCDM) procedure is connected to discover the significance level of components with respect to improvement in the product organizations. 31 specialists in the ES improvement organizations decided the weight and need of the components. From the specialists' perspective, the outcomes demonstrated that CIA forerunner variables can be arranged into high need and low need gatherings. 11 factors from the removed predecessor factors were in the high significance gathering. In this way, these factors have been considered which are basic for the effective usage of CIA. In expansion, high need authoritative variables ("Customer inclusion", "Client driven culture", "CIA system advancement", "Cross-useful participation", "Top director bolster", "Hierarchical preparing") enact different factors and give the suitable condition to CIA. Moreover, high need innovative components ("Collaboration framework", "CRM innovation framework", "Information delineate") CIA in the association. Additionally, high need human components ("Individual capabilities and aptitudes", "Trust amongst client and friends")

Table 1. The Frequency of CIA Antecedent Factors in the Literature

CIA Antecedent Factors	Frequency
Customer-centric culture	38
Collaboration system	29
CRM technology infrastructure	29
CIA Strategy development	28
Individual competences and skills	25
Community of practice	24
CK oriented business process	20
Reward system	20
Key customer support	18
Top manager support	18
Individual motivation	17
Training	17
Cross-functional cooperation	14
Customer involvement	12
Integrated knowledge repository	12
Social media	11
Customer knowledge quality	8
Knowledge map	7
Provide privacy for customers	5
Trust between customer and company	5
Program champion	4
Respect to the intellectual property	4

are actuated and impacted by the authoritative and mechanical conditions (see Table 2).

- In this investigation, the Generic CIA Framework is utilized to build up the exploration show. This system demonstrates the grouping impact of three angles (Enablers, Processes and Outcomes). What's more, in this inquire about, the primary result of utilizing CIA is programming quality change. Accordingly, the examination demonstrate is created in light of the high need CIA factors which are separated from the writing also, assessed by the ES advancement specialists (see Figure 4)

- In the wake of building up the hypothetical model and characterizing the examination theories, estimation things were removed from the writing to assess the model whether the exploration speculations are upheld or rejected

Table 2. Final Ranking of CKM Antecedent Factors

CIA Antecedent Factors	Rank
Customer involvement	0.593590
Customer-centric culture	0.590937
CIA strategy development	0.590003
Collaboration system	0.587413
Cross-functional cooperation	0.580199
Individual competences and skills	0.572135
Trust between customer and company	0.568038
Top manager support	0.564566
CRM technology infrastructure	0.558364
Training	0.547299
Knowledge map	0.543385
Key customer management	0.390853
Reward system	0.383553
CI oriented business process	0.383275
CI quality	0.375244
Individual motivation	0.368001
Program champion	0.341885
Integrated knowledge repository	0.341851
Community of practice	0.334415
Social media	0.326380
Provide privacy for customers	0.309822
Respect to the intellectual property	0.308688

(see Table 1 in Appendix A). To accomplish this target, this investigation created substantial and solid estimation things for the conjectured builds and the connections in the proposed examine display. Hair et al. (2013) gave a few criteria to recognize the build sort which can be in two classes, developmental or intelligent. As indicated by Hair et al. (2013), CIA and Programming Quality as appeared in Fig. 4 are multi-dimensional builds and developmental and the other builds are intelligent. The vast majority of the contemporary specialists utilized the current estimation things in the writing and reconsidered them with respect to the reason and the setting of their exploration (Ramirez et al., 2013). A similar approach is taken after. In this manner, the estimation things are received from the past approved sources. The poll was assessed utilizing content legitimacy what's more, a pilot thinks

Figure 4. Research Model

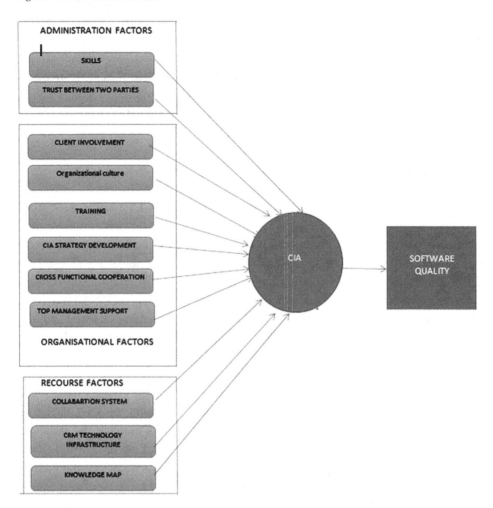

about. Content legitimacy distinguishes that to what degree estimation things mirror the operational meaning of a build. A Content Validity Index (CVI) approach was utilized to approve the estimation things in term of importance and straightforwardness. Amid the substance legitimacy, the number of estimation things was diminished from 50 to 46. A few inquiries were refined in their demean or what's more, wording. The pilot ponder surveyed the unwavering quality and legitimacy of the estimation things. The pilot testing has a part in guaranteeing that the outlined instrument works well. In the pilot examine, 48 finished surveys from the ES improvement organizations were gathered. In this progression, two 10 instrument things were dispensed with as a result of low external stacking. All other instrument things were affirmed for the information gathering.

- In the wake of planning a substantial and solid estimation instrument and in view of the objective populace, overview information were gathered. The information were broke down utilizing the Partial Least Squares Structural Condition Modelling (PLS-SEM) strategy with the guide of SmartPLS 2.0 measurable programming. The outcomes of the examination were utilized to conclude the reasonable model.

Hypothesis Formulation

In light of the chose precursor factors that impact on the CIA and the connection between the CIA and the product quality, 12 investigate theories were created which are clarified as takes after. Singular Competences and Skills. This relates to every one of the aptitudes and abilities of laborers in acquiring, sharing and using the client information. Past exact examinations found a positive relationship between singular capabilities and aptitudes and CIA (Tseng and Fang, 2015; Attafar et al., 2013; Hair et al., 2013; Wu et al., 2013; Wilde, 2011). The more elevated amounts of individual capabilities and aptitudes are related with the effective CIIA in the ES advancement setting (Aho and Uden, 2013). Along these lines, this prompts the accompanying speculation:

- **H1**: Individual abilities and aptitudes decidedly impact the CIA in the ES advancement setting. Trust amongst Customer and Company. As indicated by Skotis et al. (2013), put stock in alludes to the shirking of sharp practices to pick up CI and the parallel change of the company's notoriety and picture. There is an observational confirmation that trust amongst client and friends is huge and decidedly identified with the CIA (Vaezitehrani, 2013; Wu et al., 2013; Lin et al., 2006). In this manner, the accompanying theory is recommended:
- **H2**: Trust amongst client and friends decidedly impacts the CIA in the ES advancement setting. Client Involvement. Client association alludes to the interest and collaboration of the clients in the prelaunch period of an advancement or improvement of item/benefit, which has four stages: (1) Idea Generation, (2) Concept Development, (3) Product Design and (4) Prototyping/ Testing. Client association is a significant hotspot for the CKM since the measure of client contribution can enhance the level of learning that would be assembled from the client. Hence, the client association is emphatically identified with the CK improvement. As needs be, the accompanying theory is proposed:

- **H3**: Customer contribution decidedly impacts the CIA in the ES improvement setting. Client Centric Culture. The CIA as a client situated business approach is one of the noteworthy assets in firms that help them to change themselves into a client driven circumstance. Al-Shammari and Global (2009) noticed that effective CKM requires change of the associations from product– driven to client driven and from storing to a sharing society. Consequently, the following theory is proposed:

- **H4:** Customer-Centric Culture decidedly impacts CIA in ES advancement setting. CIA Strategy Development. This relates to the hierarchical approach that examines CI as a prized wellspring of item and process upgrade, and rearranges the way toward sharing, securing and executing purchaser information (Aho and Uden, 2013). Khodakarami and Chan (2014) specified that a powerful technique can be a critical hierarchical factor that impact the CI creation endeavors. Henceforth, the accompanying speculation is proposed:

- **H5**: CIA technique advancement decidedly impacts the CIA in the ES improvement setting. Top Management Support. This relates to the procedures through which the best administration demonstrates its sponsorship for the age and digestion of the CI inside the association (Campbell, 2003). The support of best administration has been observed to be basic for the CIA accomplishment in many examinations (Salojärvi et al., 2010; Rollins and Halinen, 2005). In this way, the accompanying speculation is recommended:

- **H6**: Top administration inclusion emphatically impacts the CIA in the ES advancement setting. Hierarchical Training. This alludes to the CIA preparing program for the workers to engage them, to retain, share and apply the CI adequately. It was commented by Lyu et al. (2009) that, using the CK relies upon the faculty preparing. The past examinations demonstrated that worker preparing has emphatically related with the CIA upgrade in the organizations (Garrido-Moreno et al., 2014; Khodakarami and Chan, 2014; Talet, 2012; Garrido-Moreno and Padilla-Meléndez, 2011; Shieh, 2011; Gebert et al., 2002). In like manner, the accompanying speculation is proposed:

- **H7:** Training program emphatically impacts CIA in ES advancement setting. Cross-Functional Cooperation. This alludes to the collaboration among the distinctive offices in an organization. Shieh (2011) and Nejatian et al. (2011) contended about the significance of cross-utilitarian participation for the CIA. Khodakarami and Chan (2014) specified that the independency of the collective frameworks inside interior offices and the absence of cross-utilitarian collaboration are the hindrances of the CIA. At that point, the accompanying theory is proposed:

- **H8**: Cross-utilitarian participation emphatically impacts the CIA in the ES advancement setting.
- CRM Technology Infrastructure. This alludes to the data innovation foundation, for example, CRM what's more, other programming and equipment frameworks that encourage the administration of the client information and data (Salojärvi et al., 2010; Rollins and Halinen, 2005). The CRM specialized foundation can help the association not just by organizing the information about and from the clients, yet additionally offer assistance the administration worker to give the information to the clients and take care of their issues (Skotis et al., 2013; Talet, 2012; Dous et al., 2005). Consequently, we propose the accompanying speculation:
- **H9**: CRM innovation emphatically identified with the CIA in the ES improvement setting. Coordinated effort System. Cooperation framework is a data framework which is utilized to encourage productive sharing of the records and information between the groups and people in a venture (Chan, 2009; Bueren et al., 2004; Gebert et al., 2002). Shieh (2011) demonstrated that the productivity of the joint effort framework and the group operation has a positive association with the CIA. Smith and McKeen (2005) noted that building up a coordinated effort framework that help groups of training for clients is essential for fruitful CIA. Along these lines, we propose the accompanying speculation:
- **H10**: Cooperation framework decidedly identified with the CIA in the ES advancement setting. Information Map. A client learning map is a route help to find the wellsprings of express and inferred CK by delineating how CI courses through the associations. The learning guide would go about as a reference in the improvement of IA to help CRM (Talet, 2012). The past investigations found a positive connection between information outline fruitful CKM in the associations (Bagheri et al., 2015; Mukherji, 2012; Smith and McKeen, 2005; Gebert et al., 2002). At that point, the accompanying speculation was proposed:
- **H11**: Information delineate impacts the CIA in the ES improvement setting.
- CIA and Software Quality. CI assumes a crucial part in building up the quality programming (Prabhu et al., 2011). Yeung et al. (2008) noticed that CI improves the item quality in the production network condition. The past investigations found a positive connection amongst CIA and item quality in the associations (Aho and Uden, 2013; Al-Busaidi, 2013; Wu et al., 2013; Talet, 2012; Kannabiran and Sankaran, 2011; Prabhu et al., 2011; Yeung et al., 2008; Lin et al., 2006; Stefanou et al., 2003). At that point, the accompanying theory is proposed:

- **H12**: CKM decidedly impacts the Software Quality in the ES advancement setting.

INFORMATION ANALYSIS AND DISCUSSION

Profile of Respondents

The present examination concentrates on the product organizations in Iran that create ES, for example, CRM, Accounting Frameworks, and Enterprise Resource Planning (ERP). The respondents in this examination are engaged with the basic leadership and taking care of client request, for example, the Chief Customer Officer, Chief Commercial Officer, Chief Product Officer, and Chief Executive Officer, who are very learned about the 12 administrations of CI and item quality. The Computer Trade Organization (CTO) in Iran is mindful for approving the organization abilities. Organizations that need to work in the field of PC equipment also, programming need to get a permit from the CTO before working here. CTO works under the Preeminent Council of Informatics (SCI). The SCI is an abnormal state government body that screens and positions every single dynamic organization in the Iranian informatics area. As per the most recent insights from the CTO site, 283 programming organizations are dynamic in the field of ES advancement. This examination utilizes the CTO database. The contact number, mail address, and email of these organizations are accessible in the CTO database. The International Exhibition of Electronic Computers and IT (ELECOMP) is a major yearly ICT presentation in Tehran. This occasion features the items like hardware and programming items from the maker and retailer related administrations organizations. In this investigation, the information accumulation started at ELECOMP 2015. 52 ES improvement organizations were introduced at the show, which were all given an overview survey. An aggregate of 33 (64%) substantial surveys were gathered. For the following period of information gathering, whatever is left of the ES advancement organizations were called by phone. 166 of these organizations consented to collaborate with this investigation. On the whole, 166 surveys alongside an introductory letter, prepaid return envelope, and a CTO's consent letter were dispatched to the sharing firms. The respondents were requested to consider their CIA conditions and the client input in their reactions. An organized mail poll was utilized as an overview instrument. A few calls were made to the organizations as an update. A sum of 109 reactions were gotten, and the reaction rate was 65 percent at the organization level (109/166). Be that as it may, just 95 reactions were legitimate. An underlying notice by telephone, CTO's letter of authorization for social occasion information, and affirmation of protection and classification were utilized to upgrade the rate of reaction. Besides, the scientist guaranteed to offer a graphic synopsis of the examination results to respondents. In the last period of information gathering, to enhance the reaction rate, organizations were called by phone. The specialists went by the site of a few organizations to gather information up close and personal. 36 legitimate polls were gathered in this stage. An aggregate of 164 substantial surveys were gathered from 283 programming organizations (a reaction rate of 57.9%). The base number of respondents was ascertained utilizing G*Power programming. All perceptions with the missing information were avoided from the investigation on the grounds that the number of cases was adequate to be utilized as a part of the chose factual methods. The quantity of the substantial cases was bigger than the required number of 123 cases as controlled by the G*Power examination. The activity work announced by the respondents was generally disseminated between the Chief Commercial Officer (43%) to Chief Executive Officer (15%), and the dominant part of them (53%) had over 10 years working knowledge in the field of programming improvement. Most respondents announced (72%) 50-250 fulltime workers in their association. In this investigation, the meaning of SMEs gave by the European Commission (2005) was embraced, which stipulates that small scale endeavors have less than ten workers; little undertakings have 10-49 workers, medium-sized firms have 50-250 representatives, and enormous associations have more than 250 workers (Durst & Runar Edvardsson, 2012). In this way, in this think about, 72% of the organizations were medium-sized firms and 18% of them were little undertakings. Just 10% of the respondents were from the enormous organizations. The CRM encounter factors speak to what extent an organization has executed CRM techniques (Garrido-Moreno and Padilla-Meléndez, 2011). What's more, most of the product organizations (72%) utilized the CRM techniques for over 5 years. The lion's share of the respondents was male (52%), hold Bachelor degrees (76%), and were inside the 26-35 age gathering (49%). A diagram of statistic attributes is given in Table 3.

Assessment of Measurement Model

In this examination, the information investigation is isolated into two stages, which is proposed by Hair et al. (2013). In the beginning stage, the estimation show is inspected with respect to the legitimacy and dependability. After the affirmation of the estimation show, in the following stage, the auxiliary model ought to be evaluated by evaluating the connection amongst builds and the prescient capacity of the model. In this way, in this area, the estimation display is surveyed to ensure that each build is measured properly. Hair et al. (2013) noticed that intelligent measures should be assessed for the marker dependability, inside consistency, discriminant legitimacy and focalized legitimacy. Interior consistency is evaluated utilizing Cronbach's alpha and composite unwavering quality. Marker dependability is assessed in term

Table 3. Profile of Survey Respondents

Gender	%			Education	%	Age	%
Respondents profile							
Male	52			Bachelor's	76	26-35	49
Female	48			Master's	19	36-45	39
				Higher	5	46-55	9
						>55	3
Job Title	%					Working Experience	%
Chief Executive Officer	15					<5	4
Chief Commercial Officer	43					5-10	43
Chief Customer Officer	25					10-15	27
Chief Product Officer 17 Over 15 26							
Employees	%				CRM Experience		%
>250	10				<5		28
50-250	72				5-10		50
<50	18				>10		22

of thing stacking, while focalized legitimacy is assessed utilizing the estimation of Average Variance Extracted (AVE). Fornell Larker paradigm together with assessment of cross-factor stacking were utilized to survey the discriminant legitimacy. The developmental builds are assessed for their co linearity issue utilizing the resistance and Change Inflation Factor (VIF) together with checking the hugeness and importance of their pointers' external weights. The proposed demonstrate in this investigation comprises of two endogenous idle factors (subordinate) which are developmental and 11 exogenous (autonomous) factors that are intelligent. Tables 4 introduce the legitimacy and unwavering quality appraisal of intelligent builds.

As introduced in Table 4, the external stacking of all pointers met the limit of 0.7. The estimations of Composite Reliability (CR) and Cronbach's alpha of every single intelligent build is well over the adequate edge of 0.7. Besides, all the AVE esteems surpass the edge of 0.5.

Table 4. Factor Loadings and Reliability of Reflective Constructs Using PLS-SEM

Construct	Item	Outerloading	Cronbach's α	CR	AVE
Trust	TR01	0.833			
	TR02	0.815	0.777	0.871	0.692
	TR03	0.845			
Competencies and Skills	CO 01	0.919			
	CO 02	0.848	0.859	0.914	0.780
	CO 03	0.881			
Client Involvement	CI01	0.899			
	CI02	0.816	0.841	0.904	0.759
	CI03	0.895			
Organizational Culture	OC01	0.824			
	OC02 OC03	0.875 0.815	0.833	0.889	0.667
CKM Strategy Development	OC04 SD 01	0.746 0.832			
	SD 02	0.910	0.844	0.906	0.763
	SD 03	0.875			
Cross-Functional Cooperation	CF01	0.827			
	CF02 CF03	0.838 0.843	0.845	0.895	0.681
Senior Management Support	CF04 TS 01	0.789 0.866			
	TS 02	0.858	0.834	0.900	0.751
	TS 03	0.874			
Training	TN 01	0.856			
	TN 02	0.857	0.859	0.900	0.750
	TN 03	0.775			
CRM Technology Infrastructure	TI01	0.806			
	TI02	0.855	0.782	0.873	0.696
	TI03	0.840			
Collaboration System	CS 01	0.786			
	CS 02	0.773	0.767	0.867	0.686
	CS 03	0.916			
Client Knowledge Map	KM01	0.814			
	KM02	0.901	0.843	0.904	0.759
	KM03	0.896			

Note: CR = Composite Reliability and AVE = Average Variance Extracted.

To survey the discriminant legitimacy, the estimation demonstrate is inspected by the criteria of cross loading values and the more traditionalist approach of Fornell-Larcker. Table 5 exhibited the Fornell Larcker appraisal, in which the square roots AVE of each develop ought to be more noteworthy than its relationship with alternate develops. Table 2 in Appendix A presents the estimations of cross-stacking of marker things, in which a pointer's external loadings on the related build ought to be more noteworthy than of all its stacking on different develops (Hair et al., 2013). Subsequently, the two criteria of cross-stacking and Fornell-Larcker appraisal were met. Along these lines, the estimation display mirrored the legitimate and dependable inward consistency, pointer unwavering quality, discriminant also, joined legitimacy in regard to the estimations of their external stacking, composite unwavering quality, Cronbach's alpha, AVE, cross-stacking and Fornell-Larcker, individually. The developmental builds of the CIA and Software Quality were evaluated in regard to their co linearity issue and furthermore the importance and significance of their pointers' external weights. The after effects of legitimacy and dependability of these develops are represented in Table 6.

As per Table 6, the outcome demonstrates that there are no co linearity issues with the developmental develops as the estimation criteria of resistance and VIF both met the limits of more than 0.2 and under 5, individually, for every marker of the developmental builds (Hair et al., 2013).

Table 5. Fornell-Larcker Criterion Results

	CF	CI	CI	CO	CS	KM	OC	SD	SQ	TI	TN	TR	TS
CF	**0.825**												
CI	0.666	**0.871**											
CI	0.758	0.756	F										
CO	0.675	0.610	0.735	**0.883**									
CS	0.713	0.610	0.730	0.630	**0.828**								
KM	0.321	0.340	0.375	0.406	0.289	**0.871**							
OC	0.402	0.414	0.511	0.437	0.407	0.264	**0.817**						
SD	0.391	0.403	0.484	0.459	0.438	0.080	0.290	**0.874**					
SQ	0.541	0.484	0.629	0.493	0.459	0.269	0.307	0.222	F				
TI	0.574	0.582	0.666	0.628	0.552	0.149	0.395	0.528	0.327	**0.835**			
TN	0.017	0.078	0.081	0.177	-0.001	0.243	0.122	0.175	0.029	0.166	**0.866**		
TR	0.694	0.706	0.726	0.592	0.661	0.306	0.311	0.385	0.371	0.496	0.067	**0.832**	
TS	0.223	0.275	0.334	0.274	0.183	0.119	0.152	0.146	0.152	0.143	0.033	0.236	**0.867**

Note: F indicates formative construct.

Table 6. Validity and Reliability Assessment for Formative Constructs

	Measure	Tolerance	VIF	Significance of Outer Weight
Construct	CIACI1	.406	2461	3.0351
	CI2	.394	2.539	3.0864
	CI3	.442	2.265	3.9312
	CI4	.373	2.679	5.7806
Software Quality	SQ1	.946	1.057	4.0313
	SQ2	.878	1.139	3.3079
	SQ3	.936	1.068	2.293
	SQ4	.916	1.091	4.1632
	SQ5	.922	1.084	2.6378

Assessment of the Structural Model

In the initial step, the basic model should be assessed for the co linearity issues by evaluating the estimation of Variance Inflation Factor (VIF) and the level of resistance. At that point, the noteworthiness and significance of the basic model ought to be inspected utilizing way coefficient esteems and standard mistakes (t-values) which are acquired through the utilization of bootstrapping system. Subsequently, the level of R-square (R2) ought to be accounted for. R2 mirrors the measures of difference of the reliant variable, which is clarified by its indicator develops in the basic model (Hair et al., 2013). The estimation of R2 ranges from 0 to 1 what's more, the higher esteems demonstrate the better forecast capacity of the model through PLS way modelling.(Lin et al., 2012; Ifinedo, 2011; Chow and Chan, 2008). Table 7 represented the after effect of the co linearity evaluation. The outcomes demonstrate that the estimations of resistance are more than 0.20 and the estimations of VIF are under 5. In this way, they passed the edges. Thusly, every one of the builds incorporated into the proposed show were not related and no develop is should have been wiped out from the model.

The following stage for assessing the auxiliary model is the appraisal of way coefficients that are the consequence of the PLS calculation. The way coefficient (β) has standard esteems between - 1 and +1, in which a esteem more like +1 takes after a solid positive relationship and an esteem nearer to - 1 mirrors a solid negative relationship. Likewise, to look at the essentialness of way coefficients the t-values are evaluated utilizing the criteria of p-values. While there was no immediate approach to get p-values. In this examination, the p-values are ascertained by utilizing worked in capacity of MS Excel named as TDIST in which its contentions are the t-esteem, level of opportunity, and the quantity of tails for the circulation

Table 7. Co linearity Assessment for the Structural Model

Construct	Tolerance	VIF
CF	0.352	2.839
CI	0.382	2.615
CO	0.384	2.604
CS	0.397	2.518
KM	0.721	1.388
OC	0.755	1.325
SD	0.650	1.538
TI	0.454	2.201
TN	0.859	1.164
TR	0.379	2.638
TS	0.898	1.114

(for this situation two-followed test), and the yield of this capacity is the p-esteem. The path coefficient (β) demonstrates the qualities of the connection between the autonomous and subordinate factors (Ko et al., 2005). The speculation testing is finished by following the rules proposed by Chin (1998). He suggested that the way hugeness can be evaluated through t-tests values by utilizing the bootstrapping method. Ordinarily, t-esteem >1.96 implies noteworthy level. Moreover, in light of past investigations, p-value<0.05 affirms that related speculation is noteworthy (Ifinedo, 2011). The PLS bootstrapping strategy was used to gauge noteworthiness as demonstrated by t-values in the PLS yield (Hair et al., 2013). The PLS bootstrapping calculation utilizes mean trade for the missing values. The outcomes revealed in Table 8 incorporate (1) the way coefficients (β), (2) the way's comparing t value with a documentation of the related level of importance, and (3) the p-values are utilized to show regardless of whether the relationship of the builds is altogether or irrelevantly associated. Since the PLS strategy does not offer essentialness tests as a piece of the general assessment method, this approach is steady with the suggestions in the past investigations distributed in the data frameworks diaries (Lin et al., 2012). As indicated by Backhaus et al. (2003, 2009), there isn't any understanding with respect to adequate edge estimations of R2. Notwithstanding, the bigger R2 is, the bigger the level of difference clarified (Götz, 2010). Jaw and Dibbern (2010) depicts R2 estimations of 0.67, 0.33, and 0.19 in the PLS way models individually as generous, direct, and powerless.

The R2 estimations of "CIA" and the "Product Quality" which are two ward develops of this look into are 0.797 and 0.693, which are generally considerable and

Table 8. Summary of the Structural Model

Hypothesis	Description	Path Coefficient	*t*-Value	*p*-Value	SignificanceLevel	Results
H1	CO -> CK	0.130	2.416	0.017	**	Supported
H2	TR-> CK	0.156	2.227	0.027	**	Supported
H3	CI-> CK	0.181	2.721	0.007	***	Supported
H4	OC -> CK	0.113	2.523	0.013	**	Supported
H5	SD -> CK	0.044	0.948	0.344	NS	Not Supported
H6	TS-> CK	0.101	2.638	0.009	***	Supported
H7	TN -> CK	-0.035	0.653	0.514	NS	Not Supported
H8	CF-> CK	0.147	2.187	0.030	**	Supported
H9	TI-> CK	0.152	2.349	0.020	**	Supported
H10	CS-> CK	0.144	2.489	0.014	**	Supported
H11	KM-> CK	0.065	1.397	0.164	NS	Not Supported
H12	CK ->SQ	0.629	11.486	0.000	***	Supported

Note: NS = not significant.

* $p < .10$. ** $p < .05$. *** $p < .01$. (Hair et al., 2013)

direct, separately. As exhibited in Fig. 5, all the way coefficients were noteworthiness ($p<0.01$) aside from the way coefficient of connections amongst "CIA" and "Methodology Development" ($p = 0.344$), "Authoritative Training" ($p = 0.514$), and "Client Knowledge Map" ($p = 0.164$).

DISCUSSION

The after effects of this investigation affirmed that "Individual Competences and Skills" significantly affects CIA in the ES improvement. This finding is in accordance with the current examinations by Khodakarami and Chan (2014) and Skotis et al. (2013), which distinguished the critical part of abilities and skill to adequately deal with the CI. Speculation 2 predicts that the "Trust amongst client and friends" is decidedly identified with the CIA. Affirmation of this speculation demonstrates that the most programming organizations concurred that giving a putting stock in condition amongst organization and clients urges clients to share their learning and involvement with the organization. This empowers clients to easily share information, counsel with organization's specialists, and give new plans to deliver inventive items and enhance the product\service quality. This finding is predictable with Vaezitehrani (2013), Stefanou et al. (2003) and Skotis et al. (2013), who showed that trust amongst organizations and clients upgrades the ability of associations to recognize, retain, share, and convey important client learning. The outcome for Speculation 3 demonstrated a positive connection between the "Client Involvement" and the CIA. Besides, the "Client Involvement" had the most elevated effect on the CIA in this examination. This demonstrates that the "Client Involvement" is the most vital factor for enhancing the CIA in the ES advancement setting. The after effects of this investigation are steady with those of earlier examinations, which expressed that client inclusion is an unfair variable for the CIA frameworks, which considering the degree of client association builds the volume of data/information gathered from a client. Likewise, at the point when client association is high, it is less demanding to produce and accumulate intelligent information (Lorenzo-Romero et al., 2014; Kruse, 2013a; Kruse, 2013b; Mukherji, 2012). Theory 4, which anticipated that the "Client Centric Culture" positively affects the CIA, was affirmed in this examination. This outcome is predictable with the discoveries from Salojärvi et al. (2013), Gibbert et al. (2002) and Tseng and Fang (2015), who noticed that CIA is decidedly influenced by the "client centred culture".

The outcomes for Hypothesis 5 did not affirm a positive connection between the "CIA Strategy Advancement" and the CIA. This implies, according to hierarchical leaders, the technique of the most programming organizations won't not bolster the CIA. The statistic information demonstrates that the most programming organizations in Iran are SMEs (90%). The SMEs confront asset requirements (Durst & Runar Edvardsson, 2012). As indicated by Durst and Runar Edvardsson (2012), the greater part of SMEs is shy of unequivocal and comprehensive IA procedures, and subsequently tend to manage the IA on an operational level, accentuating just the frameworks and instruments. In examination with the vast estimated organizations, SMEs have an inclination to be more disposed towards the administration of certain learning, and their ways of correspondence regularly include different firms, rather than just inside the association. The SME area does not appear to be exceptionally created with regards to information development, for which it embraces just exceedingly unthinking methodology and is less occupied with social cooperation (Durst & Runar Edvardsson, 2012). Besides, to formulate a successful methodology design, the essential advance is to advance objectives of CIA that are steady with the objectives of an association. Nonetheless, most little organizations don't have enough time, spending plan, and experience to give the reasonable key designs with respect to the CIA. As per an examination of 22 programming advancement organizations that proposed items in ELECOMP 2014 (Khosravi et al., 2017), 69% of them didn't have any arrangements or rules for get-together client learning. Along these lines, lacking orderly procedures for CIA in many organizations (Salojärvi et al., 2010) also, disregarding the usage of CI in a few firms (Davenport et al., 2001), connoted that building up a clear CIA technique in the majority of programming organizations in Iran are not solid.

The after effects of this investigation uncovered a noteworthy relationship between the "Best administration bolster" and the CIA in the ES advancement setting. Therefore, it could be inferred that the best administration bolster identifies with and adds to the change in CIA. The best administration bolster is a broadly acknowledged condition for the fruitful usage of CIA as said in the past examinations (Attafar et al., 2013; Campbell, 2003) and affirmed by the present investigation.

The examination discoveries inferred that authoritative preparing did not essentially add to the CIA. This implies, according to the hierarchical chiefs, authoritative preparing did not bolster the CIA in the ES improvement setting in Iran. The SMEs don't have enough spending plan for worker preparing, particularly as they don't contribute for preparing programs that are not specifically identified with their centre business. Durst and Runar Edvardsson (2012) revealed that the most SMEs show a casual short-term approach towards the authoritative learning. The SMEs attempt to urge representatives to self-prepare. In these organizations, representatives attempt to take in required abilities from alternate colleagues, sites, web-based social networking, clients, and other learning sharing channels. The representatives upgrade their insight and abilities in related territories by learning sharing. Accordingly, coordinate authoritative preparing in these associations isn't solid. Hence, programming organizations ought to make a self-learning condition where the staff approaches learning that empowers them to get certain aptitudes and capabilities (Tseng and Fang, 2015). This might be the motivation behind why the hierarchical preparing does not essentially add to the CIA.

The after effect of this examination showed that a positive relationship between the "Cross-Functional Participation" and the CIA was found. Affirmation of this speculation delineated that participation between the diverse offices in an association significantly affects improving the CKM. In line with the after effects of past investigations (Garrido-Moreno et al., 2014; Salojärvi et al., 2013; Nejatian et al., 2011; Campbell, 2003), our discoveries give exact help of the significance of the "Cross Functional Participation" in the CIA. The Hypothesis 9 recommended that the "CRM Technology Foundation" significantly affects the CIA. The information investigation comes about affirmed a solid positive connection between the "CRM Technology Infrastructure" and the CKM. The after effects of this theory are reliable with the outcomes found by Tseng and Wu (2014) and Salojärvi et al. (2010), who proposed that CRM frameworks are important to help the CIA. Innovation can encourage the route in which clients and workers can get in touch with each other to talk about and share the information. The after effects of this contemplate connoted a positive relationship between the "Coordinated effort System" and the CKM in the ES improvement. Affirmation of this speculation exhibited that the "Joint effort

System" in associations significantly affects upgrading the CIA. These discoveries were affirmed by the consequences of the past investigations identified with the CIA. (Skotis et al., 2013; Mukherji, 2012; Buchnowska, 2011; Gebert et al., 2002).

The Hypothesis 11 suggested that the "Learning Map" significantly affected the CIA. As opposed to our desires, the "Learning Map" did not contribute essentially to the CIA. It implies that, according to the hierarchical chiefs, the "Learning Map" does not bolster the CIA in the ES improvement setting in Iran. In this way, as per our outcomes, utilizing the "Learning Map" to deal with the specialists' registries and sort out the implicit and express CI in the product organizations in Iran does not really prompt a dynamic and methodical CIA. This implies, notwithstanding the better than average nearness of CIA in the product firms, overseeing understood and additionally unequivocal learning is all the more specially appointed or, on the other hand intuition construct than situated in light of the methodical administration of information. Moreover, the "Learning Guide" might be emphatically connected with the before phases of handling, accomplishment and sharing the CIinside a venture, yet the undertaking might not have the aptitudes to utilize this. As indicated by Tao et al. (2006), their review demonstrated that 30 percent of the associations have an "Information Map". The way that the selection of "Information Map" is the second to the last among the 15 things of IA execution is a genuine concern (Tao et al., 2006). A similar outcome was accounted for on an examination of the 22 programming advancement organizations in Iran that proposed their item in ELECOMP 2014 (Khosravi et al., 2017). 41% of these organizations did not have a rundown of qualified specialists (index) and just 9% of them utilized the "Information Map" to deal with the client learning. This demonstrates the rate of utilizing the "Learning Guide" in the product organizations is low in light of the fact that the most programming organizations are little and face constraints in the HR, time, spending plan and ability to oversee and make the "Information Guide". In this way, obviously the most programming organizations in Iran did not adjust any sort of the "Learning Map".

The Hypothesis 12 placed that the CKM is decidedly identified with the "Product Quality". The consequences of this examination bolster the contention that the CKM impressively improves the "Product Quality" in the ES improvement. All through this investigation, the positive effect of the CKM on the product quality is exhibited. Thus, it can be presumed that once an association can get and share client data in a successful way, upgrading the item quality through the utilization of the CK can be achieved.

Implications and Limitations

Theoretical Implications

This study makes the following theoretical contributions:

Displaying the Generic CIA Framework is the primary hypothetical commitment that elucidated how the CIA precursor factors prompt the product quality. This system has defended that CIA is a profitable what's more, uncommon resource for organizations, which will enable them to react rapidly to the client needs and adjust to changing the business sectors (Shi and Yip2007). It ought to be noticed that gathering data from and about the clients through relationship and offering a better an incentive than those clients in view of this information will give a non-imitable favorable position (Garrido-Moreno and Padilla-Meléndez, 2011). In this way, information can be dealt with as an imperative asset for associations according to KBV of the firm (Wernerfelt1984). The KBV of the firm suggestion expresses that the association exists to make, exchange and change information into the upper hand (Alamgir and Quaddus, 2012). In this manner, this hypothetical structure reveals insight into the general instrument to effectively empower the CIA in the associations and the conditions by which the CIA upgrades programming quality.

To discover the CIA predecessor factors, a far reaching orderly writing audit was directed what's more, 22 CIA forerunner factors were separated. Subsequently, another hypothetical commitment of this examination that helps the specialists for additionally investigate is the consciousness of the importance of these separated factors.The weight and need of the variables were dictated by the specialists. Along these lines, this investigation gives a noteworthy commitment with regards to CIA by positioning the CIA forerunner factors for the ES advancement organizations. What's more, this examination made an imperative commitment in characterizing a model for CIA keeping in mind the end goal to actualize CIA effectively to enhance the item quality. The exhaustive examine that demonstrates the Human, Organizational and Technological condition for improving CIA in the programming organizations have been a missing bit of CIA baffle.

At last, this examination gave a hypothetically grounded focal point through which to better comprehend the condition for overseeing CI and incorporating it in the hierarchical business procedures to enhance the programming quality and therefore, accomplish the business change.

Practical Implementation

CI is turning into an undeniably basic vital preferred standpoint for the organizations. In any case, the CI has been frequently difficult to oversee by and by. Overall, this investigation makes the accompanying handy commitments:

For effectively actualizing and organization the CIA in the product organizations, two stages are recommended. In the main stage, the accentuation ought to be on the high need CIA precursor factors gathering so as to start and execute the CIA adequately. Additionally, professionals need to consider the high huge factors more than others. At that point in the following stage, the directors can concentrate on the low need variables to enhance the execution of CIA and finish the arrangement of CIA. Considering the reality that the most programming organizations in Iran are SMEs, the HR and the financial plan in these organizations are restricted. In this manner, committing the financial plan and human asset for CIA is exceptionally troublesome. Thusly, utilizing the after effect of this investigation encourages them to concentrate on the high need CIA achievement factors that can diminish the danger of CIA execution disappointments.

This investigation has fascinating ramifications for the supervisors in that it gives a valuable model to the fruitful usage of the CIA. The after-effects of the experimental trial of the model demonstrated that "Client Involvement", "Trust amongst Customer and Company" and "CRM Infrastructure" are the high huge components, while "Hierarchical Training", "CIA Strategy Development" and "Information Map" have not huge effect on the CIA with regards to ES advancement organizations in Iran. In this way, the after effect of the examination demonstrates that "Client Involvement" is crucial for the fruitful execution of CIA in the product organizations, since the client association gives a significant what's more, viable information for the organizations. In this manner, the part of the client to give the valuable learning for the organizations is featured more in the current item advancement writing. In like manner, this examination has recommended that organizations need to give the solid relationship lead clients in request to assimilate and utilize more CI and grow high caliber and inventive programming items that fit the client requests. It is emphatically prescribed that product organizations give enough assets and plans for including the main clients during the time spent the product advancement.

The finding of this examination demonstrates that creating and keeping up a framework that can encourage a dependable condition in which the two clients and the representatives could impart legitimately and trade their relative information in a productive path for improving the CIA. The discoveries of this investigation additionally demonstrate that how cultivating a proper CRA innovation foundation creates an incentive for the clients, upgrading the CIA and engaging the change of the items and administrations.

At long last, this investigation demonstrates that a top of the line item quality is positively and enormously impacted by the rate of the CIA, and at the appropriate time, there can be a change in the operational execution (Anderson et al., 2004). Considering that clients now and again can't expressive their requests, the associations should sustain themselves with the extraordinary correspondence capacity to practically connect with the buyers to accomplish the information relating to their requests. The after effects of this experimental think about rejected the immediate impact of the preparation on the CIA. Along these lines, the direct hierarchical preparing in the product associations in Iran isn't solid. Thus, programming organizations need to give a self-learning condition where the representative's approach learning that empowers them to obtain the certain aptitudes and skills.

Suggestions for Future Studies

In the first place, the setting of this examination is ES improvement organizations in Iran. The discoveries can be tried in the different settings and nations to broaden and additionally confirm the consequences of this examination.

Second, this exploration investigated the effect of the CIA on the product quality in light of the organization's recognition. In this way, it is proposed that future research can concentrate on a particular organization and examine the impact of the CI on the product quality from the clients' view of the organization.

Third, proposing the new procedures and strategies in light of the CIA predecessor factors that assistance the associations to diminish the danger of CIA usage is an open door for additionally explore. In expansion, it positively affects the economy all in all.

Fourth, because of the originality of the present research point, considering fitting factors that can encourage the connection between the CIA and the product quality is an open door for the further look into. Thus, the future research can broaden the exploration model of this examination and research the impact of the arbitrators, for example, organization measure, industry sort and CRA encounter on the connection between the CIA and the product quality. At long last, despite the fact that it was perceived that information is either implicit or unequivocal, the experimental examination of the examination did not make a refinement between these two sorts of learning. Accordingly, the future examinations ought to inspect in more detail the impact of the idea of the information on the CIA and its relationship with the product quality.

CONCLUSION

To reveal insight into the point, a model was produced that draws on the Generic CKM Framework to demonstrate connects between the CKM empowering agents and the CKM and also the CKM and the product quality. In this investigate, the proposed show was affirmed with regards to the ES improvement organizations. Of 12 conjectures, 3 of them (CKM Strategy Development, Organizational Training and Knowledge Map) were rejected. The outcomes affirmed that the CKM empowering agents are arranged into the Organizational, Human and Technological variables that effectively affect the CIA. The connection between the CIA (Processes measurement) and programming quality (Outcomes measurement) is factually noteworthy. Subsequently, the after effects of this examination emphatically affirmed and bolstered the Generic CIA Framework.

The KBV empowered us to expect that the utilization of Human, Organizational and Technological abilities enhances the IA procedures and expands the item and administration adequacy. As per IBV, when creating items and administrations from unmistakable assets, the blend and use of those assets assumes an indispensable part, which is identified with the capacity of an undertaking's skill. In this way, the Human factors, for example, Competencies and Skills, Trust between the Customer and Company and Hierarchical factors, for example, Organizational Culture, Cross-Functional Cooperation, Customer Contribution, Top Management Support and in addition Technological factors, for example, CRM Infrastructure and joint effort system empowers and impacts the CKM in the product associations.

In this examination, 8 CKM empowering influences were factually endorsed that can improve the CIA and the CIA altogether prompt one of the fundamental yields for the product advancement organizations. This result is predictable with the KBV hypothesis, which explains that learning is an unmistakable asset and that the execution of an association (as far as business, advancement, operations, item and administration quality) is subject to how soundly individuals from a business element can enhance their insight base, acclimatize new learning and data inside the business element and in addition the outside sources to the business element, and apply the information to the definition of items with superb quality and oddity.

REFERENCES

Aho, A.-M. & Uden, L. (2013). Customer knowledge in value creation for software engineering process. In *Proceedings of the 7th International Conference on Knowledge Management in Organizations: Service and Cloud Computing*. Springer. 10.1007/978-3-642-30867-3_13

Al-Busaidi, K. A. (2013). Empowering Organizations through Customer Knowledge Acquisition: A pilot investigation.

Al-Shammari, M. & Global, I. (2009). Customer knowledge management: People, processes, and technology.

Alamgir, M. & Quaddus, M. (2012). Customer Relationship Management Success Model: A Conceptual Framework. In *Proceedings of the 26th Australian and New Zealand Academy of Management Conference (ANZAM)*, Dec 5- 7.

Attafar, A., Sadidi, M., Attafar, H., & Shahin, A. (2013). The Role of Customer Knowledge Management (CKM) in Improving Organization-Customer Relationship. *Middle East Journal of Scientific Research*, *13*(6), 829–835.

Bagheri, S., Kusters, R. J., & Trienekens, J. (2015, September). The Customer Knowledge Management lifecycle in PSS Value Networks: Towards process characterization.

Belkahla, W., & Triki, A. (2011). Customer knowledge enabled innovation capability: Proposing a measurement scale. *Journal of Knowledge Management*, *15*(4), 648–674.

Buchnowska, D. (2011). Customer Knowledge Management Models: Assessment and Proposal.Research in Systems Analysis and Design: Models and Methods 25-38, Springer.

Bueren, A., Schierholz, R., Kolbe, L., & Brenner, W. (2004). Customer knowledge management improving performance of customer relationship management with knowledge management. In *Proceedings of the 2013 46th Hawaii International Conference on System Sciences*. IEEE Computer Society.

Campbell, A. J. (2003). Creating customer knowledge competence: Managing customer relationship management programs strategically. *Industrial Marketing Management*, *32*(5), 375–383. doi:10.1016/S0019-8501(03)00011-7

Chan, J. O. (2009). Integrating Knowledge Management and Relationship Management in an Enterprise Environment. *Communications of the IIMA.*, *9*(4), 37.

Cho, W., Subramanyam, R., & Xia, M. (2013). Vendors' incentives to invest in software quality in enterprise systems. *Decision Support Systems*, *56*, 27–36. doi:10.1016/j.dss.2013.04.005

Choi, S. and Ryu, I. (2013). Leveraging Customer Knowledge in Electronic Knowledge Repositories for Service Expertise. In *PACIS 2013 Proceedings* (pp. 132-145).

Chow, W. S., & Chan, L. S. (2008). Social network, social trust and shared goals in organizational knowledge sharing. *Information & Management, 45*(7), 458–465. doi:10.1016/j.im.2008.06.007

Davenport, T. H., Harris, J. G., & Kohli, A. K. (2001). How do they know their customers so well? *MIT Sloan Management Review, 42*(2), 63–73.

Dous, M., Salomann, H., Kolbe, L. and Brenner, W. (2005). Knowledge Management Capabilities in CRM: Making Knowledge For, From, and About Customers Work. In *AMCIS 2005 Proceedings*.

Durmuşoğlu, S. S., & Barczak, G. (2011). The use of information technology tools in new product development phases: Analysis of effects on new product innovativeness, quality, and market performance. *Industrial Marketing Management, 40*(2), 321–330. doi:10.1016/j.indmarman.2010.08.009

Durst, S., & Runar Edvardsson, I. (2012). Knowledge management in SMEs: A literature review. *Journal of Knowledge Management, 16*(6), 879–903. doi:10.1108/13673271211276173

Eisenhardt, K. M., & Santos, F. M. (2002). Knowledge-based view: A new theory of strategy. In Handbook of strategy and management (Vol. 1, pp. 139-164).

Feher, P., & Gabor, A. (2006). The role of knowledge management supporters in software development companies. *Software Process Improvement and Practice, 11*(3), 251–260. doi:10.1002pip.269

Fidel, P., Cervera, A., & Schlesinger, W. (2015a). Customer's role in knowledge management and in the innovation process: Effects on innovation capacity and marketing results. *Knowledge Management Research and Practice, 9*(1), 132–146.

Fidel, P., Schlesinger, W., & Cervera, A. (2015b). Collaborating to innovate: Effects on customer knowledge management and performance. *Journal of Business Research, 68*(7), 1426–1428. doi:10.1016/j.jbusres.2015.01.026

Garrido-Moreno, A., Lockett, N., & García-Morales, V. (2014). Paving the way for CRM success: The mediating role of knowledge management and organizational commitment. *Information & Management, 51*(1), 1031–1042. doi:10.1016/j.im.2014.06.006

Garrido-Moreno, A., & Padilla-Meléndez, A. (2011). Analyzing the impact of knowledge management on CRM success: The mediating effects of organizational factors. *International Journal of Information Management, 31*(5), 437–444. doi:10.1016/j.ijinfomgt.2011.01.002

Gebert, H., Geib, M., Kolbe, L., & Riempp, G. (2002). Towards customer knowledge management: Integrating customer relationship management and knowledge management concepts. *In Proceedings of the Second International Conference on Electronic Business (ICEB '02).*

Ghobadi, S. (2015). What drives knowledge sharing in software development teams: A literature review and classification framework. *Information & Management, 52*(1), 82–97. doi:10.1016/j.im.2014.10.008

Gibbert, M., Leibold, M., & Probst, G. (2002). Five styles of customer knowledge management, and how smart companies use them to create value. *European Management Journal, 20*(5), 459–469. doi:10.1016/S0263-2373(02)00101-9

Grant, R. M. (1996). Toward a knowledge-based theory of the firm. *Strategic Management Journal, 17*(S2), 109–122. doi:10.1002mj.4250171110

Hair, J. F., Hult, G. T. M., Ringle, C., & Sarstedt, M. (2013). *A primer on partial least squares structural equation modeling (PLS-SEM).* Sage Publications.

Hammami, S. M., & Triki, A. (2011). Exploring the information technology contribution to service recovery performance through knowledge based resources. *Vine, 41*(3), 296–314. doi:10.1108/03055721111171627

Ifinedo, P. (2011). Examining the influences of external expertise and in-house computer/IT knowledge on ERP system success. *Journal of Systems and Software, 84*(12), 2065–2078. doi:10.1016/j.jss.2011.05.017

Kannabiran, G., & Sankaran, K. (2011). Determinants of software quality in offshore development–An empirical study of an Indian vendor. *Information and Software Technology, 53*(11), 1199–1208.

Khodakarami, F. and Chan, Y. E. (2014). Exploring the role of customer relationship management (CRM) systems in customer knowledge creation. *Information & Management, 51*(1), 27–42.

Khosravi, A., Ab Razak, C.H. & Minaei-Bidgoli, B. (2017). Customer Knowledge Management in Software Development: A Descriptive Field Survey. *Journal of Theoretical and Applied Information Technology, 96*(1).

Khosravi, A., Ismail, M. A. B., & Najaftorkaman, M. (2014). A Taxonomy of Knowledge Management Outcomes for SMEs. In PACIS 2014 Proceedings.

Ko, D.-G., Kirsch, L. J. and King, W. R. (2005). Antecedents of knowledge transfer from consultants to clients in enterprise system implementations. *Management Information Systems Quarterly*, 59–85.

Korhonen-Sande, S., & Sande, J. B. (2016). Improving customer knowledge transfer in industrial firms: How does previous work experience influence the effect of reward systems? *Journal of Business and Industrial Marketing*, *31*(2), 232–246. doi:10.1108/JBIM-03-2014-0048

Kruse, P. (2013a). Customer Involvement in Organizational Innovation–Toward an Integration Concept. In *Proceedings of the Nineteenth Americas Conference on Information Systems, Chicago*, IL, August 15- 17.

Kruse, P. (2013b). External knowledge in organisational innovation-toward an integration concept. In *Proceedings of the 21st European Conference on Information Systems*.

Kumar, R. (2012). *Research Methodology: A Step-by-Step Guide for Beginners*. SAGE Publications.

Liao, S.-H., & Wu, C. (2010). System perspective of knowledge management, organizational learning, and organizational innovation. *Expert Systems with Applications*, *37*(2), 1096–1103. doi:10.1016/j.eswa.2009.06.109

Lin, H.-F. (2007). Knowledge sharing and firm innovation capability: An empirical study. *International Journal of Manpower*, *28*(3/4), 315–332. doi:10.1108/01437720710755272

Lin, T. C., Wu, S., & Lu, C. T. (2012). Exploring the affect factors of knowledge sharing behavior: The relations model theory perspective. *Expert Systems with Applications*, *39*(1), 751–764. doi:10.1016/j.eswa.2011.07.068

Lin, Y., Su, H.-Y., & Chien, S. (2006). A knowledge-enabled procedure for customer relationship management. *Industrial Marketing Management*, *35*(4), 446–456. doi:10.1016/j.indmarman.2005.04.002

Lohan, G., Lang, M., & Conboy, K. (2011). Having a customer focus in agile software development. In Information Systems Development (pp. 441-453). Springer. doi:10.1007/978-1-4419-9790-6_35

Lorenzo-Romero, C., Constantinides, E., & Brünink, L. A. (2014). Co-creation: Customer Integration in Social Media Based Product and Service Development. *Procedia: Social and Behavioral Sciences*, *148*, 383–396. doi:10.1016/j.sbspro.2014.07.057

Lyu, J.-J., Yang, S.-C., & Chen, C. (2009). Transform customer knowledge into company value—case of a global retailer. In *Proceedings of the 6th International Conference on Service Systems and Service Management ICSSSM '09*. IEEE.

Mukherji, S. (2012). A framework for managing customer knowledge in retail industry. *IIMB Management Review*, *24*(2), 95–103. doi:10.1016/j.iimb.2012.02.003

Nagati, H., & Rebolledo, C. (2012). The role of relative absorptive capacity in improving suppliers' operational performance. *International Journal of Operations & Production Management*, *32*(5), 611–630. doi:10.1108/01443571211226515

Nejatian, H., Sentosa, I., Piaralal, S. K., & Bohari, A. M. (2011). The influence of customer knowledge on CRM performance of Malaysian ICT companies: A structural equation modeling approach. *International Journal of Business and Management*, *6*(7), 181. doi:10.5539/ijbm.v6n7p181

Nonaka, I., Von Krogh, G., & Voelpel, S. (2006). Organizational knowledge creation theory: Evolutionary paths and future advances. *Organization Studies*, *27*(8), 1179–1208. doi:10.1177/0170840606066312

Prabhu, N. A., Latha, R., Sankaran, K., & Kannabiran, G. (2011). Impact of knowledge management on offshore software development: An exploratory study. In *Proceedings of the 2011 Third International Conference on Advanced Computing (ICoAC)*. IEEE.

Ramirez, E., David, M. E., & Brusco, M. J. (2013). Marketing's SEM based nomological network: Constructs and research streams in 1987–1997 and in 1998–2008. *Journal of Business Research*, *66*(9), 1255–1260. doi:10.1016/j.jbusres.2012.02.022

Ranjan, J., & Bhatnagar, V. (2011). Role of knowledge management and analytical CRM in business: Data mining based framework. *The Learning Organization*, *18*(2), 131–148. doi:10.1108/09696471111103731

Rollins, M., Bellenger, D. N., & Johnston, W. J. (2012). Does customer information usage improve a firm's performance in business-to-business markets? *Industrial Marketing Management*, *41*(6), 984–994. doi:10.1016/j.indmarman.2012.01.004

Rollins, M., & Halinen, A. (2005). Customer knowledge management competence: towards a theoretical framework. In *Proceedings of the 38th Annual Hawaii International Conference on System Sciences HICSS '05*. IEEE. 10.1109/HICSS.2005.180

Salojärvi, H., Saarenketo, S., & Puumalainen, K. (2013). How customer knowledge dissemination links to KAM. *Journal of Business and Industrial Marketing*, *28*(5), 383–395. doi:10.1108/08858621311330236

Salojärvi, H., & Sainio, L.-M. (2015). CRM Technology and KAM Performance: The Mediating Effect of Key Account-Related Knowledge. *Journal of Business Marketing Management.*, *8*, 435–454.

Salojärvi, H., Sainio, L.-M., & Tarkiainen, A. (2010). Organizational factors enhancing customer knowledge utilization in the management of key account relationships. *Industrial Marketing Management*, *39*(8), 1395–1402. doi:10.1016/j. indmarman.2010.04.005

Schaarschmidt, M., Bertram, M., Walsh, G. and von Kortzflieisch, H. F. (2015). Customer Knowledge and Requirements Engineering in Customization Projects: A Multi-Method Case Study. *ICIS 2015 Proceedings*, *12*(1), 111-126.

Shieh, C.-J. (2011). Study on the relations among the customer knowledge management, learning organization, and organizational performance. *Service Industries Journal*, *31*(5), 791–807. doi:10.1080/02642060902960818

Skotis, A., Katsanakis, I., Macris, A., & Sfakianakis, M. (2013). *Creating Knowledge within a C-Business Context: A Customer Knowledge Management View. In Collaborative, Trusted and Privacy-Aware e/m-Services (pp. 264- 277).* Springer.

Smith, H. A., & McKeen, J. D. (2005). Developments in practice XVIII-customer knowledge management: Adding value for our customers. *Communications of the Association for Information Systems*, *16*(1), 36.

Sofianti, T., Suryadi, K., Govindaraju, R., & Prihartono, B. (2010). Customer Knowledge Co-creation Process in New Product Development. In *Proceedings of the World Congress on Engineering.*

Stefanou, C. J., Sarmaniotis, C., & Stafyla, A. (2003). CRM and customer-centric knowledge management: An empirical research. *Business Process Management Journal*, *9*(5), 617–634. doi:10.1108/14637150310496721

Talet, A. N. (2012). KM Process and CRM to manage Customer Knowledge Relationship Management. *International Proceedings of Economics Development & Research IPEDR.*, *29*, 60–67.

Tao, Y.-H., Wu, Y.-L., & Li, J.-K. (2006). A taxonomy of knowledge maps in business application. In *Proceedings of the Thirty-Fifth Annual Meeting of Western Decision Institute*, Big Island, Hawaii, April 11-14 (pp. 72-81).

Theriou, G. N., & Chatzoglou, P. D. (2008). Enhancing performance through best HRM practices, organizational learning and knowledge management. *European Business Review*, *20*(3), 185–207. doi:10.1108/09555340810871400

Tseng, S.-M., & Wu, P.-H. (2014). The impact of customer knowledge and customer relationship management on service quality. *International Journal of Quality and Service Sciences*, *6*(1), 77–96. doi:10.1108/IJQSS-08-2012-0014

Tseng, S. (2016). The effect of knowledge management capability and customer knowledge gaps on corporate performance. *Journal of Enterprise Information Management*, *29*(1), 34–71. doi:10.1108/JEIM-03-2015-0021

Tseng, S. M., & Fang, Y. Y. (2015). Customer Knowledge Management Performance Index. *Knowledge and Process Management*, *22*(2), 68–77. doi:10.1002/kpm.1463

Vaezitehrani, S. (2013). Customer Knowledge Management in Global Software Projects [Master thesis]. Northumbria University Gothenburg, Sweden.

Van Den Brink, P. (2001). Measurement of conditions for Knowledge Sharing. In *Proceedings 2nd European Conference on Knowledge Management*, Bled.

Wang, H., & Yu, Z. (2010). The Research of Customer Knowledge Management in CRM. In *Proceedings of the 2010 International Conference on Intelligent Computation Technology and Automation (ICICTA)*, May 11-12.

Wang, M.-L. (2015). Learning climate and customer-oriented behaviors: The mediation of customer knowledge. *Journal of Managerial Psychology*, *30*(8), 955–969.

Wilde, S. (2011). *Customer Knowledge Management*. Springer.

Wu, J., Guo, B., & Shi, Y. (2013). Customer knowledge management and IT-enabled business model innovation: A conceptual framework and a case study from China. *European Management Journal*, *31*(4), 359–372. doi:10.1016/j.emj.2013.02.001

Yang, L.-R., Huang, C.-F., & Hsu, T.-J. (2014). Knowledge leadership to improve project and organizational performance. *International Journal of Project Management*, *32*(1), 40–53. doi:10.1016/j.ijproman.2013.01.011

Yeung, A. H. W., Lo, V. H. Y., Yeung, A. C. L., & Cheng, T. C. E. (2008). Specific customer knowledge and operational performance in apparel manufacturing. *International Journal of Production Economics*, *114*(2), 520–533. doi:10.1016/j.ijpe.2007.06.011

Bhullar, R. K., Pawar, L., & Kumar, V. (2016, October). A novel prime numbers based hashing technique for minimizing collisions. In *Proceedings of the 2016 2nd International Conference on Next Generation Computing Technologies (NGCT)* (pp. 522-527). IEEE.

Bhullar, R. K., Pawar, L., Bajaj, R., & Manocha, A. K. (2017). Intelligent stress calculation and scheduling in segmented processor systems using buddy approach. *Journal of Intelligent & Fuzzy Systems, 32*(4), 3129–3142. doi:10.3233/JIFS-169256

Taneja, K., Taneja, H., & Kumar, R. (2017). Multi-channel medium access control protocols: review and comparison. *Journal of Information and Optimization Sciences*.

Taneja, K., Taneja, H., & Bhullar, R. K. (2016, March). Cross-platform application development for smartphones: Approaches and implications. In *Proceedings of the 2016 3rd International Conference on Computing for Sustainable Global Development (INDIACom)* (pp. 1752-1758). IEEE.

Kumar, R. (2018). *DOS Attacks on Cloud Platform Their Solutions and Implications.* In *Critical Research on Scalability and Security Issues in Virtual Cloud Environments*. doi:10.4018/978-1-5225-3029-9.ch008

Kumar, R., Kumari, N., & Bajaj, R. (2018). Energy Efficient Communication Using Reconfigurable Directional Antenna in MANET. *Procedia Computer Science*.

Kaur, D., Kumar, R.V.K.M., Brar, S.S., & Kumaresan, K. (2015). Named entity recognition, extraction and classification using conditional random field with kernel approach. *International Journal of Applied Engineering Research*.

Zhang, Z. J. (2011). Customer knowledge management and the strategies of social software. *Business Process Management Journal, 17*(1), 82–106. doi:10.1108/14637151111105599

Zogaj, S. & Bretschneider, U. (2012). Customer integration in new product development-a literature review concerning the appropriateness of different customer integration methods to attain client information. *ECIS 2012 Proceedings, 15*(2), 12-18.

Chapter 11
Risk Management in Web Development

Anu Priya Sharma
Chandigarh University, India

Sugandha Sharma
Chandigarh University, India

ABSTRACT

This chapter describes how risk management is the identification, assessment, and prioritization of risks followed by coordinated and economical application of resources to minimize, monitor, and control the probability or impact of unfortunate events or to maximize the realization of opportunities. The National Institute of Standards and Technology, actuarial societies, and ISO standards has developed various risk management standards. The standards (methods, definitions and goals) are created in the context of project management, security, engineering, industrial processes, financial portfolios, actuarial assessments, or public health and safety.

INTRODUCTION

Risk word is derived from the Italian verb "Risicare." In the 16th century; the science of risk management was discovered. The root of risk management is the concept of probability that was developed to help better estimate human's chances in games. There is variety of description for the term "risk" but none is generally accepted. All definitions implicitly include two features: uncertainty (an event may or may not occur) and loss (an event has undesired effects).

DOI: 10.4018/978-1-5225-6029-6.ch011

- **Risk Management:** To maximize the awareness of opportunities by minimizing, monitoring and controlling the probability of unfortunate events is known as Risk Management. It's the procedure to identify, assess and prioritize the risk followed by synchronized and inexpensive application of resources.

The improbability in financial markets, fear from project failures (at any phase such as during designing, development, production, or life-cycles), legal liabilities, credit risk, accidents, natural causes and disasters, purposeful attack from an opponent, or events of uncertain or unpredictable root-cause are the main sources of risk. The two types of events are considered during risk management process are: (a). Negative events (b). Positive events. These can be classified such as the events that are negative falls into the category of Risk whereas the positive events are classified as opportunities.

The National institute of Standards and Technology, actuarial societies, and ISO standards has developed various risk management standards. The standards such as methods, definitions and goals are created in the context of project management, security, engineering, industrial processes, commercial portfolios, actuarial analyses, or public health and safety.

To lessen, observe, and constrain the probability or impact of tactless events or to increase the realization of opportunities. Risk management is the recognition, estimation, and arrangement of risks followed by coordinated and commercial application of resources.

There are assorted levels of risks that are evolved during the life cycle of a product. At every stage, be at planning, designing, development or implementation there is risk involved. Thus at is always advised to access the risk at the early stages so that at can be avoided to large extent.

The majority risks that are encountered during the development of a project are:

- Cost risk
- Schedule risk
- Performance risk
- Governance risk
- Strategic risks
- Operational risk
- Market risks
- Legal risks
- Risks associated with external hazards

There are various internal risks associated with each stage of the project, where as some risk are beyond the scope of project team. Such risks are external risks that could be arising from outside the organization.

There are various phases following which the risk can be identified, assessed, analyzed, evaluated and finally treated as shown in Figure 1.

Before the start of any project various risk factors should be considered so that preventive measures could be taken before it may lead to a serious problem. List of risk factors are encountered in real life cases and their preventive measures are discussed in Table 1.

Boehm's Risk-Management Process

Boehm's Risk-Management Process: Risk management was introduced as an explicit process in software development in the 1980s. The father of software risk management is considered to be Barry Boehm, who defined the risk-driven spiral model - a software-development lifecycle model - and then described the first risk-management process. Most of the processes defined since then stem from his basic process. As shown in Figure 2, the risk-management process consists of two sub-processes, "risk assessment" and "risk control."

Figure 1. Various types of Risk

Table 1. Boehm's ten risk factors

S.no.	Risk Factors	Preventive Measures
1.	Human errors are the first and most common issue	The best people should be employed. Tamely training, rewards should be given. Team with best people should be employed.
2.	Impractical schedule and unreasonable budget	Analyses of Business-case; incremental development; the modification and reuse of software; scheduling and budget.
3.	Incompatibility of standard software external components	Compatibility analyses, review of suppliers should be done with proper benchmarking; prototyping and review of reference installations.
4.	Improper Requirements analyses that ultimately leads to miss match of developed functions and requirements.	Business analyses and prototyping should be done with a win-win agreement between parties concerned.
5.	Unmatched User interfaces according to the needs	Description of all the system users, Prototyping by making various scenarios;
6.	Inadequate and insufficient architecture, poor performance and quality	Adequate and sufficient architecture and quality must be assured for best performance.
7.	Constant and rapid alteration of requirements	The threshold should be increased for changes; incremental development and change management must be supported
8.	Legacy systems related problems	It should support Design, recover and restructuring
9.	Problems related to Externally performed task	Parallel design or prototyping by several suppliers should be done following with regular audits
10.	Much risk is involved when there is overestimation of possessed IT capabilities	This could be concurred by cost benefit analyses, Technical analyses and prototyping

Figure 2. Bohem's Risk Management Process

Risk Management Strategies and Processes

The steps that combine to make up the overall risk management process are as follows:

- **Risk Identification:** The Company identifies then defines potential risks that may negatively influence a specific company process or project.
- **Risk Analysis:** The analyses are done to further understand the risk involved, and how at could influence the company's projects and objectives.
- **Risk Assessment and Evaluation:** The risk is evaluated after determining the risk's overall likelihood of occurrence and with its overall consequence.
- **Risk Mitigation:** Companies assess their highest-ranked risks. Further they develop a plan to improve them using specific risk control methods. These plans include risk mitigation processes, risk prevention tactics and contingency plans in the event the risk comes to fruition.
- **Risk Monitoring:** To continuously monitor and track new and existing risks the part of the mitigation plan includes following up on both the risks and the plan. The overall risk management process should also be reviewed and updated accordingly.

Risk Management Approaches

The risk management process is implemented after the specific risks are identified. There are number of strategies as shown in Figure 3, which companies' follows in context to different types of risk. Following are the various risk management approaches followed by companies:

Figure 3. Step by Step Process of Risk Management

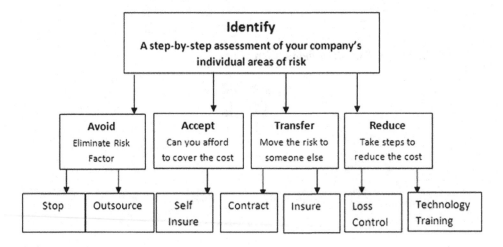

- **Risk Avoidance:** To avoid the costly, disruptive side effects to the project risk avoidance strategy is designed. Though complete elimination of risk is completely impossible still at can be avoided up to some extent.
- **Risk Reduction:** The amount of effect that certain risk can have on the processes, companies sometimes are able to reduce that effect by adjusting certain aspects of an overall project plan or by reducing process scope.
- **Risk Sharing:** The consequences of a risk could be shared or distributed among various project participants or departments. The risk cloud also be shared with vendors or business partners.
- **Risk Retaining:** Sometimes companies decide to retain the risk and deal with at. This is the case when project's anticipated profit is greater than the cost of its potential risk.

Other than banking systems there are lots of risk involved in other project such as in case of web development. Here are the various issues that are encountered during web development or in website projects.

Various Risks to a Website Project

These are not necessarily in order of severity as certain risks can be more damaging to certain projects. It isn't an exhausted last either. There are n number of risk involved in website development. Some of the most common website risk (Danielle, 2007) are discussed in Table 2.

Table 2. List of Risk to a website project

	Risk to Website Project
Risk 1:	Incomplete preparation at onset of project
Risk 2:	Indecisiveness
Risk 3:	Limited Accessibility to Project Lead
Risk 4:	Incompetent Authority
Risk 5:	Conflict of thought of Decision Makers
Risk 6:	Undue attention to low priority tasks
Risk 7:	Colossal adaptive maintenance
Risk 8:	Improper project planning
Risk 9:	Low bowling
Risk 10:	Flaws

Risk Number 1: Incomplete Preparation at Onset of Project

Before contacting a web developer client should gather all the available information such as:

- Objectives of the website
- Familiar functional requirements
- Ideas and invocation consulted within the organization
- Design details such as copes of images, logos, and banners that will display on the website
- Promoting information
- Content inventory like types of content to be on website and a database of existing content.
- Gather information regarding existing service providers.

Risk Number Two: Indecisiveness

The developer should be clear with the requirements before start of the implementation. The preliminary designing also couldn't be started until the designers are not provided with the basic visual details. if all the functional requirements are clear at the preliminary phase serious delays can be avoided.

Risk Number Three: Limited Accessibility to Project Lead

While stepping into the development phase, client must assign a single point of contact (SPOC) within the organization that will be responsible for communicating, approving and detailing about the requirements of new website to the development team.

Risk Number Four: Incompetent Authority

The project Lead should be competent enough to answer the queries of development team during the designing process. The decision taken by the project lead should be final.

Risk Number Five: Conflict of Thought of Decision Makers

There are more chances of conflict when too many people are involved in decision making process. Longer time for decision making will lead to longer delays. The long delays can be avoided by proper management of time and resources.

Risk Number Six: Undue Attention to Low Priority Tasks

Maximum risk is involved when low priority task is given more attention than the higher priority task. it's better to categorize the low and high priority task before the beginning of implementation phase.

Risk Number Seven: Colossal Adaptive Maintenance

Large change request in the later stages of development life cycle will lead towards missing deadline and thus leads to possible breach of contract.

Risk Number Eight: Improper Project Planning

Generally, a website takes 4 weeks for the completion, but according to a research in the real time scenario, most of the time while a website is being developed at exceeds the timeline, due to improper planning. Minimum risk is involved in case of the website project that had given maximum time for planning phase.

Risk Number Nine: Low Bowling Causality

As we know that in the software development life cycle the output of one phase is the input to another. Thus, each phase is affected by the development of its previous phase. A small enhancement or delay in the previous phase may affect the schedule of its next phase, thus leads to the overhead of project timeline.

Risk Number Ten: Flaws

There are some scenarios where the things do not work as they were supposed to do.

A little code error sometimes creates such a conflict that may consumes much of the development time, thus leads to the delay in timely completion of project (Danielle, 2007).

Risk in the field of websites is not only encountered by the developers but also by the client or the end users. The most common risk that affects the performance of any project and the revenue of any business (mostly e-commerce websites) is the implementation of payment gateways. Mostly customers prefer to use the websites with secure payment gateways. Let's discuss some issues related to payment gateways.

Secure Payment Gateways

While working on e-commerce websites at the time of payment the most important issue that is to be considered is Security. Most of the time the clients/users get offended when they are redirected to an insure payment gateways. The payment gateway is one of the most impactful tools to show trustworthiness to your client. The payment gateway allows the client to assess its credit/debit cards or net-banking through a website. A website may suffer with great loss if its payment gateways are not implemented correctly. On the other hand, it can bring a great success to your website if its payment gateways are made secure. While using e-commerce websites or other sites where payment gates are used for online payments, secure payment gateways should be used. Following are the list of secure payment gateways that can be used during online transactions:

- Authorized.net
- PayPal
- SecurepPay.com
- Checkout.com
- First Data Corporation
- Blue Pay Processing LLC
- Pay Simple
- Fastcharge.com
- Paynov
- ChronoPay.

Since all the gateways do not function in the same scenario thus being an alert user the payment methods should be used cautiously. The most sensitive area where maximum risk is involved is the field of Banking and online transaction processing. Numerous risk are involved in online banking and online transaction processing and there preventive measures are discussed below:

Risk Management in Online Transaction Processing

In banking sectors Transaction Processing System (TPS) plays vital roles in financial transactions. TPS (Transaction Processing System) helps an organization to improve and manage the business performance. In order to deal with threats, information security systems are mandatory.

The process in which the information is divided into individual, indivisible operations is called as Transaction processing. The underlying principal of transaction processing is that the transaction cannot be committed in an intermediate state. In any case each transaction must be in any of the two states either successful or fail as a complete unit. The transaction processing makes the computer system more reliable and accurate, as the system is never left in an intermediate state, either the complete transaction will be successful or it will completely failed. Thus makes the system more independent and reliable. That's the reason why all the banking systems are dependent on transaction processing systems.

While analyzing the banking system various categories of Risks were identified. That may affect the performance of the system. Following are the areas where there is high probability of risks encountered in real time banking systems (Ilmudeen A et al., 2014):

- While depositing money
- While withdrawals of cash
- Clearance of cheque
- Transactions of credit cards
- Bank to bank transactions
- Foreign money exchange
- ATM systems
- E-banking facilities

Let's discuss some of the real life scenarios that involve a high amount of risk during transaction processing.

- Power failure
- Low bandwidth or internal breakdown
- Outside/human attacks
- Staff errors
- Cash transports
- Natural disasters

Following are 8 different types of Risks in banking sector that are octenyl faced in day to day life:

1. **Credit Risk:** Most likely caused by loans, inter-bank transactions, trade banking, foreign exchange transactions etc.
2. **Market Risk:** Depending on the potential cause of the risk market risk can by classified into 4 categories:
   a. Interest rate risk
   b. Equity risk

     c.   Currency risk

     d.   Commodity risk

3.   **Operational Risk:** A risk where the expected value differs from the actual loss. There are various reasons that may lead to operational risk such as:

     a.   Human risk

     b.   IT/system risk

     c.   Process Risk

4.   **Liquidity Risk:** A situation when an investor or person is unable to convert an asset into cash.

5.   **Reputational Risk:** Risk of damage and associated risk to the earnings.

6.   **Business Risk:** There are various types of business risk:

     a.   Strategic Risk

     b.   Financial Risk

     c.   Reputational Risk etc.

7.   **Systemic Risk:** Risk of disintegration of whole financial system.

8.   **Moral Hazard:** When an organization has provided misleading information about it product, processes, liabilities, or assets, etc.

To deal with these risks in various real-time systems, some approaches are used to detect and prevent risk. Before applying the risk prevention techniques, we need to identify and categorize the risk. Thus, numerous indicators of risk are used to recognize the risk.

Indicators of Transaction Risk

According to studies the transactional risk analysis can be defined as a function of probability and impact of risk. There are various important measures to gauge the impact and likelihood. Almost every organization defines a scale, to measure the degree and impact of risks. The measurements and degree are defined by making some standard comparisons. It is always recommended to use the descriptive scales, as at may lead to more clear results.

IMPACT refers to the degree up to which the risk can affect the organization. The impact includes almost every aspect of business such as security, health, financial, employee, customer etc. The impact scale is represented in Figure 4.

Figure 4. The Representation of Impact Scale

IMPACT SCALE

Probability Scale represents the possibility of the occurrence of the event. The probability can be expressed by various qualitative terms. Figure 5 illustrates the Probability scale that is represented by various levels.

PROBABILITY SCALE

Let's take an example of a banking system. The risk can be categorized into diverse levels according to the level of ranges. There are various indicators used to represent the probability of risk and its impact. In the following example a real-life banking scenario is considered where the impact and probability of risk is categorized according to their level of affect in the system.

While assessing the quality of transaction risk various indicators are used as shown in Figure 6.

Figure 5. The Representation of Probability Scale

Frequent   Likely   Possibility   Unlikely Rare

Figure 6. Transaction Risk indicators

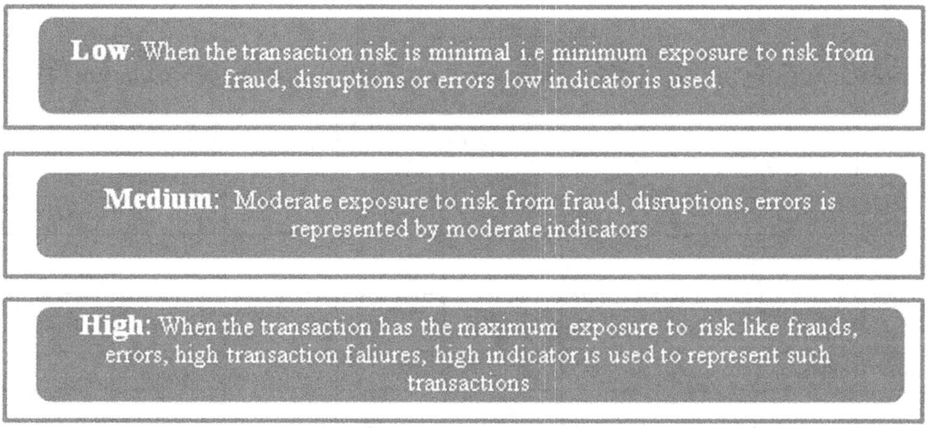

Low: When the transaction risk is minimal i.e minimum exposure to risk from fraud, disruptions or errors low indicator is used.

Medium: Moderate exposure to risk from fraud, disruptions, errors is represented by moderate indicators

High: When the transaction has the maximum exposure to risk like frauds, errors, high transaction faliures, high indicator is used to represent such transactions

199

Categorization of Risk

The categorization of Risk can be explained with a real-life example where data is considered by analyzing the real time banking system.

The data collected for categorization (Almaden et al., 2014) is presented in Table 3. The categorization is done by the Probability impact matrix using original scale that ranges from: Low, Medium, and High.

The Table 4 represents the probability and impact of risk in online transaction processing systems (TPS). The data considered in Table 4 shows numerous categories of risk that usually encountered during online transactional processing.

Final Results Analyzed by Probability – Impact Matrix for Transaction (TPS)

The data in Table 4 and 5, has been analyzed using probability- impact Matrix

From the findings shown in the Table 5, the probability of risk is higher for the transactions A, B, D, E, F i.e. A->while depositing money, B->Withdrawals,

Table 3. Categorization of risk with reference to general Transaction (TPS)

	Transaction	Probability of Risk			Impact of Risk		
		Low	Medium	High	Low	Medium	High
A	On Depositing money	✓					✓
B	Withdrawals	✓					✓
C	Clearance of Chequeen	✓				✓	
D	Credit Card Transactions, e-transaction		✓				
E	Foreign Exchange - Money Gram	✓					✓
F	ATM	✓					✓
G	E-banking		✓				✓

Table 4. Categorization of risk with reference to Online Banking Transaction (TPS)

	Transaction	Probability of Risk			Impact of Risk		
		Low	Medium	High	Low	Medium	High
A1	Power failure	✓					✓
B1	Low bandwidth or internet breakdown		✓				✓
C1	Outside/Human Attacks	✓					✓
D1	Staff errors	✓			✓		
E1	Transport of Cash		✓				✓
F1	Natural Disasters	✓					✓

Table 5. Results of probability of risk in TPS

Probability of Risk		Impact of Risk		
		Low	Medium	High
	High			
	Moderate			G
	Low	C		A, B, D, E, F

Table 6. Difference between Qualitative Risk Analysis and Quantitative Risk Analysis

Qualitative Risk Analyses	Quantitative Risk Analyses
Risk-Level	Project-Level
All the risk is considered that are identified during the process	Considers the risk those have high impact on the project objectives
Stake holder's input or expert judgments are used for the calculation of probability and impact.	It uses project model for the analyses. To calculate the probability and impact mathematical and simulation tools are used.
The ranking of probability and impact is used to access individual risk (Rank 0,1)	The estimation is done on the likelihood of meeting targets. The project outcomes are predicted in terms of money or time based on combined effects of risk.
Qualitative Risk Analyses is quick and easy to perform	Quantitative Risk Analyses is time consuming.
It's a subjective evaluation approach	It's a probabilistic estimation approach
in case of Qualitative Risk Analyses there is no need of special software or tool	This approach may require specialized tools.

D->Credit Card Transactions, E-> e-transaction, F->Foreign Exchange -Money Gram, Whereas the transaction C i.e. C-> Chequeen Clearance has the probability of lower Risk (Almaden et al., 2014). According to a research the real obstacles which exist in the bottom line financial transactions of banking sectors can be identified by performing Quantitative and Qualitative Risk Assessment in Transaction Processing system (iZenbridge, 2014). The difference between the qualitative and qualitative Risk Analyses is explained in Table 6.

In studies it has been discovered that there are three main underlying causes of failures of risk management.

The three causes for recent failures are:

1. Dysfunctional culture
2. Unmanaged and uncontrolled knowledge of organization
3. Ineffective controls.

Thus it is emphasized that there should be a more structured approach to transferring knowledge to the business decision makers before it is needed and enabling the access of information, and about the firm's changing risk management requirements and testing of new knowledge.

Risk management standards have been developed by several organizations, including the National Institute of Standards and Technology and the ISO. The standards are designed to help organizations:

1. Identify specific threats,
2. Assess unique vulnerabilities to determine their risk,
3. Identify ways to reduce these risks and then implement risk reduction efforts according to organizational strategy.

Risk management is disciplined environment in which processes, methods and tools are used for managing risk in a project. The risk management helps to assess what could go wrong that leads to a higher risk for the project, it determines the priority of various risk and decides the accordingly the strategies to deal with those risks. Thus, for the success of any project its risk management activities must be assured.

REFERENCES

Bhullar, R. K., Pawar, L., Bajaj, R., & Manocha, A. K. (2017). Intelligent stress calculation and scheduling in segmented processor systems using buddy approach. *Journal of Intelligent & Fuzzy Systems*, *32*(4), 3129–3142. doi:10.3233/JIFS-169256

Bhullar, R. K., Pawar, L., & Kumar, V. (2016, October). A novel prime numbers based hashing technique for minimizing collisions. In *Proceedings of the 2016 2nd International Conference on Next Generation Computing Technologies (NGCT)* (pp. 522-527). IEEE.

Boukhris, S., Andrews, A., Alhaddad, A., & Dewri, R. (2016). A Case Study of Black Box Fail-Safe Testing in Web Applications. *Journal of Systems and Software*.

Danielle. (2007). Top Ten Risks to Your Website Project. Retrieved May 31, 2007, from http://becircle.com/top_ten_risks

Ismail, M. B. M., & Aboobucker, I. (2014). Risk Assessment (RA) in Transaction Processing System (TPS).

IZenbridge. (2014). Difference between Qualitative and Quantitative Risk Analysis. Retrieved February 11, 2014, from https://www.izenbridge.com/blog/differentiating-quantitative-risk-analysis-and-qualitative-risk-analysis

Taneja, K., Taneja, H., & Kumar, R. (2017). Multi-channel medium access control protocols: review and comparison. *Journal of Information and Optimization Sciences*.

Taneja, K., Taneja, H., & Bhullar, R. K. (2016, March). Cross-platform application development for smartphones: Approaches and implications. In *Proceedings of the 2016 3rd International Conference on Computing for Sustainable Global Development (INDIACom)* (pp. 1752-1758). IEEE.

Wallmüller, E. (2011), Risk Management for IT and Software Projects. In *Business Continuity* (pp. 165-178). Springer.

Chapter 12
Use of Software Metrics to Improve the Quality of Software Projects Using Regression Testing

Arshpreet Kaur Sidhu
Chandigarh University, India

Sumeet Kaur Sehra
GNDEC, India

ABSTRACT

Testing of software is broadly divided into three types i.e., code based, model based and specification based. To find faults at early stage, model based testing can be used in which testing can be started from design phase. Furthermore, in this chapter, to generate new test cases and to ensure the quality of changed software, regression testing is used. Early detection of faults will not only reduce the cost, time and effort of developers but also will help finding risks. We are using structural metrics to check the effect of changes made to software. Finally, the authors suggest identifying metrics and analyze the results using NDepend simulator. If results show deviation from standards then again perform regression testing to improve the quality of software.

INTRODUCTION

Testing of software is fundamental and central part of software development process. UML is the most prevailing standard language used in modeling test cases (A. K. Jena et al, 2014). Therefore, if it is pleasingly exploited it will reduce the cost and

DOI: 10.4018/978-1-5225-6029-6.ch012

effort of testing as well as modification in code. Activity diagrams can improve the quality of the generated test cases as well as use these test cases for regression testing because it shows the overall flow of control between activities and object using activity-based relationships (Ye et al., 2011).

Testing of Software

Before moving to the details of work done in this chapter, we are focusing on testing first. Testing of software in a simple language is a method to find out errors and missed requirements as specified by the user. Testing can be performed by developers as unit testing and can be performed by software testing professionals to get good quality product.

Testing can be started from the early phase of software i.e. requirement phase and can be done up till deployment. Early start of testing will help in reducing the cost and time of developers because the errors and gaps can be removed as earliest possible. Testing is one process which is not confined at testing phase only. At requirement phase testing is performed in the form of analyzing and verifying the requirements. At design phase reviewing the design documents with gathered requirements is also a part of testing. At coding phase, the part of unit testing performed by developer at completion of code is also a part of testing.

Testing and Quality Assurance

Testing and Quality Assurance are interrelated terms. Testing insures the identification of errors and bugs in software whereas quality assurance focuses on accomplishment of processes and standards in the direction of verification of software. Testing is error and bug identifying technique and do not fixes bugs. To fix bugs at coding level developers can use debugging which is a part of white box and black box testing.

Types of Testing

Testing is categorized as manual and automated. In manual testing software is tested manually and end users take the role of testers to test software for bugs and unforeseen behavior. Stages at which manual testing is done are unit, integration, system and user acceptance testing. In automated testing also known as test automation the tester writes script and uses different software to test the functionality of given software. In this testing test scenarios are re-run repeatedly which were performed manually for time saving. It is assumed that automated testing improves test coverage and accuracy. GUI items, connections can be effectively tested with the help of test automation (Rathi et al., 2015; Bhullar et al., 2017).

Methods of Testing

Black Box Testing

It is a technique of testing software without knowing the internal details and working of software. Generally, in black box testing testers interact with the user interface of system by giving inputs to the system and analyzing the outputs. They hardly have details about where the inputs are working in code. This method is preferred for large segment of code but has limited coverage of test cases.

White Box Testing

In this method of testing, code and logic is tested in detailed. Also known as Open box or Glass testing. To perform this type of testing, tester must have all the knowledge of code and internal working of software. For this type of testing skilled tester is required to look into each nook and corner of code.

Grey Box Testing

In this method of testing, tester has limited knowledge of code but unlike black box testing where only user interface is tested; grey box testing has access to design documents and database. This knowledge helps tester to plan better test cases.

Levels of Testing

Different methodologies can be used for defining levels of testing. Mainly it is categorized as

Functional Testing

It is a type of black box testing in which tester tests the specifications of software. The obtained results are compared with actual functionality of software which is expected as per requirements of user.

Steps to test the functionality of software

- Find the functionality of software which is expected.
- Generation of test data according to the specification of software.
- Output based on test data and specifications.
- Execution of test cases obtained from test data.
- Comparison of expected and actual results.

These steps help in maintaining software quality and ensures that standards are been followed. Some common functional testing is unit testing, integration testing, system testing, regression testing, acceptance testing, alpha testing and beta testing (M.A. Jamil et al, 2016).

Unit Testing

This testing is performed by developers on each unit of code before handing over to professional testers. The purpose of unit testing is to check that each individual part is working correct in terms of functionality and requirements.

Integration Testing

This testing is performed when two individual parts are combined to check they are working functionally correct or not. It is carried out by two methods bottom up approach and top down approach.

System Testing

System testing is used to test the complete system as a whole after integration, to see that system is meeting the requirements and quality standards.

Regression Testing

Regression testing is the most widespread method for ensuring the quality of altered software. It examines whether altered parts of software behave as expected. The unaffected parts remain in their original behaviors. It mitigates risks and suggests selecting and executing only a set of test cases that are altered.

Acceptance Testing

Acceptance testing is most important testing to be carried out by quality assurance team to check whether software is meeting the user requirement and satisfying expected conditions. It is performed at two stages Alpha Testing and Beta Testing.

Alpha Testing

It is a first stage of testing and is performed by the team of developers and quality assurance. All the functional testing except regression testing when combined together is called as alpha testing. Latency problem, load time, spelling mistakes, broken lines, etc., are checked at low specifications in alpha testing.

Beta Testing

It is a second stage of acceptance testing after alpha testing is performed successfully. A sample group of audience tests the application at real time.

Nonfunctional Testing

Nonfunctional testing is performed on nonfunctional attributes of software which are important from the quality perspective of software. Commonly used nonfunctional testing are performance testing, load testing, stress testing, security testing.

Performance Testing

It is a method of testing which mainly focuses on performance of software such as response time, network delay. It is further classified into two types stress testing and load testing.

Load Testing

Load testing tests the behavior of software at maximum load in terms of input and at peak conditions.

Stress Testing

Stress testing tests the behavior of software in abnormal conditions like shutting down of system, network failure.

Security Testing

Security testing is used test the check points where security of software can be breached. It mainly focuses on authentication, authorization and confidentiality of software.

Probability Testing

Probability testing focuses on reusability of software and its code. The software is able to build on different platforms.

In this chapter, we are using regression testing to test the changes in behavior of software. Again to apply regression testing, identification of altered parts and to generate test cases for those altered parts of the software is difficult task. So, we can use model based generation of test cases to recount changes in test cases.

Model based approach which is used to identify the changes in the software. We generated Activity Flow graph from activity diagram. Depth first search algorithm is used traverse the graph and to generate test cases.

Metric is a quantitative gauge of degree to which a system, component or process possesses a given attribute. Using Ndepend, we can evaluate 12 metrics on application, 18 metrics on assemblies, 13 metrics on namespaces, 22 metrics on types, 19 metrics on methods, 2 metrics on fields.

Broadly we took following metrics to analyze the results using metric values.

Application Metrics

- **Number of Lines of Code (NbLOC):** This metric will compute the quantity of lines of code.
- **Number of Methods (NbMethods):** It will compute the number of methods in a class. A method can be an intangible, virtual or non-virtual method. Method can be declared in an interface, a constructor, a class constructor, a property/indexer getter or setter, an event adder or remover.
- **Number of Intermediate Language Instructions (NbILInstructions):** Computes the number of instructions inside the intermediate file which is created after compiling the source code.
- **Number of Types (NbTypes):** Computes number of types used which are defined for application, assemblies and namespaces. A type can be conceptual or an actual class, a structure, or an interface.

Dependency Metrics

- **Afferent Coupling (Ca):** The number of types outside this assembly that depend on types within this assembly. High afferent coupling indicates that the concerned assemblies have many responsibilities.
- **Efferent Coupling (Ce):** The number of types outside this assembly used by child types of this assembly. High efferent coupling indicates that the concerned assembly is dependent.

Inheritance Based Metrics

- **Depth of Inheritance (DIT):** The Depth of Inheritance Tree for a class or a structure is its number of base classes.
- **Number of Children (NOC):** The number of children for a class is the number of sub-classes. The number of children for an interface is the number of types that implement it.

Metric Showing Project Readability

- **Percentage Comment:** The amount of comments available for the code explanation.

If the percentage of comment in code is lower than 20% then it should be more commented. However, if code is commented more than 40%, is not considered a blessing as it is an insult to the intelligence of the reader.

Percentage Comment= 100*NbLinesofComment / (NbLinesofComment + NbLinesofCode)

- **Lack of Cohesion of Methods (LCOM):** The single responsibility principle states that a class should have only a single objective. Different classes should be created for implementing different scenarios and objectives. Such a class is said to be cohesive. A high LCOM value generally points to a poorly cohesive class.

LCOM= 1-(sum(MF)/M*F)

Where:

M is the number of methods in class.

F is the number of instance fields in the class.

MF is the number of methods of the class accessing a particular instance field.

Further the objective to write this chapter is to select and use software metrics for improving the quality of software projects based on results of calculated metrics with the help of Ndepend simulator and regression testing.

BACKGROUND

According to American Programmer, 31.1% of computer software projects get canceled before they are completed. In other words we can say that defects in projects leads to failures. When we try to perform changes on software projects (regression testing), quality of project decreases in most of the cases due to changes in dependency metrics, inheritance based metrics, metrics stating project objectivity. Figure 1 shows the reasons due to which a project leads to failure or defects occur while testing of software.

Metrics help in determining, predicting and improving the quality of software process. Few are the factors listed which motivated us to use metrics for software projects at early stages.

- It helps to estimate the cost & schedule of future projects
- It improves software quality
- It forecast future staffing needs
- It reduces future maintenance needs

Figure 1. Causes and Origin of Defects
Source: slideshare.net/Softwarecentral/software-metrics

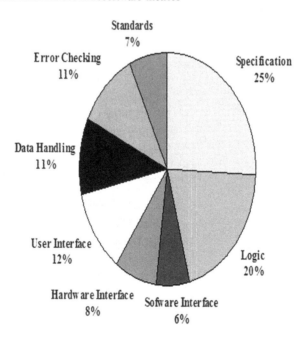

PROPOSED WORK

In this section the chapter is categorized into the following steps to analyze the effect of alterations made in the project at design phase or by applying regression testing. Steps are shown in figure 2.

1. Categorization of metrics based on software into Size Based Metrics, Dependency Metrics, Inheritance Based Metrics, Project Readability Metrics.
2. Selected metrics are calculated with the help of Ndepend Simulator.
3. Assessment of calculated metrics with the Threshold values of Metrics.
4. Improve the quality of software projects based on results of computed Metrics with the help of Ndepend Simulator and by performing regression testing.

Figure 2. The proposed workflow diagram

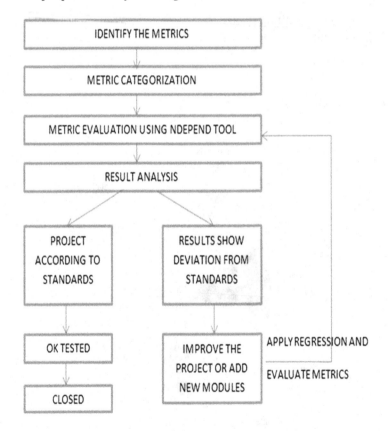

Activity Diagram

We considered a simple website of student management system in our approach. Activity diagrams are considered due to their dynamic behavior. It can construct, visualize and specify dynamic aspects of objects. Figure 3 shows the activity diagram of Student management system.

Figure 3. Activity diagram of online student management system

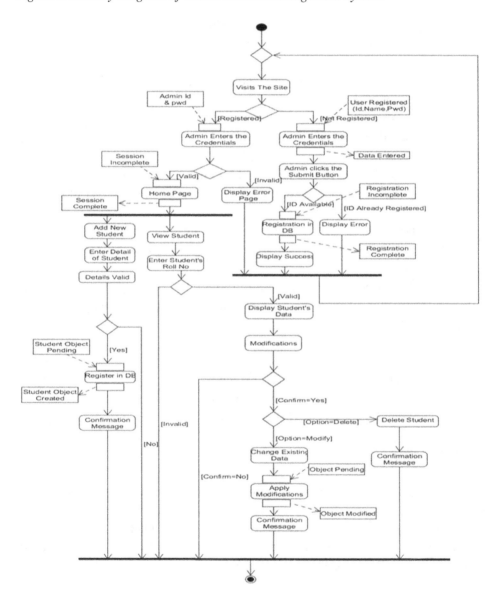

Description of Activity Diagram

1. User Login Section
    a. User visits website by entering valid domain name.
    b. If user is already registered, then will proceed to login section.
    c. If user is a new user, then will go for registration section before login.
2. Registration Section
    a. User enters his/her credentials like user ID, Name, Password, Gender, Address, etc., for registration.
    b. All the data is send to server by clicking submit button.
    c. If it is already registered with some-one else, then server generates error message.
    d. Else server will proceed with the registration process by inserting user's data in the database.
    e. On successful registration, server will display success message and will proceed for login section.
3. Login Section
    a. User enters the ID and password for login.
    b. On pressing Login button, the request is sent to the server along with user data.
    c. The server retrieves user data and validate with database.
    d. If the authentication is successful then server will take to the home page of website.
4. **Home Page Section:** After successful login, the administrator can manage the information of students of an organization online. User is authorized to perform following tasks:
    a. Add new student in the database.
    b. View student of available students.
    c. Search the data of a particular student.
    d. Modify the details of existing students.
    e. Delete the details of existing student

Activity Graph

Here, in this section, we construct the activity graph shown in figure 4 from activity diagram.

We have divided the work into three projects and evaluating metrics at each project level. At each level we are performing regression testing to check effect on metric values when we make changes to the software.

Figure 4. Activity Graph of online student management system

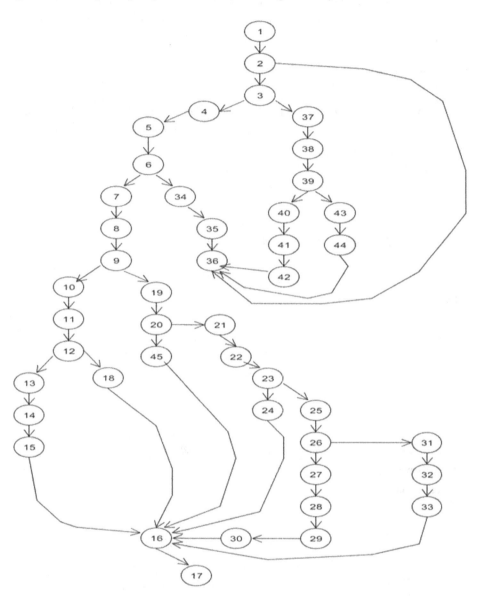

- **Project 1:** Only modules are being added without testing and validation of paths.
- **Project 2:** At Login Session validate inputs for emptiness (username and password), valid email, and length. At Regression Session validate contact number length and data type, email, emptiness. Two new modules are added.

- **Project 3:** Changes in modify and delete module. It includes the code of project 2 along with all the test sequences from regression testing and functional testing.

Test Cases (Suit1)

In our approach graph is traversed through depth first search algorithm (DFS) which visits all the nodes of graph. After traversing the graph, we will generate the possible test cases using path coverage criteria.

Possible test paths are generated after traversing graph are as follows:

- **TC1:** $1 \to 2 \to 3 \to 4 \to 5 \to 6 \to 7 \to 8 \to 9$
- **TC2:** $1 \to 2 \to 3 \to 4 \to 5 \to 6 \to 34 \to 35 \to 36$
- **TC3:** $1 \to 2 \to 3 \to 37 \to 38 \to 39 \to 40 \to 41 \to 42$
- **TC4:** $1 \to 2 \to 3 \to 37 \to 38 \to 39 \to 43 \to 44$

Results

Metric values on Test Suit

It can be clearly observed from metric result values from table 1 to table 4 that Ce values are increasing with changes made in projects which mean dependency is

Table 1. Dependency metric values on three projects

METRIC	PROJECT 1	PROJECT 2	PROJECT 3
Afferent Coupling	0	0	0
Efferent Coupling	21	23	26

Table 2. Inheritance based metric values on three projects

METRIC	PROJECT 1	PROJECT 2	PROJECT 3
Depth of Inheritance	8	28	22
Number of Children	2	7	7

Table 3. Project readability based metric values on three projects

METRIC	PROJECT 1	PROJECT 2	PROJECT 3
Comment %	24	7	7

Table 4. Project objectivity based metric values on three projects

METRIC	PROJECT 1	PROJECT 2	PROJECT 3
Lack of Cohesion Over Methods	.87	.87	.87

increasing. Also values of DOI (Depth of Inheritance) and NOC (Number of Children) are increasing which clearly shows that software might be hard to maintain. The values of LCOM (Lack of Cohesion over Methods) are constant that shows there is no effect of changes on cohesiveness of methods of the class.

From the results above we can improve the software quality at earliest phase with the help of metric values. With every change we can check the effect on stability and quality of software before performing those changes.

FUTURE WORK

This chapter purposes a metric based evaluation of web applications to improve the quality. By comparing metric values of different projects, with changes we found that application has become difficult to maintain. The values of coupling and inheritance become high due to regression. This gives developers a clear idea about direction of changes to be made at earliest stage. Future work involves developing a tool or mechanism to provide optional paths for changes and comparison in terms of metric values so that developers can boost the quality of software.

CONCLUSION

In this chapter we tried to calculate the effects on quality of software or web application when changes are made in accordance to the user. With the case study of simple web application of student management system, by applying regression at early stage of project results showed deviation in metrics. So, in future we can suggest use of such methods for ensuring and improving the quality of software projects. Also, this will reduce the efforts of developers in testing phase and maintenance phase.

REFERENCES

Ajay Kumar Jena., Santosh Kumar Swain, & Durga Prasad Mohapatra, A. (2014). A novel approach for test case generation from UML activity diagrams. In *Proceedings of the International Conference on Issues and Challenges in Intelligent Computing Techniques*. IEEE.

Bhullar, R. K., Pawar, L., Bajaj, R., & Manocha, A. K. (2017). Intelligent stress calculation and scheduling in segmented processor systems using buddy approach. *Journal of Intelligent & Fuzzy Systems, 32*(4), 3129–3142. doi:10.3233/JIFS-169256

Frederiksen, H. D., & Iversen, J. H. A. (2003). Implementing Software Metric Programs: A Survey of Lessons and Approaches. Hershey, PA: IGI Global.

Jamil, M. A., Arif, M., Normi, S. A. A., & Ahmad, A. A. (2016). Software Testing Techniques: A Literature Review. In *Proceedings of the 2016 6th International Conference on Information and Communication Technology for The Muslim World (ICT4M)*. IEEE.

Rathi, P., & Mehra, V. (2015). Analysis of Automation and Manual Testing Using Software Testing Tool. *International Journal of Innovations & Advancement in Computer Science, 4*.

Sapna PG, & Arunkumar, A. (2015). An approach for generating minimal test cases for regression testing. *Procedia computer science, 47*, 188-196.

Rawat, M. S., Mittal, A., & Dubey, S. K. (2012). Survey on Impact of Software Metrics on Software Quality. *International Journal of Advanced Computer Science and Applications, 3*(1).

Verma, V. & Sona Malhotra, A. (2011). Applications of Software Testing Metrics in Constructing Models of the Software Development Process. *Journal of Global Research in Computer Science, 2*(5).

Ye, N., Chen, X., Jiang, P., Ding, W., & Li, X., A. (2011). Automatic Regression Test selection based on activity diagrams. In *Proceedings of the Fifth International Conference on Secure Software Integration And Reliability Improvement*. IEEE. 10.1109/SSIRI-C.2011.31

Chapter 13
Gamification:
An Effectual Learning Application for SE

Samiksha Sharma
Chandigarh University, India

Rimsy Dua
Chandigarh University, India

ABSTRACT

This chapter describes how gamification is a technique which is used to bring the gaming methods and elements into the working environment of the company to make the allocated tasks more interesting for the user. Gamification helps in improving the performance, interest, involvement and motivation towards a specific goal. In software engineering, while applying gamification, all the software projects are made into challenges that require certain skills to get fulfilled with the integrated effort of the working team. This chapter will introduce the structure of the gamification application used in software engineering. A real scenario is presented where the gamification is applied in a company for different working fields like project management, testing and management of requirements. As a result, after applying the gamification technique, the performance has been improved to a greater extent, improved design and increased development effort by the user team. The chapter will bring out the insight of gamification in software engineering and how it helps in creating the intellectual working atmosphere.

INTRODUCTION

A software process can be refined by number of methods and standards that helps in improving the software process at various stages. One of the common standards used for enhancing the software process is CMM known as capability maturity model.

DOI: 10.4018/978-1-5225-6029-6.ch013

CMM Model was developed in the month of august 1990 by software engineering institute (SEI). Companies developing product has to undergo different set standard guidelines under CMM that starts from the beginning i.e., development process to the implementation phase (M. Yadav, 2014). Quality ontology signifies the quality of the characteristic features related to the software system such as traceability, completeness, reliability, robustness, simplicity, accuracy, expandability, precision, maintenance and correctness (Beniwal, 2016). So CMM as quality ontology check the software product for different defined levels starting from level 0 to level 5. Every CMM level has different bounded description to it that tells about what kind of process a software product will undergo under that specific defined level.

When a software product is under development stage, it is checked for quality assurance under different levels of capability maturity model which starts from level 0 as beginning level defined as "incomplete processes", then level 1 which is "the initial level," level 2 is defined as "the repeatable level", level 3 termed as "the defined level", level 4 is called "the managed level" and at last level 5 "the optimizing level". Let's have a brief preface to all these defined levels of CMM with their detailed description. The given table 1 below defines all the five levels of capability maturity model with their description regarding process they hold to measure the quality of the software.

CMMI is developed after CMM by addition of superior guidelines and various components of CMM. CMMI can be applied for people management and software

Table 1. Different Levels in Capability Maturity Model

S. no	Level	Depiction
Level 0	Incomplete Processes	Processes that get failed to achieve certain goal of objectives or no product realization
Level 1	The initial level	At the initial level there's no process defined so the overall product development depends upon the individual work effort and thus the outcomes in initial phase are unpredictable
Level 2	The repeatable level	At repeatable level different software processes are planned according to the project management functions and they are traced throughout the development using documentation. Processes repeat the same set of rules for similar projects
Level 3	The defined level	In the defined level, all the processes are standardized and defined thought the complete organization. Different software activities become consistent and guidelines are prepared specific to project development
Level 4	The managed level	A quantitative analysis is performed at managed level for the quality of the product and processes, risks are discovered and managed
Level 5	The optimizing level	The highest level of CMM where the processes are improved at each and every stage in a continuous process. Making diverse range of goals, updating accordingly with the new techniques and tests.

development. CMMI is better approach as it gives better functionality than CMM because in CMMI the use of multiple CMMs is not required. CMMI follows iterative type of life cycle model and identify risks at the beginning stage of product development. The other well-known method is PSP commonly stated as personal software process that helps in improving the software process by enhancing the individual effort towards a particular objective. PSP acts as a basic foundation that evaluates the individual skills for developing software (A. Marcus, 2001). CMM works for individual software processes i.e. it improves a software process but the PSP works for individuals in improving their effort for effective team work. User under PSP gain knowledge of the below mentioned points (Prechelt, 2001)

- How each and every user will work according to the defined process.
- How process refinement is to performed and make them able to define the process.
- To estimate the time or to re-plan the time required by individual in their developing effort.
- For improving the software process quality, how the reviews have to be considered in the restricting of the software process by the development team.
- How to effectively avoid the development risks and defects.
- How to identify different variety of process deficiency.

Gamification is documented as "use of gaming element in non-gaming framework" (Deterding, 2011). Gamification introduces the tactics of gaming element into the non-gaming environment to make the working tasks as different challenges for enhancing the interest and motivation of the employees of the organization. Some of the software tasks are boring and monotonous because of which users lose interest and become lethargic, this probably lower down their performance hence the overall efficiency of the team will reduce. Gamification make use of gaming techniques to make each assigned task in the workplace interesting as each task is considered as challenge. Every individual has to complete the given task challenge that will rate his performance and improves their skills. Gamification thus helps in bringing the best quality products and projects with high performance. For making Gamification application more adopted sometimes a framework is used, one of such Gamification is proposed in (Garcia, 2017). The framework proposed is GOAL (Gamification Focused on Application Life Cycle) which comprise of gaming and software engineering integration. GOAL framework will provide organization the basic set of rules of gaming and to guide about how to apply gaming with the help of technical support within an organization. The given GOAL framework has been applied to one of the company in Spain. Let's have a brief look at the GOAL framework, how it supports the Gamification in software engineering.

GOAL Framework

Goal comprise of three main elements named as ontology, technology and the Gamification methodology. Ontology refers to bringing application related to Gamification in an organization and sharing of knowledge. Methodology component comprise of terminology regarding how Gamification will be introduced by considering certain business objectives, their resolution and efficacy. In today's era Gamification framework is used in the companies from which software engine is build up. The software engine helps in traducing the Gamification into the projects owned by the company. The Gamification architecture thus helps in integrating the software tools with the Gamification methodology. Let's have a look at different Gamification elements that are stated above diagrammatically represented in figure 1 below.

Ontology Used for Gamification

The first step is to identify the domain in which the Gamification can be applied by looking at the concept and association between the elements of the domain. While building up the ontology for a Gamification architecture specific features are considered, let's briefly introduce those features.

Figure 1. Goal Framework

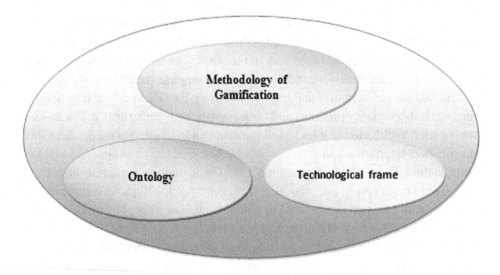

Gamification Span and Functions

There are some tasks in workplace that a user will handle and the performance of the user will be evaluated by the gaming tools. The quality of the work done by the user can be measured by the SE tools used in gaming. In Gamification, a user has to achieve some of the targets that have a valid score related to it. User's main aim or goal is to achieve that target that will score his performance. The first goal is to define the players of the team. An employee of an organization can play individually or can be a part of a group or team.

Different teams can interact with each other or can have a relationship between team members as friends. Players can be categorized into socializers, killers, explorer and achievers (R. Bartle, 1996). Killers are those types of players who provoke other team members and they create disturbance for others in achieving the objectives of the tasks.

Achievers take on the tasks confidently and try to beat each and every level of the game given to them. On the other hand, the explorers will try to get into the game mechanics and explore further the gaming tactics. Socializers maintain the relations with the members of the gaming community.

Gamification Procedure

Procedure of Gamification includes the part of ontology that gives the insight about the activities, practices and methods that are required for the interaction of employee with the tools of SE. Gamification involves set of activities that are converted into challenges

By following certain set of rules. Various set of activities related to practitioners that can be evaluated for getting the results. The set of activities includes players' conduct that gives the interaction of player with the tools of SE. The features of the player than can be evaluated and measured, contribute towards the performance of players. To enhance the efforts of a player mission is set, which is a complete journey that consists of set of obstacles that must be covered by the player.

Gamification Aesthetic

This includes the presentation of different tasks, players and the results they have achieved visually. It represents the GUI through which user will interact with the Gamification tools and the more superior skill set it will develop. Then the performance of the user will be displayed in his profile along with the other related information. At the end the user dashboard will provide the details and other related information in a customized manner.

Gamification Dynamics

Gamification dynamics includes the set of actions that are performed by players as a result of interaction with the gaming tools. Players behavior is evaluated and reflected into its profile, on the basis of which rewards will be given to the players. Evaluation of achievements must be performed and kept as a log for future reference.

Methodology Related to GOAL

This defines the role of the designers in the gaming that must be included as a part of gaming system development for making it more interactive with the practitioners. For making the environment of gaming more intellectual and interesting for the user, there is a need of certain steps to be followed:

- **Player Centered:** The most important factor for any gaming system will be the player who will participate. So, a player will hold a greater impact in the Gamification.
- **Creativeness:** Different challenges of the gaming system must possess high creativity that is necessity of a system in making it more interactive for a user.
- **Based on Some Prototype and Should be Iterative:** A prototype must be there because of frequent changes. Iterations needs to be there because of the frequent changes made to the system.

So in all Gamification methodology includes all the tactics and techniques that are required to build up the gaming framework. To fulfill the abovementioned characteristics there are specific methods and tactics that need to be considered while building a methodology for a gaming system. The below mentioned table 2 represents the set of activities along the description their tasks and the resource that supports these set of activities.

Identifying the Objectives

The first step towards defining the methodology of the GOAL is to make specific set of objectives that are required to fulfill all the challenges of the Gamification. For defining the objectives future and present scenario are considered. According to the scenario the objectives for business are defined. Whatever objectives are defined must be realistic, specific, real time bound and should be measurable.

Table 2. GOAL Tactics

S no	Action	Depiction	Related Resource
1	Look for the objectives	The first step towards Gamification is to identify the objectives and the resources that will fulfill those objectives.	(Kumar, 2013)
	Mission: 1.1 Taking into consideration the present state 1.2 Taking into consideration the future state 1.3 Establishing mission		
2	Analyzing the Player	Player analysis is performed in order to check whether the profile matches with the objectives of Gamification	(Kumar, 2013) or they can be categorized according to the (Bartle, 1996) type
	Mission: 2.1 identification of different types of players 2.2 addition of player related information to the profile		
3	Gamification span and practicability	To define the scope of the Gamification and feasibility that includes technical, economic and operational feasibility	(Burke, 2016) Various kinds of extrinsic motivators and built-in motivators depicted in (Zichermann, 2011)
	Mission: 3.1 To check the game span and motivators 3.2 Run the feasibility analysis and to get the best alternative solution out of that study		
4	aim of the Game and investigation	Finding out all the requirements of the tools that are required for the Gamification and to automate the gaming components	(Dignan, 2011)
	Mission: 4.1 Selecting gaming elements 4.2 Selecting the game methodology 4.3 Economy of the game 4.4 Selection of gaming rules 4.5 Setting up the principles 4.6 Selecting the use cases for the game		
5	Developing the platform	Different iterations are carried out for the gaming platform periodically to check for the business objectives that needs to be fulfilled	Agile approach that integrates the scrum and kanban dynamics (Keith, 2010)
	Mission: 5.1 Sprint organization 5.2 Testing and development of sprint consisting plan, investigation, foundation and completion		
6	Administration, Supervision and Evaluation	Administrating the gaming tools, supervising and evaluating the challenges to know about the performance and the achieved business objectives	(Canossa, 2016)

Analyzing the Player

Gamification is player centered so analysis of player is performed that categorize players to different types. Players can be categorized into socializers, killers, explorer and achievers (R. Bartle, 1996). Killers are those types of players who provoke other team members and they create disturbance for others in achieving the objectives of the tasks. Achievers take on the tasks confidently and try to beat each and every level of the game given to them. On the other hand, the explorers will try to get into the game mechanics and explore further the gaming tactics. Socializers maintain the relations with the members of the gaming community.

Game Span and Practicability

After identifying all the objectives and player analysis is performed; after the analysis phase scope of the solution is checked. Scope of Gamification tells about the solution and the extent to which it can affect the tools and different build up processes. From the beginning task goals of Gamification are identified and then user's profile from the second task is created according to which the Gamification environment is created and different alternatives are chosen. Feasibility analysis of the chosen alternatives is performed in terms of operational, legal, economic and technical facet.

Aim of the Game and Investigation

In this phase analysis is carried out along with the design of the rules required for Gamification. This includes which set of activities needs to be rewarded and what type of rewards will be given to the practitioners. It also represents the gaming environment along with the rules that are designed for each task given as a challenge to the practitioner. Use cases are designed that signify the role of each interacting team element along with the standard procedures that will be followed as a base of the game.

Developing the Platform for Gamification

In this phase the designed solution for the Gamification is carried to the working platform of the organization. For making the designed solution more effective and working, the organization's tools and processes needs to be examined. The maturity level of processes within an organization should be evaluated before implementing the solution on the working platform.

Administration, Supervision and Evaluation

The task of this component is to monitor the developed gamified environment. What effects can exist for the processes that have been developed for the gamified system. After developing the Gamification platform, what can be problems or risk threats from which the system's working platform can suffer are monitored. The alternatives are refined at each stage and the problems that are discovered in the gaming platform are recovered with better design of prototype with the help of monitoring. Figure 2 given below demonstrate the steps of GOAL methodology.

Figure 2. Goal Methodology

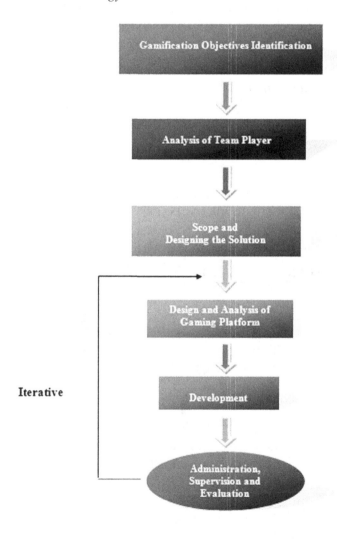

Tool Design for GOAL

The figure 3 presented below depicts the architecture of GOAL tool. Tool architecture consists of different component, the main one is Gamification engine. Role of Gamification engine is to monitor the behavior of all the users that are interacting with the GOAL tools, based on that their performance is evaluated and they are decided for reward. Gamification engine thus holds all the actions of users or maintains a log of user's performance along with their rewards. The game designer maintains a set of actions or activities that needs to be followed by the practitioners in the gaming environment. Rules of Gamification act as a function that decides for the reward according to the action performed by the practitioner. Players will perform set of actions that needs to get communicated with the Gamification engine using an API that can be executed as web service. REST web service can be used to integrate the tools with the Gamification engine. The integration can be made using the plug-in

Figure 3. Design of GOAL Tool

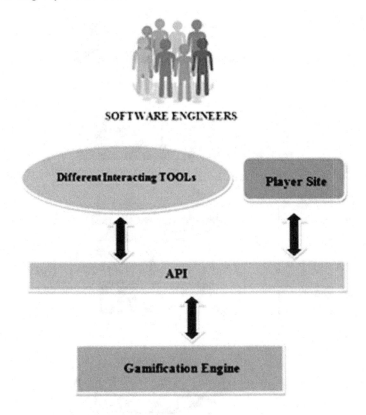

between the tools and the Gamification engine and if that connection through plug-in is not possible then connector can be used as intermediate between the GOAL tools and Gamification engine.

GOAL Application in Software Company

The GOAL framework is practically implemented on a company cited by (F. Garcia, 2017), and it has been observed on the basis of results that the work environment quality is enhanced after applying Gamification. The company named as SWcomp in which the Gamification is applied gave positive feedback regarding the framework. The employees stated that after introduction of Gamification to their work environment tasks allocated to them are of more fun and are more interactive. The Gamification framework helps them to improve their routine as they can monitor their performance on regular basis. Gamification provides each user a profile that consists of user tasks and corresponding rewards earned by that user. The employees thus can compare their performance with other teammates and can improve also based on their previous performance. So, a complete log is provided by Gamification framework that consists of various tasks performed by a user.

About SWcomp

SWcomp is a medium sized Spanish company that develops software, provide IT services and operations. The company operates internationally and founded in 2004, the current personnel employed is 25 from which 19 are engaged in software development, managers and project analysts. SWcomp focuses on areas such as GIS (geographic information system), maintaining the education content digitally, publishing quarters, business related systems and commerce. This firm has also contributed to the quality management. The company has implemented successfully security management system (SMS) which is an ISO certified standard.

Tool Used by SWcomp

With the improvement in the process, the tools have been developed and are being used by the company. The tool used by the company for the project management is the custom developed software. With the help of these tools the project managers create projects, decide the start and finish time of the project, to specify the tasks to the employees and to calculate the effort required by each employee. With the help of these tools employees can see their devoted effort in performing the tasks allocated to them. In this way the design tools give real-time information, past reports and estimate about the upcoming project finishing points

Design

The design of tool is decided and applied to SWcomp is based on certain research questions. For designing the GOAL tool, few questions need to be taken care of, like is it feasible to apply the GOAL for supporting the Gamification into software engineering? Is the idea of GOAL methodology clear in promoting the efforts of the Gamification into the working environment, is the software design and the tool is suitable for Gamification and the effort whether it is suitable according to the pros and outputs. Below given table 3 gives the brief preface to the research questions required to be framed for designing the tool for Gamification.

CONCLUSION

The Gamification framework helps them to improve their routine as they can monitor their performance on regular basis. Gamification provides each user a profile that consists of user tasks and corresponding rewards earned by that user. The employees thus can compare their performance with other teammates and can improve also based on their previous performance. So, a complete log is provided by Gamification framework that consists of various tasks performed by a user. Gamification has gained popularity in both the domains of industry as well as research. Many companies have applied this framework in their workplace environment and the framework has been proved successful in making the better interaction among workplace users. This chapter presented different components of framework that includes ontology, methodology and the GOAL tool.

Gamification Ontology

Ontology refers to the concepts that can be applied or used for the gaming environment. Also, it holds the relationships between the concepts related to different context of the Gamification environment.

Table 3. Research questions for effective tool design

RESEARCH QUESTIONS
Is the GOAL framework feasible to apply to the software engineering?
Is the idea of GOAL framework clear in promoting the efforts of gamification into software engineering?
Is the software design and the tool suitable for the gamification approach?
Is the effort required by gamification suitable according to the results and benefits it gives?

Methodology

Gamification methodology includes identification of objectives, analysis of player, deciding the aim and scope, developing a Gamification platform and administration of Gamification environment.

Gamification Tool

A tool will be used that will be integrated with the Gamification engine. With the help of Gamification tool players' performance and accomplishments can be recorded as per the designed rules of the gaming environment.

The designed framework is according to the software industry life cycle models that cover almost all the phases starting with the feasibility phase, analysis phase, design phase, test and maintenance. The role of designer in Gamification is to identify the fields where the framework cam be applied. Gamification can also be applied to the area such as operational as well as development in software industry.

So the given chapter brought the insight of Gamification in software engineering and how it helps in creating the intellectual working atmosphere for the users. The concept of ontology is also introduced with a brief look up to demonstrate the idea of used methodology and to support the Gamification working technique engine. In previous researches a case study is carried out for a company that proved all the results to be more positive the Gamification approach.

FUTURE WORK

In future, analysis can be carried out further for the solutions obtained from the Gamification. Enhancements can be performed on the Gamification design. New case studies can be designed for which the commitment, inspiration, performance and efficiency can be considered. The Gamification framework can be applied to the education field also and that can become a future most promising research area.

REFERENCES

Bartle, R. (1996). Hearts, clubs, diamonds, spades: Players who suit MUDs. *Journal of MUD research, 1*(1), 19.

Bhatia, M. P. S., Kumar, A., & Beniwal, R. (2016). Ontologies for software engineering: Past, present and future. *Indian Journal of Science and Technology, 9*(9). doi:10.17485/ijst/2016/v9i9/71384

Bhullar, R. K., Pawar, L., Bajaj, R., & Manocha, A. K. (2017). Intelligent stress calculation and scheduling in segmented processor systems using buddy approach. *Journal of Intelligent & Fuzzy Systems, 32*(4), 3129–3142. doi:10.3233/JIFS-169256

Bhullar, R. K., Pawar, L., & Kumar, V. (2016, October). A novel prime numbers based hashing technique for minimizing collisions. In *Proceedings of the 2016 2nd International Conference on Next Generation Computing Technologies (NGCT)* (pp. 522-527). IEEE. 10.1109/NGCT.2016.7877471

Burke, B. (2016). *Gamify: How gamification motivates people to do extraordinary things*. Routledge.

Deterding, S., Dixon, D., Khaled, R., & Nacke, L. (2011, September). From game design elements to gamefulness: defining gamification. In *Proceedings of the 15th international academic MindTrek conference: Envisioning future media environments* (pp. 9-15). ACM. 10.1145/2181037.2181040

Dignan, A. (2011). *Game frame: Using games as a strategy for success*. Simon and Schuster.

El-Nasr, M. S., Drachen, A., & Canossa, A. (2016). *Game analytics*. Springer London Limited.

García, F., Pedreira, O., Piattini, M., Cerdeira-Pena, A., & Penabad, M. (2017). A Framework for Gamification in Software Engineering. *Journal of Systems and Software, 132*, 21–40. doi:10.1016/j.jss.2017.06.021

Keith, C. (2010). *Agile Game Development with Scrum (Adobe Reader)*. Pearson Education.

Kumar, J. (2013, July). Gamification at work: Designing engaging business software. In *Proceedings of the International Conference of Design, User Experience, and Usability* (pp. 528-537). Springer. 10.1007/978-3-642-39241-2_58

Maletic, J. I., Howald, A., & Marcus, A. (2001). Incorporating PSP into a traditional software engineering course: an experience report. In *Proceedings of the 14th Conference on Software Engineering Education and Training* (pp. 89-97). IEEE. 10.1109/CSEE.2001.913825

Prechelt, L., & Unger, B. (2001). An experiment measuring the effects of personal software process (PSP) training. *IEEE Transactions on Software Engineering, 27*(5), 465–472. doi:10.1109/32.922716

Taneja, K., Taneja, H., & Bhullar, R. K. (2016, March). Cross-platform application development for smartphones: Approaches and implications. In *Proceedings of the 2016 3rd International Conference on Computing for Sustainable Global Development (INDIACom)* (pp. 1752-1758). IEEE.

Taneja, K., Taneja, H., & Kumar, R. (2017). Multi-channel medium access control protocols: review and comparison. *Journal of Information and Optimization Sciences*.

Yadav, M., & Kumar, K. (2014). CMM or CMMI, which is more appropriate for a software industry? *International Journal in IT & Engineering, 2*(1), 24–33.

Zichermann, G., & Cunningham, C. (2011). *Gamification by design: Implementing game mechanics in web and mobile apps.* O'Reilly Media, Inc.

Chapter 14

A New Approach for Reinforcement of Project DEMATEL–FMCDM–TODIM Fuzzy Approach

Rajshree Srivastava
Chandigarh University, India

Shiv Kumar Verma
Glocal University, India

Vikas Thukral
Charles River Development, USA

ABSTRACT

This chapter describes how an effective work towards software project risk plays a vital role in determining the accomplishment of any project. In this chapter, the aim is to associate fuzzy criteria decision-making based on the approaches for the development of an assessment framework. This framework will be helpful in terms of identification and ranking the software risk according to its characteristics which will be helpful in decision-making of a software lifecycle. For the assessment for the risk of a project, there is an integration of fuzzy decision-making trial, evaluation laboratory trial and fuzzy multi-criteria decision. This new method proposed will be effective in terms of ranking and as well as to measure the software risk factors.

INTRODUCTION

In order to handle any software project and make it successful it goes to through various processes such as documentation, application maintenance, debugging and testing. As a result of acute research attention, several works were proposed

DOI: 10.4018/978-1-5225-6029-6.ch014

to improve software project management techniques. To measure any software product for designing any software the factors which are considered are scope of the project, the technology used, team development and quality of the products (Boehm et al., 1978). While working in the software development life cycle several unavoidable risks like business, technical and project risk occur so there is urgent requirement of project management in a project. Now, the challenging situation which arises is to manage the risk factor and performance of the software product throughout the development of software project life cycle (Kahneman et al., 1979). The new approach which is introduced in this chapter is based on statistical based predictive techniques. Further many approaches were designed but where having some limitations. To overcome this problem (MCDM) multi-criteria decision-making technique is introduced (Arshadi et al., 2014). MCDM techniques such as Fuzzy Multi-Criteria Decision Making (FMCDM), Decision Making Trial and Evaluation Laboratory (DEMATEL)approaches have combined for project risk evaluation. Earlier in the study fuzzy TOPSIS and fuzzy DEMATEL approach were used for evaluating risk factors which are based on global software development project outcome (Heitkotter et al., 2013). In the recent study hybrid based technique such as TODIM and fuzzy DEMATEL were used for the evaluation of risks in supply chain projects (Mahmoodi et al., 2014). TODIM technique is never been integrated with FMCDM and DEMATEL to address the problem of bounded reality in software project risk evaluation. In this chapter, the proposed multi-technique approach "DEMATEL-FMCDM-TODIM "gives focus on providing an assessment scheme which can be used to classify risk on the basis of software project performances. The variables used for fuzzy linguistic are computed on the scale of [0, 1] by using the technique triangular fuzzy numbers. By using this approach, risk can be controlled at an early stage in any project which will be helpful to improve the performance of the software.

STUDY

Fuzzy DEMATEL Method

Having an accurate value in a complex system is very difficult during the preceding of decision making. The main objective of using this method is to evaluate the interrelationship among numerous criteria, multiple attributes, handling uncertainty and having subjective ambiguity with the decision-making process.

DEMATEL approach had achieved success in various contexts namely in the cases of knowledge management strategies, global managers competencies, assessment of project outcome and in the planning of industrial (Kahneman et al., 1979). According to prior studies DEMATEL has been engaged with the subjective weights of each decision criteria. Hence for the computation of weights and ranking risk factors, fuzzy DEMATEL method is used (Wang et al., 2008).It involves some steps to compute weight and ranking risk factors these are setting up direct-relation matrix; defining the fuzzy linguistic variables; transformation of initial direct-relation matrix to TFNs; then obtaining the average value; having a direct-relation matrix; then setting up total-relation matrix; obtain the sum of columns and rows of each criterion and last obtaining the weight of the individual based on its weight.

FMCDM Approach

This approach helps in decision making to evaluate, select and rank problems according to its weights having some defined criteria. According to (Sangaiah et al., 2005) FMCDM deals with inadequate information and uncertain thoughts in the process of decision making. In the real time, it is hard to give preference for efficient risk assessment in software projects that generally group decision making process. In order to handle all this, concept of fuzzy set theory will be best (Wang et al., 2008). There are four steps which FMCDM follows for the operational process these are firstly determine the fuzzy rating for the software risk factors; secondly, aggregate the fuzzy rating which can be possible based on the effectiveness of software risk factors; thirdly, defuzzifying the rating for the effectiveness of software risk factors and finally calculating the risk factors based on the efficiency of software project performance.

Approach of TODIM

This method is used to measure the dominant degree of each other by establishing a multi-criteria value function based the theory of prospect (Li et al., 2015). Earlier study shows that Euclidean distance is used for both TODIM and DEMATEL for defuzzification. The DEMATEL –FMCDM approach is used for determining the weights and rank of the risk which are laid down. Further, the weights of criterion obtained through DEMATEL have been initially weighted in TODIM that represents the hybrid approach and then use both in order to determine the final weights of the risk (Fan et al., 2013). The operational and data analysis approach used are first determine and normalize the decision matrix; secondly compute overall dominance degree; thirdly compute the overall prospect value and finally rank the overall prospect values.

Materials and Methods for Evaluating Software Risks

In the earlier studies the dataset used was OMRON data set in order to classify the efficiency and effectiveness of their methodology. The dataset used was for the prediction of software project risk by Software Engineering Process Group. The dataset contains 40 projects and 22 project risk-related attributes as shown in Table 1. The work is being experimented on 40 employees from the organization to determine the effectiveness of each risk factor based on the software performances.

In this chapter hybrid fuzzy DEMATEL- FMCDM –TODIM approach is used for evaluating software risk factors and it follows the following steps:

Table 1. Data set attributes

Criteria and Measurement Of Sources	Its Code Used	Software Risk Based on the Evaluation Criteria
	Requirements	
	R1	Ambiguous requirements
	R3	Misunderstanding of the requirements
	R5	Changes which are on frequent basis
	R4	Lack of commitment regarding fulfillments of requirement between
	R2	members of project and customer
	Estimation	
	E1	Unawareness of importance of estimation
	E3	Lack of assessment for the implicit requirement
	E4	Lack of assessment for the issues related to technical problem.
	E5	Insufficient cost estimation.
	E2	Lack of skill for the estimation method
	Planning	
	P1	Improper management audit for the plan of the project
	P5	Breakdown of the work products
	P3	Planning of project controlling and monitoring is not unavailable.
	P2	Improper management of responsibilities distribution.
	P4	Unspecified reviews of project
	Team Organization	
	T1	Inexperienced and unplanned skills.
	T2	Limited allocation of resources
	T3	Inadequacy self-confidence
	Management of project	
	M1	Inadequacy of resources during the completion of project.
	M2	Improper monitoring of project
	M3	Less amount of data to fulfill the objective of project

1. **Research Methodology Process:** In this step the objective, scope and the evaluation criteria is defined for the project.
2. **Applying Fuzzy DEMATEL:** In this the setup is being initialized based on direct relational matrix, then total relational matrix is being calculated; prominence and relation values is calculated and being recorded and at last the criteria to obtain weights is calculated as shown in Table 2.

Applying FMCDM

Initially setup the direct relational matrix based on the subjective decision; then aggregating and de-fuzzy the possible ratings of risk factors with reference to performance of the project; then obtain the marks based on the final indexes and finally compute the FMCDM ranking based on the DEMATEL weights. The risk assessment criteria are summarized in Table 3. The result achieved by the last step of FMCM is summarized in Table 4.

Table 2. Result of the DEMATEL based on priority weights of risk assessment criteria

Criteria	Sum of the row(r_n)	Sum of the column (c_n)	$(r_n) + (c_n)$	$(r_n) - (c_n)$	Weights based on priority
R1	3.2	2.5	5.7	0.7	0.096
R2	3.22	3.1	6.32	0.12	0.106
R3	3.24	3.23	6.47	0.01	0.097
R4	3.26	3.24	6.5	0.02	0.097
R5	3.38	3.35	6.63	0.03	0.104
E1	2.7	2.65	5.35	0.05	0.091
E2	2.5	2.44	4.94	0.06	0.085
E3	2.4	2.32	4.72	0.08	0.076
E4	2.3	2.21	4.51	0.09	0.081
E5	2.1	2	4.1	0.1	0.099
P1	2.6	2.4	5	0.2	0.085
P2	2.55	2.43	4.98	0.12	0.100
P3	2.42	2.36	4.78	0.06	0.087
P4	2.32	2.25	4.57	0.07	0.096
P5	2.30	2.26	4.56	0.04	0.095
P6	2.22	2.19	4.41	0.03	0.073
T1	2.7	2.1	4.8	0.6	0.99
T2	2.1	1.9	4	0.2	0.10
T3	3.4	3.1	6.5	0.3	0.08
M1	2.23	2.20	4.43	0.03	0.85
M2	2.45	2.30	4.75	0.15	0.76
M3	1.22	1.15	2.37	0.07	0.06

Table 3. Weights of risk assessment criteria of FMCDM

Factors	Synthesized fuzzy ~ importance weights(w_i)	Factors based on FMCDM weights (Q_i)	Final weights of FMCDM
R= 2.121			
R1	(0.25, 0.33, 0.31)	0.3140	0.1413
R2	(0.44, 0.50, 0.30)	0.4221	0.1996
R3	(0.40, 0.52, 0.43)	0.4400	0.2060
R4	(0.40, 0.53, 0.42)	0.4200	0.1995
R5	(0.49, 0.63, 0.41)	0.5122	0.2206
E=1.6242			
E1	(0.15, 0.26, 0.31)	0.2272	0.1305
E2	(0.26, 0.36. 0.30)	0.3444	0.1623
E3	(0.35, 0.50, 0.35)	0.4200	0.2205
E4	(0.32. 0.42, 0.37)	0.3765	0.2214
E5	(0.20, 0.32, 0.38)	0.3088	0.1591
P=2. 1616			
P1	(0.33, 0..45, 0.39)	0.3902	0.1656
P2	(0.51, 0.67, 0.30)	0.4977	0.2167
P3	(0.32, 0.43, 0.35)	0.3601	0.1577
P4	(0.32, 0.44, 0.33)	0.3604	0.1533
P5	(0.35, 0.48, 0.38)	0.4566	0.1746
P6	(0.26, 0.38, 0.32)	0.3457	0.1332
T=0.924			
T1	(0.33, 0.44, 0.37)	0.3777	0.4322
T2	(0.22, 0.33, 0.37)	0.2973	0.3033
T3	(0.17, 0.28, 0.28)	0.2491	0.2734
M=0.961			
M1	(0.22, 0.33, 0.31)	0.3031	0.2558
M2	(0.28, 0.39, 0.35)	0.3357	0.3341
M3	(0.24, 0.36, 0.33)	0.3234	0.3222

Apply Fuzzy TODIM

In this work firstly identify and normalize the fuzzy decision matrix; secondly, obtain the relative weights of the criteria, thirdly calculate the dominance value and finally determine and sort the overall prospect value. The overall prospects values of the alternatives can be determined through the process of normalization of the corresponding to the dominance measurement is presented in Table 5. The relative weights and criteria of projects based on ranking is summarized in Table 6.

Table 4. Fuzzy weights and risk an assessment ranking criterion which is obtained by DEMATEL, FMCDM and DEMATEL-FMCDM integration.

Criteria	DEEMATEL		FMCDM		DEEMATEL-FMCDM	
	Wj	Rank (R)	Qj	Rank (R)	Wj * Qj	Rank (R)
R1	0.096	07	0.3140	01	0.0301	06
R2	0.106	10	0.4221	06	0.0447	09
R3	0.097	11	0.4400	11	0.0426	03
R4	0.097	15	0.4200	16	0.0407	15
R5	0.104	09	0.5122	20	0.0532	20
E1	0.091	03	0.2272	07	0.0206	01
E2	0.085	14	0.3444	02	0.0292	05
E3	0.076	19	0.4200	12	0.0319	07
E4	0.081	21	0.3765	15	0.0304	11
E5	0.099	08	0.3088	19	0.0305	16
P1	0.085	02	0.3902	08	0.0331	04
P2	0.100	06	0.4977	13	0.0497	12
P3	0.087	04	0.3601	17	0.0313	17
P4	0.096	12	0.3604	03	0.0345	02
P5	0.095	15	0.4566	18	0.0433	13
P6	0.073	20	0.3457	21	0.0252	21
T1	0.99	01	0.3777	09	0.3739	08
T2	0.10	17	0.2973	04	0.0293	14
T3	0.08	18	0.2491	14	0.0199	09
M1	0.85	05	0.3031	05	0.2576	10
M2	0.76	13	0.3357	10	0.2551	18
M3	0.06	22	0.3234	22	0.0194	19

Table 5. Overall prospect values and DEMATEL and TODIM ranking obtained by integrating

Projects	Overall Prospect Value	Rank of the Project
P1	0.8571	03
P2	0.0011	20
P3	0.3688	18
P4	1.0001	01
P5	0.3107	19
P6	0.6338	10
P7	0.5078	15
P8	0.8214	02
P9	0.4104	14
P10	0.3281	17
P11	0.7883	04
P12	0.4108	13
P13	0.6700	06
P14	0.5645	12
P15	0.4357	11
P16	0.3875	08
P17	0.4682	09
P18	0.3499	05
P19	0.8771	07
P20	0.7662	16

Table 6. Relative weights, ranking of criteria of projects obtained by applying TODIM

Risk Factors	Overall Prospect Value	Criteria Rank
R1	0.7227	07
R2	0.9187	02
R3	0.3262	17
R4	0.7970	05
R5	0.8834	04
E1	0.4057	14
E2	0.7273	06
E3	0.9932	01
E4	0.9016	03
E5	0.2180	20
P1	0.5404	11
P2	0.5781	09
P3	0.2062	21
P4	0.6894	08
P5	0.4866	12
P6	0.3354	16
T1	0.4856	13
T2	0.2692	18
T3	0.1580	22
M1	0.5553	10
M2	0.2294	19
M3	0.3748	15

DISCUSSION

In the result of fuzzy DEMATEL there are 22 risks factors which are characterized in the terms of performance of software project. It shows the analysis of the degrees and relation in terms of risk factors.

In the chapter of FMCDM, both the OMRON data set were used for the comparison of the result. This comparison helps us to carry out the evaluation based on 5 dimensions of the software risk.

In the study of TODIM, there is integration of hybrid DEMATEL-FMCDM approach with TFN's while considering the decision-making concept. One of the advantage of DEMATEL-FMCDM-TODIM is that it can handle uncertainty while during in the decision-making phase. This approach is considered best in the terms of the risk factors. By looking and considering these factors, any organization can obtain effective goals in the terms of risk management.

The overall study finds the key factors for determining the risks of software projects. In order to find the software risk factors based on project performance 5 dimensions and 22 evaluation criteria were used. The present approach helps in decision making with more than one optimum means for calculating the risk factors, thereby considering human behavior in decision making process. There are two contributions concluded after the study first a comprehensive framework of the risk factors which influence the performance of software project and a hybrid DEMATEL-FCMCDM-TODIM approach that is used to determine the relative importance of the risk factor.

CONCLUSION

In the software development industry effective management of software risk plays an important role. The DEMATEL – FMCDM – TODIM fuzzy approach gives a clear vision of logic and shows effectiveness of risk factors in the performance of software project. The chapter also presents an intense picture which affirms that software risk factors are key-determinant for the success of project performance. Further, this study provides a precise analysis of the significance of risk factors in the performance of software project.

FUTURE WORK

For the future work, there can be an extension to integrate the approach of MCDM with the information of fuzzy. Further there can be collaboration with MCDM on the intelligence technique namely support vector machine, neural network and adaptive fuzzy system.

REFRENCES

Arshadi Khamseh, A., & Mahmoodi, M. (2014). A new fuzzy TOPSIS-TODIM hybrid method for green supplier selection using fuzzy time function. *Adv. Fuzzy Syst.*

Bhullar, R. K., Pawar, L., Bajaj, R., & Manocha, A. K. (2017). Intelligent stress calculation and scheduling in segmented processor systems using buddy approach. *Journal of Intelligent & Fuzzy Systems, 32*(4), 3129–3142. doi:10.3233/JIFS-169256

Boehm, B. W. (1978). *Characteristics of software quality*. NorthHolland.

Charland, A., & Leroux, B. (2011). Mobile application development: Web vs. native. *Communications of the ACM, 54*(5), 49–53. doi:10.1145/1941487.1941504

Fan, Z. P., Zhang, X., Chen, F. D., & Liu, Y. (2013). Extended TODIM method for hybrid multiple attribute decision making problems. *Knowledge-Based Systems, 42*, 40–48. doi:10.1016/j.knosys.2012.12.014

Gopal, J., Sangaiah, A.K., Basu, A., & Gao, X.Z. (2015). Integration of fuzzy DEMATEL and FMCDM approach for evaluating knowledge transfer effectiveness with reference to GSD project outcome. *Int. J. Mach. Learning cybernetics.* doi:.10.1007/s13042-015-0370-5

Kahneman, D., & Tversky. A. (1979). Prospect theory: an analysis of decision under risk. *Econometrica: J, Econ. Soc.*, 263–91.

Mahdi, M., & Gelayol, S.F. (2014). A new fuzzy DEMATEL-TODIM hybrid method for evaluation criteria of knowledge management in supply chain. *Int. J. Manag. Value Supply Chains*, 5(2), 29–42. doi:10.5121/ijmvsc.2014.5204

Marcu, M., Tudor, D., & Fuicu, S. (2010). A view on power efficiency of multimedia mobile applications. In K. Elleithy (Ed.), Advanced Techniques in Computing Sciences and Software Engineering (pp. 407–412). Springer. doi:10.1007/978-90-481-3660-5_70

Robertson, S., & Robertson, J. C. (2006). *Mastering the requirements process* (2nd ed.). Boston, MA: Addison-Wesley.

Roman, G. (1985). A taxonomy of current issues in requirements engineering. *IEEE Computer*, 18(4), 14–23. doi:10.1109/MC.1985.1662861

Sangaiah, A.K., Gopal, J., Basu, A., & Subramaniam, P.R. (2015). An integrated fuzzy DEMATEL, TOPSIS, and ELECTRE approach for evaluating knowledge transfer effectiveness with reference to GSD project outcome. *Neural computing and applications.* doi:.10.1007/ s00521-015-2040-7

Tiwana, A., & Keil, M. (2004). The one-minute risk assessment tool. *Communications of the ACM*, 47(11), 73–77. doi:10.1145/1029496.1029497

Wang, Y.J. (2008). Applying FMCDM to evaluate financial performance of domestic airlines in Taiwan. *Expert Syst. Applic.*, 34(3), 1837-1845.

KEY TERMS AND DEFINITIONS

Risk: Any exposure to some specific factor which will create hindrance while achieving the expected outcomes of a project.

Risk Management: It is defined as set of principles and practices whose aim is to identify, analyze and handle risk factors so as to deliver a best software project.

Chapter 15
Role of Attacker Capabilities in Risk Estimation and Mitigation

Deepshikha Chhabra
Chandigarh University, India

Isha Sharma
Chandigarh University, India

ABSTRACT

This chapter describes how the impacts of risk, or we may say risk exposure, are dependent upon the losses already occurred by the risk and probability to occur. There are various methods for estimating the risks and its impacts. The loss created by the threat can be reduced if the attacker does not have access to the system's objects or resources which are vulnerable to the risk. Attacker capabilities play the major role in the risk estimation and mitigation approach. Use of appropriate knowledge, skill and time to exploit the system or to create the threat comes under Attacker Capability. In this chapter, we will discuss how to include attacker capabilities when the risk estimation or mitigation plan is made. We will conclude the chapter with an appropriate study of various examples which indicate that impacts of risks can be minimised or reduced if we include the attacker capability while estimating the risk impacts and preparing the risk mitigation approach.

INTRODUCTION

In today's world producing the secure information systems is the main agenda of business. The focus of experts is to make the information system with no loopholes and highly accurate and secure. This can be achieved if there is accuracy and precision

DOI: 10.4018/978-1-5225-6029-6.ch015

in the estimation of risk exposure. There are various risk estimation techniques. In the previous risk estimation techniques all the attack scenarios were identified and risk related to each attack was estimated. These types of approaches need high budget. The other approaches such as Octave in which the subset of factors such knowledge, expertise, availability of resources is considered (Octave, 2002). On the other hand, NIST uses factors such as capabilities of attacker and intention of attacker. The drawback of these methods is high difference between estimated and actual value of risk exposure. In these methods the assumption is that attacker has the capability of performing an attack with a condition that he has complete knowledge of the system and availability of the resources. There are basically two types of threats insider and non-insider threats. Insider threats are created by the persons within the organization or the ones who have access to all the resources of the system. This includes stealing the confidential or valuable information. On the other hand, the non-insider threats are created by the persons who do not have direct access to the resources but intend to do so. The key principle of the severity of threat lies in the capability of attacker if he can access the resources or has the capability to reach to the sensitive information. The various examples of threats are illustrated below:

- **Computer Virus:** It acts as an agent who has the capability to corrupt and steal data on our personal computer.
- **Rogue Security Software:** In this security attack, Attackers (cyber criminals) attempted to hinder the confidentiality of end users banking account.
- **Botnet:** In this attack hacker hacks the system connected in an internet using some virus
- **Phishing:** Phishing scams refers to fraudulent attempts done by cybercriminals to a private

In this chapter we will first discuss the related work which is done in the software estimation and mitigation field, method for incorporating attacker capabilities in the estimation of the threats, demonstration and evaluation by considering the attacker capabilities. The organization of chapter is done as follows: In the start we have given the related work information and then the discussion is done on the capabilities of attacker. Afterwards we incorporate the attacker capabilities and propose a risk estimation method. Then the risk mitigation is discussed by incorporating the attacker capabilities. After that we have discussed the two methods that include attacker capabilities for risk mitigation. At the end we have discussed the impacts and results.

Table 1. Related terms

Access	It refers to the flow of information from source which is susceptible to risk to the target which is attacker in this case (National Computer Security Center (NCSC), 1988)
Asset	The sensitive information or the data which is attacked
Attacker capability	The expertise or the ability of the attacker to access or to reach to the set of resources (objects) of the IS to create threat.
Impact	The loss or the consequences which are incurred when the attack happens. The financial or legal loss which is borne when the attack happens (Dubois et al., 2010)
Means	The factors such as tools, expertise, and knowledge which are needed to perform actions that cause the threat (Alberts and Dorofee, 2002).
Resource	Files, data, programs which contains some valuable information.
Opportunities	This refers to the chance to perform the attack.
Risk	Uncertainty leading to loss or we may say threat of an attack.
Risk exposure	A function of the likelihood of the threat and the severity of its impacts (Wheeler, 2011).
Security Policy	The rules which decide the legal and illegal things in a security attack.
Threat	It is something which has power to cause serious harm to the sensitive data.

RELATED WORK

Risk assessment technique provides decision-makers and business parties with a better understanding of risks and its impact. Also, it helps to control the impact of threat if it is likely to happen. The figure 1 shows the various activities involved in risk estimation and risk mitigation plan. We have reviewed various risk assessment methods which are developed basically to address InfoSec risk.

- **CORAS:** It is based on UML model. This approach defines the UML language for various security concepts including threat, asset which are applied to analyze the unwanted risks or the security threat.
- **The CCTA Risk Analysis and Management Method the CCTA Risk Analysis and Management Method (CRAMM v.5):** Is a qualitative ISRA method. CRAMM focuses on the establishment of objectives, risk assessment, and identification and selection of countermeasures. The method is mainly built around the supporting tool which has same name and also refers to descriptions which are provided in the repositories and databases present in the tool.
- **FAIR (Factor Analysis of Information Risks):** This is the rare used approach. FAIR provides a risk taxonomy which breaks down the risk into twelve specific factors. Further each factor contains four well-defined factors for the loss and probability calculations.

Figure 1. Activities Involved in risk estimation and Risk mitigation

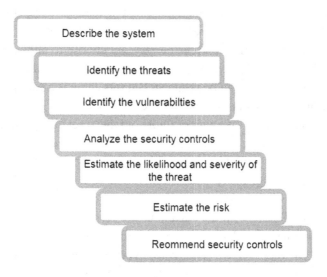

- **The Norwegian National Security Authority Risk and Vulnerability Assessment (NSMROS) Approach:** This approach mainly focuses on cyber security and was designed for helping organizations in their effort to become compliant with the Norwegian Security Act. NSMROS has been written in Norwegian and also it provides a general description of the risk management process and associated activities.
- **OCTAVE (Operationally Critical Threat, Asset, and Vulnerability Evaluation):** Allegro methodology is the latest method of the OCTAVE-family. It aims at being less extensive as it is a lightweight version of the original OCTAVE and it is mainly designed as a streamlined process which focus on facilitating risk assessments without the need for InfoSec experts and still aim at production of robust results.
- **The ISACA (Information Systems Audit and Control Association):** Risk IT Framework and Practitioner Guide which is an ISRM/RA methodology which focuses on providing the practical guidance, benchmarks and other effective tools for the enterprises which are using IS (Information systems)

ATTACKER CAPABILITIES

Risk likelihood is the Measurement of the frequency and possibility the threat occurs. The key point of any kind of security attack is the motivation level of the attacker. The benefits or rewards they will get after doing the attack and the resources which they are spending to perform the attack mainly decides the impact or severity of the attack. It is the perception of an attacker that he feels he will get undue benefits after the security attack, which motivates him to attack. But in a situation where the attacker has insufficient resources he may not choose to attack. If the attacker capabilities are incorporated while risk estimation and mitigation process then the harmful effect of the threat can be reduced. But this again is a tricky process. Some adversaries can be easily understood like we know that bank robbers want money. But in most of the situations we cannot figure out the exact objectives of an attacker. The most common example is terrorist attack in which we cannot list the exact reason because they attack on something which is inexpensive but costs a large number of lives (Kumar, 2017). Capability is the "ability to do something" and the "number of weapons, soldiers, etc. that a country has for fighting a war (Macmillan Dictionary). This definition is aligned with the current use of term attacker capability. It means the given attacker has knowledge or expertise to do an attack.

As per the OCTAVE if we talk about cyber security attacker then his main motives would be means and opportunities which are used to cause the threat. If we talk about NIST then it would be means and intents. In a nutshell the attacker can perform the attack if he has access to the resources.

For example, if an attacker has an intention to access the messages which are exchanged between two parties, he cannot do so unless and until he has access to the communication link between the two parties or he has the source or the target terminal used in the communication. So, we may say that attacker capability not only includes information related to the attack but also it includes the conditions which the attack feasible. If we combine all the features we can summarize that security policy can be represented by the use of following features:

1. S_i (set of subjects)
2. O_i (set of objects)
3. A_i (set of Actions)
4. C_i (set of conditions)

If all these above security policies are in reach of an attacker then only an attack is possible (Bishop et al., 2010). In practical implementation we sometimes ignore the C_i because conditions may vary for and insider or non-insider attacker. For example, if a bank person who is working inside the organization and has the access to the sensitive data of the customers, can misuse this privilege to create the threat. Also in case of airline reservation the insider employees can attack the system by simply shutting down the server by unplugging the power cable. Therefore, we consider the tuple <SOA>.

Dubious proposed the ISRRM domain model which is represented in below figure 2. In the below diagram motive, capability, means and opportunity which are highlighted by the shaded area are the additions which are given by Dubious (Dubious, 2010).

The key features of attacker capability are:

1. Motive
2. Means
3. Opportunity
4. Capability (Dubious 2010)

The event refers to the state when threat has already occurred. Attack mainly happens when the system's vulnerability is exploited or may be the weak or the loopholes of the system are exploited. This can be best explained with the help of an example in which the messages between the two parties are exchanged without application of any encryption algorithm. This vulnerability (easily prone to attack) can be misused. The idea of motive, means and opportunity were already linked with attack but introduction of capability along with the three mentioned concepts is new in this chapter. The attacker which has the capability to perform the attack or

Figure 2. ISRRM Domain Model

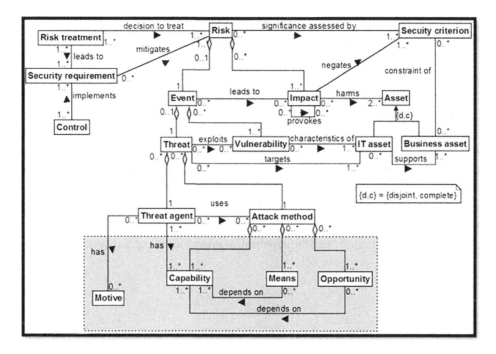

we can say the attacker has the ability to use proper skill and tools or other means at right time and in right direction leveraging the opportunity to perform an attack. As far as motives of attacks are vary from Espionage (stealing information related to national security), Sabotage (aim of destruction), Information Theft (stealing the sensitive information). Sometimes the motives of attacks could not be clearly understood.

HOW TO DIAGNOSE ATTACKER'S CAPABILITY?

There are various studies which help us to identify or determine the Attacker's capabilities. Attack is associated with unwanted access to any of the objects like hardware device, sensitive data or any software product. In order to determine the attacker capabilities, we need to consider the group of objects represented by Oi and group of Actions represented by Ai. The capabilities can be represented by summation of:

$$Ci = \sum Ai*Oi \qquad (1)$$

Note-We have not given importance to S i.e. subjects as discussed earlier because here the assumption made is that all the attackers are capable (potential).

Ci here refers to the Capabilities.

Algorithm to Calculate Attacker Capability

1. List down the objects related to information system.
2. Bifurcate the objects into software or of database types.
3. Identify all the possible scenarios in which the objects can be accessed.

Determination of capability likelihood: It implies the amount or the measure of the capability an attacker has to perform any particular attack. It can be considered like a score or a value which tells how much effective is the attacker based on the capability value. We can consider a scale of (0-5) where 0 considers zero chance the attacker has the capability and 5 representing maximum chance the attacker has the capability. The summation of all the capabilities provides the capability of an attacker.

$$CA = \sum ci \qquad (2)$$

Table 2. Objects and type of possible Access

Objects	Access/Attack possible
Hardware components	Physical Access
Software products/Software components	Deletion of some files by some virus attack
Database/data	Modification or updating of data related to business or any sensitive information.
Communication channel/link	Updating, deletion, modification of the messages or read the messages shared via a communication link

**Also, there is concept of Attack tree in which is constructed which contains all the attack scenarios. All the realistic and non-realistic scenarios are covered. In this approach we assume the attacker is most capable and can do the worst. But in actual in the real life the scenarios are not that worst. After that the attacker profile is applied to the tree and all the nodes which are not in reach of an attacker are removed. Thus, the risk estimation and mitigation is done based on the resultant tree in which we study only feasible attacks.

CA Represents the Likelihood of Capability for a Particular Attack

Incorporating Attacker Capability in Risk Assessment Process

Steps incorporated:

1. We consider an IS which has the domain boundaries.
2. Threats are identified
3. We then consider and identify motivation and capabilities as discussed in section (Attacker capabilities).

After that risk estimation done keeping in account risk severity, frequency of the threat and likelihood of the threat.

Role of Attacker Capability in Risk Mitigation

As discussed in the precious sections an attacker can perform a risk if he has the capabilities needed for doing an attack. If we focus to change the capability of the attacker then there are great chances that attacker is unable to cause the threat. Therefore, if we work in direction of changing the hardware and software architecture of the IS then there are great chances that Attacker is not able to do his task. For example, an employee of an organization who can remotely connect to the system via VPN or some other method and after office hours he tries to fetch and manipulate the sensitive data then in that case the privileges to do so should be given only to

Figure 3. Risk Assessment process

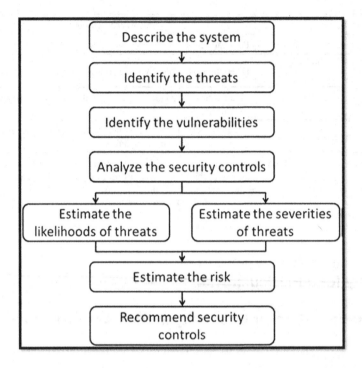

Table 3. Representing the factors and Attacker capability examples

Areas(Factors)	Scaling (Attacker Capability) Examples
Expertise in knowledge	Scale from 2 to 10 where 2 refers the deep knowledge and 10 refers to the normal person with zero knowledge
Elapsed time (Time required to identify and perform the attack)	2 to 10 where 2 is for time>=1 year and 10 for few days.
Sample opportunity (number of times an attacker can avail the opportunity to explore the system)	2 refers to unlimited and 10 refers to few minutes

the system administrator. Thus, changing the privileges is one method by which we can control the threat. The other way around is changing the architecture of the system. Suppose there is an online chat server. In order to access the system, the attacker needs to get the secret code present in the server. Therefore, if we inculcate sensors n the servers that automatically the capability of an attacker is hampered.

ELABORATION OF THE TOPIC WITH
THE HELP OF AN EXAMPLE

Banking System

Consider an online banking system which stores the customer's information, account details, transaction details and personal information. It contains all the information related to finance, loan, etc. The customers can perform functions like net banking, online opening of an account, opening of a recurring deposit.

The attackers may be interested to hack the password details of bank account, transaction password, etc., in order to make money. In case the attacker tries to log in and he tries to hack the password, there should be automatic message on your registered number that one account is trying to login using your user id from which particular location by giving proper location via GPS.

Video Conferencing

Consider a system in which video calls, chats, meetings cab be planned for business needs. Images, text documents, audios videos can be exchanged between the sender and receiver. An attacker can do malicious act of capturing the business details, change the meeting timings, can try to exchange the unethical data or any other can which is not favorable for the organization. If we change the capabilities or limit the capabilities of the system we can reduce the threat.

SUMMARY

In this chapter the main focus is given on attacker capabilities (ability of an attacker to use the knowledge, skill, means and opportunity) to access the resources. This chapter has completely removed the notion of not considering the attacker capabilities

Table 4. Threat and change in capability

Threat	Change in Capability
Sharing of unethical data	Sender and receiver should again exchange the copy of the data shared.
Interrupting the service by applying some automated script	Asking to enter captcha after defined time
Unauthorized access to camera	Camera should work based on voice recognition

into account for considering the risk mitigation and risk estimation plan. In this approach consideration of attacker capabilities helps us to reduce the uncertainty in the projected and actual estimates of risks. Capabilities are those favorable conditions of an attacker which helps him to perform an attack and thus denying those favorable conditions inaccessible to the attacker so that attack is impossible or it has the least impact. Thus, if the Architecture of the system is changed in such a manner that the capabilities of an attacker are hampered and thus making the attacker inefficient in performing the attack. We have discussed various examples with proper evaluation and calculation. The high difference between the estimated risk impacts and actual impacts force the business partners not to rely on the estimation and mitigation plans. Therefore, consideration of an attacker capabilities, argue their thoughts of considering estimation plan of zero practical value. Limiting or controlling the attacker capability plays a crucial role in risk estimation and mitigation approach.

CONCLUSION

In the previous methods (as discussed in section 2) of risk estimation the objective evaluation has not been done so unlike to the previous methods or techniques in this chapter we have taken various examples and done the quantitative analysis of the risk mitigation after considering the attacker capability into account. The goal of achieving secure IS (Information System) is possible by considering the attacker capabilities in the risk estimation and mitigation .It helps in reduction of uncertainty risk exposures.

REFRENCES

Alberts, C. J., & Dorofee, A. (2002). *Managing information security risks: the Octave approach*. Boston, MA: Addison-Wesley Longman Publishing Co., Inc.

Agarwal, H., Renaud, J., Preston, E., & Padmanabhan, D. (2004). Uncertainty quantification using evidence theory in multidisciplinary design optimization. *Reliability Engineering & System Safety, 85*(13), 281–294.

ben Othmane L, Weffers H, Klabbers M. (2013). Using attacker capabilities and motivations in estimating security risk. In *Workshop on risk perception in it security and privacy*, Newcastle, UK. Retrieved from http://cups.cs.cmu.edu/soups/2013/risk/Cap.-Based-risk.pdf

Bhullar, R. K., Pawar, L., & Kumar, V. (2016, October). A novel prime numbers based hashing technique for minimizing collisions. In *Proceedings of the 2016 2nd International Conference on Next Generation Computing Technologies (NGCT)* (pp. 522-527). IEEE.

Bhullar, R. K., Pawar, L., Bajaj, R., & Manocha, A. K. (2017). Intelligent stress calculation and scheduling in segmented processor systems using buddy approach. *Journal of Intelligent & Fuzzy Systems, 32*(4), 3129–3142. doi:10.3233/JIFS-169256

Macmillan dictionary. (n.d.). Capability. Retrieved Feb. 2014. from http://www.macmillandictionary.com/us/dictionary/american/capability

Dubois, E., Heymans, P., Mayer, N., & Matulevicius, R. (2010). A systematic approach to define the domain of nformation system security risk management. In S. Nurcan, C. Salinesi, C. Souveyet et al. (Eds.), Intentional perspectives on information systems engineering (pp. 289-306). Springer.

Hernan, S., Lambert, S., Ostwald, T., & Shostack, A. (2006). Uncover security design flaws using the stride approach. *MSDN Magazine*. Retrieved from http://msdn.microsoft.com/en-us/magazine/cc163519.aspx.

Kumar, R. (2017). DOS Attacks on Cloud Platform: Their Solutions and Implications. *Critical Research on Scalability and Security Issues in Virtual Cloud Environments, 167*.

Physical Measurement Laboratory of NIST. (2000). The NIST reference on constant, units, and uncertainty of measurement results. Retrieved from http://physics.nist.gov/cuu/Uncertainty/international1.html

Stoneburner, G., Goguen, A., & Feringa, A. (2002). *Risk management guide for information technology systems.* NIST. doi:10.6028/NIST.SP.800-30

Taneja, K., Taneja, H., & Kumar, R. (2017). Multi-channel medium access control protocols: review and comparison. *Journal of Information and Optimization Sciences*.

Taneja, K., Taneja, H., & Bhullar, R. K. (2016, March). Cross-platform application development for smartphones: Approaches and implications. In *Proceedings of the 2016 3rd International Conference on Computing for Sustainable Global Development (INDIACom)* (pp. 1752-1758). IEEE.

Wheeler, E. (2011). Security risk management: building an information security risk management program from the ground up. Waltham, MA: Elsevier.

Chapter 16
Risks Analysis and Mitigation Technique in EDA Sector:
VLSI Supply Chain

Lokesh Pawar
Chandigarh University, India

Rohit Kumar
Chandigarh University, India

Anurag Sharma
Chandigarh University, India

ABSTRACT

This chapter describes how as the semiconductor industry is growing at a streaming pace, it comprises a number of global business entities. The industry includes the designing of the VLSI chips, manufacturing of those chips, system integration and the distribution of the VLSI chip. With this the industry has raised the bar among its vendors to provide best possible IC solutions and a highly secure product. The authors thus present this chapter in calculating views on risk involved in this area which are prone to security risks and at the same time focuses on the VLSI supply chain with references to a recent survey that illustrates various ways to handle those risks. In the absence of an effective security mechanism, a varlet here viz. an intellectual property (IP)provider or an integrated circuit design industry, an EDA company, a foundry lab, a distributor of chips or a system integrator, may easily lead to design IP theft or tampering with a designed IC. Since these risks compromise the security system for the VLSI chips, this leads to have a sound security system for an apt risk management.

DOI: 10.4018/978-1-5225-6029-6.ch016

INTRODUCTION

In an attempt and designer's desire to design lightning fast system/network on chips within minimum possible time with best possible constraints, the digital design flow is going towards being fully automated and hence the EDA companies growing in abundance in the market. The need for automation arises because of ample of steps required for a semi/full-custom digital design. Consequently, there also arises possibility of IC theft or IC tamper by an adversary. So there is always a risk involved. To understand those possibilities, we need to generalize some of the most common CAD (Computer aided) design tools that are available in Semiconductor market (Liu B. et al., 2016).

Electronic Design Automation (EDA) Tools

Design Capture Tools

This is the first and most important category of EDA tools since it deals with the designer's specifications. By capturing here means abstracting and encapsulating a circuit description and preparing the same for further simulations as per SAE (simulation and analysis environment). Collectively, the work at this entry level can be shown by Figure 1.

Simulation Tools

The next set of tools that deal with Front-end IC design. Again these are further classified on the basis of operations performed. One type is for the functional verification of the design, and second one verifying the timing specifications, viz. STA tools, Power analyzers etc. The former one verifies the logic behavior of the IC design corresponding to entry level specification (i.e. in reference to gate level

Figure 1. Operations performed by Design capture tools

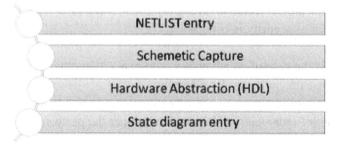

net-list). One must take care to characterize all the design primitives during formal simulation. Later tools make sure that timing constraints viz. set-up and hold time are met accordingly in proper synchronized way (Mead C. et al, 2012).

The timing simulation is performed on multiple level of abstraction so definitely it is required to be done in a careful and efficient manner. The information thus retrieved by these tools is then back-annotated for final logic simulations after the floor planning and layout of the design.

Layout Tools

These are the tool that performs the design tasks just before the actual implementation of the design for verifying inter-connects, technology parameters, floor plan, clock and data paths etc. They allows transforming the logic implementation to a physical design laying a path towards ASIC (Application specific IC) design (Zimmermann, R. et al., 1999). Now here comes the categorization based upon customization process, viz. semi and full custom design. In later the customization deals from designing a cell level ASIC representation and then combing those to form sub-components and finally having the complete design. The former one requires getting Intellectual properties from different EDA vendors and hence combining those components and verifying as a design. The physical design tools always works in conjunction with the floor planning tools showing the verified cells to go on an ASIC die (Taur, Y. et al., 2013).

Synthesis and Optimization Tools

The synthesis tools will now take on functionality descriptions from HDL tools and gate level net-lists and then mapping them with the placement and routing (layout) tools. The mapping is done targeting a specific library in a technology specific manner to obtain area, power and delay optimization.

VLSI Supply Chain Risks

In semiconductor industry, the VLSI supply chain is found to have following two major risks as far as security is concerned.

- First one is the case of an adversary who may either obtain an IP an illegally or might use the authentic IPs illegally.
- Second possibility is when the adversary could modify the functions and change their fundamental values which hamper the performance directly and

other associated functions of an IC for spiteful or unethical activities. Further Security Risks with software approach are discussed in depth.

Intellectual Property theft and maltreat: The VLSI Chips, thus developed along with IC designs through entire designing process, it can be safe guarded legally. For Safe guarding IC's/hardware intellectual property right plays a vital role and can be named as follows: trade secret, trademark, copyright and patent. Design IPs like the Verilog code, thus seek encryption so as to prevent illegal copy or misuse of the IC's. The IP theft market is flourishing at a very fast rate due to the demand to have easy IP access with minimum cost. Evidently proving the preceding statement, there is unbridled IP theft and maltreat in semiconductor/Chips industry (Sun, M. T. et al., 1989). Theft and maltreat can be explained with the help of an example of a industry which was supposed to build certain number of chips but eventually the manufacturer over builds the chips and sell them in the market. There are other types of maltreating an original IC by cloning, reverse engineering: While cloning a fake design can be built up by dishonestly passing of a part of the IC or the complete design. While reverse engineering a burglar will extract all of the IP's along with the documents stating all the details that how this design work. There is number of ways to disguise the system which directly allows the burglar to use the IP with a minor or a major change. The fact that scamp business aspirants are directly driven by monetary benefits is one very common feature of such attacks. All these attacks and scams take place at a very large scale which directly or indirectly impacts the software industry (Burg A. et al., 2005).

- The products which are developed or prone to the cloning, recycling or illegal usage of the brand name are the major cause for counterfeiting the IC industry. These imitations are ubiquitous and are larger in number which has been identified by the United States Department of Defense.

The IC's which are made up by recycling the chips are depraved of lifetime along with the performance as well as reliability issues. A burglar can imitate the chip and may tinker with the original model so as to install a "Trojan Horse" element, if this element is triggered once it may behave like a logic bomb which becomes an information leak at the backdoor. A Trojan Program can be entirely concealed in the hardware. An opponent can launch such type of attack by contacting system assembly line or anyone who has authority to access the hardware device can replace the original chip with an imitated chip. Even after this tinkered system may perform with minimal functions as expected but they cannot perform all the functions. Such type of attacks can evade system and can hamper the file system, memory or stack. Such type of IC attacks doesn't carry direct benefits but there is always a scope of hidden incentive. This inefficacy in the existing VLSI Chip design causes security risks. These problems still exists because there is no effective mechanism to identify tampered IC's except identifying that whether the IC meets all the specifications. The following section discusses various mitigation techniques for IP theft and maltreat.

TECHNIQUES AGAINST IP THEFT AND MALTREAT

Design Befog

The classical definition of design befog that has emerged as a major problem in cryptography as well as computer security can be illustrated by first creating a function f that only reveals input and output relation. The function thus reveals nothing about itself. So there is a clear inculcation that an algorithm for circuit obfuscation O is efficient. Let us suppose that there is a circuit which implements some function and gives output as another circuit. If a black-box is accessible to the burglar it can be efficiently simulated for creating the same predicate with the black box access.

Corresponding to some of the most common technologies like 3-D Integrated Circuit integration or embedded reconfigurable logic in Application Specific Integrated Circuit design for IC manufacturing, Split manufacturing is one of its kind to achieve VLSI obfuscation, which realize the afore mentioned classical property. But the mere presence of befog modules doesn't guarantee the obfuscation of whole design, since the antagonist may still attain knowledge on or tinker with that part of the design which is un-obfuscated. And the methods adopted for design obfuscation might fail to stop an antagonist, but for sure it will swell the cost of reverse engineering. Concluding the story of obfuscation, following are some of the proposed circuit obfuscation techniques.

- An elemental die should be manufactured at a trusted foundry so as to make the die less prone to the security threats. The elemental die along with the interposer should be manufactured at the trusted foundry. Other die and interposer of less importance may be manufactured at un-trusted foundry. The vital part of the trusted die manufacturing is that it contains logic gates rather than interconnections. It becomes a bit complex for the burglar to re-construct the whole design.
- In the same manner, some of the Application Specific Integrated Circuit design modules may be discern with the reconfigurable logic that may be created by a customer, user or system engineer after the manufacturing and supply process. Any one of the antagonist can have the classical abstract access to the logic.

- Numbers of logic gates are counterfeited into similar design, when talking about IC camouflaging. Where even with low resolution microscopy equipment, an antagonist can easily re-construct a façade logic gate at a certain computational complexity.

- With logic locking, input to a system may be increased by using multiplexers combining different logical units so as to keep the system secure and complex due to which an adversary will not find it easy to penetrate through the security system .In the same way, a finite state machine can also be augmented by a group of extra finite states forming an obfuscated mode, such that very specifically correct sequence of inputs transit the finite state machine out of the obfuscated mode and set the finite state machine to the correct initial state in the normal operation mode. It prevents an adversary from unethical or illegal operation of a device. However, with knowledge on the function of a protected module, e.g., from the design of the rest of the system, an adversary can recover the key, e.g., based on IC testing techniques.

Digital Watermarking

In order to safeguard IPs as a whole, including Sequential and Combinational logical circuits, Verilog codes, finite state machines, physical designs, and CAD tools, one of the easiest approaches to follow is Digitized watermarking.

It is used for the authentication purpose, watermarking is considered as self-security for the material which is not directly accessible to the adversary, the text on the page which contains watermarking must be re-written. But such type of approach cannot be directly implemented on the hardware design IP's because the importance of a design is completely based on the accurate functionality and its performance. To achieve digital watermarking in integrated chips without altering its functionality a methodology was developed in late 1990's in USA. With the help of these constraints the properties can be derived from the final design which directly claims the ownership of the designer, and everything else can be easily regenerated using the signature of the owner and the secret key which is known to the developer only.

Fingerprinting in Integrated Circuits

Integrated Chips watermarking can be used for claiming the ownership of IC. These types of watermarks are not helpful for determining the copyright flout. Here comes the requirement of some newer technique which is named as digital fingerprinting it includes buyer's signature along with the designer's watermarking. These both security traits are not invisible which are permanently embedded in the IC design for security purposes. Watermark for all the copies of the IP is same but the fingerprint for the all the copies of the IP is different/unique.

Following fundamental problems are faced by the fingerprinting technique:

- Uniqueness in Fingerprint.
- Distribution of Fingerprints to the users.

The aftermath of fingerprinting technique is plethora of problems, in terms of generating unique fingerprints and keeping track of each one of them. Each IP should be allocated with a unique fingerprint no two IPs should be allocated same fingerprint. Because of these types of scary difficulties digital watermarking is followed and fingerprinting is avoided, there is not much literature which discuses fingerprinting technique.

TECHNIQUES AGAINST IP TAMPER

There are two techniques which identifies the tampering of IC's. The following section discusses them in depth:

Integrated Circuit Design Tamper Detection

There are number of IC's in the world actually it is very difficult to identify tampering of an IC but doing rigorous practice the tampered IC's can be identified. It can be determined that an IC is tampered or not by checking the implementation of the IC if it discerns the design faithfully without any additional functionalities then it clearly states that IC is not tampered. There are number of technique which can identify this problem easily. But shortcoming of these techniques is that they cannot identify hardware Trojan.

Simulating IC's

It is one of the vital techniques to verify the IC design. There are number of constraints in simulating the IC for verification of its originality. The techniques which are used they can verify an IC design with its specification and they are not capable of identifying extra functionalities. Trojan can perform an extra function without tinker any original/fundamental functionality of the IC. Simulation can only identify the risk by prior knowledge only, a simulator triggering for a hardware Trojan is rare.

IC's Verification

Formal verification verifies that implementing an IC states that the specifications are completely met. It can be verified with the help of equivalence checking. Equivalence checking identifies no more no less than what is specified. It can be generalized with the help of finite state machines which can accept certain strings and may reject other string of same size. The specifications for an IC are predefined and IC can perform those functions only if IC performs some extra functionalities which are not specified than the extra functionalities are performed due to hardware Trojan horse or maltreat of the IC. Equivalence checking is the vital criteria to check whether the IC performing the specified functionality or not.

Signal Identification and Redundant Logic

If in a circuit the implementation of the IC is similar to the specification than also there may exist a hardware Trojan in the IC. Trojan is such a problem which can get activated due to IC aging or just because of mere event execution. To identify such type of the problem Unused Circuit Identification have been proposed earlier. Because hardware Trojans are supposed to be triggered by a rare event, another group of techniques locate hard-to-excite signals as candidates of hardware Trojan trigger. These techniques can be combined. These techniques do not need an authentic design as reference. However, these techniques are limited as a hardware Trojan may not be based on redundant logic or a hard-to-excite signal.

Integrated Circuit Chip Issues

How an IC chip can be identified whether it is performing according to the original design without counterfeiting or without several additional functionalities.

Reverse Engineering

A Verification engineer lacks complete design details of a chip cannot detect the tampering of an IC easily, though it can be done with certain difficulties and unpredicted results. To identify tampering of an IC can be achieved from IC design specifications but if these instructions are not clear so it can be achieved by IC design tamper detection technique discussed in previous section can be applied. Reverse engineering cannot be applied on all the IC chips to detect the tampering of the IC and also it cannot guarantee to find out the tampering at the foundry.

Testing Technique

To recognize an IC Trojan by testing technique, firstly, the stratagem for testing must include activation of the Integrated Circuit Trojan, and secondly, the hardware thus activated then leads to a behavioral deviation of the VLSI system which can be easily identified by an incorrect input. Though none of them is easy to achieve or incorporate. Test engineers are not aware of determining the activation of hardware Trojan, it can activate by a rare event or may not get activate easily this makes the activation of a hardware Trojan difficult to achieve. With the help of IC aging sensor, hardware Trojan cannot be activated unless and until the particular age has been achieved.

Side Channel Analysis

Apart from afore mentioned techniques, techniques like side channel analysis collects various IC characterizations. A chip consists of performance timing, consumption of the power, the associated conditions with the suitable temperature, or certain electromagnetic emission in a side channel and thus realizes those chips which has been processed/ tampered. These types of techniques are dependent on the reverse engineering to identify a tampered chip. Still a notable number of complications exist:

- The impact of a small hardware Trojan could be buried by significant parametric variations.
- Activating Hardware Trojan is not an easy task. Without being activated hardware Trojan has no sign or very less signs of being there on the IC. This makes SCA difficult to implement.

IC Design Tamper Prevention

Apart from detecting the IC tamper, the prevention is always a suitable consideration with responses like having a recovery system or use of self-destruction methodologies with proper de-facto measures, viz. recording and digital forensic. But the solution of Tamper prevention has its own ambiguities that need to be solved. Subsequently there are number of ways proposed for the same with a confined efficacy; one of them is a straight forward technique named IC design obfuscation. Now the problem arises that it is impractical for the whole VLSI world because there are number of modules which can be befog by reconfiguring the logic or a trusted die. Encrypting the instruction/data for storage is a general technique, while decryption improves the performance cost. While obfuscation seems better with modular approach rather than having coverage for whole design.

CONCLUSION

Security risks in the hardware of the system have been into lime light with the rapid growth of EDA (Electronic Design Automation) industry. These types of security risks bring the major concern of the industry just because they hampers the basic security foundation of the IC industry hence it becomes highly critical from management point of view as well as designer's perspective to maintain the Intellectual property. Furthermore, the research on mitigating and threat resolving techniques have been rigorous since last few year. The primary focus of IC industry should be on VLSI Supply chain problems and how to mitigate them using several measures. It has been discussed in depth that how to stop maltreat of the IP/IC. Few problems are still open and can be discussed further. The future scope for the article is to communicate the major IC firms with great inputs, how to resolve these issues technically using software approach where a particular IC can identify the tampering itself and directly tell its owner with such kind of tampering.

REFERENCES

Burg, A., Borgmann, M., Wenk, M., Zellweger, M., Fichtner, W., & Bolcskei, H. (2005). VLSI implementation of MIMO detection using the sphere decoding algorithm. *IEEE Journal of Solid-State Circuits, 40*(7), 1566–1577. doi:10.1109/JSSC.2005.847505

Kung, S. Y. (1988). *VLSI array processors.* Englewood Cliffs, NJ: Prentice Hall.

Liu, B., & Qu, G. (2016). VLSI supply chain security risks and mitigation techniques: a survey. *Integration, the VLSI Journal, 55*, 438-448.

Mead, C., & Ismail, M. (Eds.). (2012). *Analog VLSI implementation of neural systems* (Vol. 80). Springer Science & Business Media.

Sun, M. T., Chen, T. C., & Gottlieb, A. M. (1989). VLSI implementation of a 16*16 discrete cosine transform. *IEEE Transactions on Circuits and Systems, 36*(4), 610–617. doi:10.1109/31.92893

Taur, Y., & Ning, T. H. (2013). *Fundamentals of modern VLSI devices.* Cambridge university press.

Zimmermann, R. (1999). Efficient VLSI implementation of modulo (2/sup n//spl plusmn/1) addition and multiplication. In *Proceedings of the 14th IEEE Symposium on Computer Arithmetic* (pp. 158-167). IEEE.

Chapter 17
Why India Should Make It Compulsory to Go for BIM

Bhupinder Kaur Srao
Punjab Technical University, India

Hardeep Singh Rai
GNDEC, India

Kulwinder Singh Mann
GNDEC, India

ABSTRACT

This chapter describes how the effective tool for scheduling and controlling costs, calculating time periods and managing the technological enhancement of a construction project is project risk assessment. Projects under construction usually encounter a lot of uncertainties at different stages of work, which leads to increase of risk in terms of the expected cost of construction, delays in handing over and a poor quality of the project. The Indian built environment sector is ruined by delays and cost overruns as projects are not completed within time and within quality guidelines. Due to the increasing complexity of the design, operation, construction maintenance of modern built environmental assets, traditional construction has become an outdated paradigm. Building Information Modelling (BIM) is a multi-dimensional tool. It is a process that puts all the team members together to build a virtual design and construction methodologies all through the complete design. This extends to the full life of the project, entailing all the construction processes and maintenance of the building.

DOI: 10.4018/978-1-5225-6029-6.ch017

INTRODUCTION

The construction industry is largest industry in the world. Construction projects are interdisciplinary process. It involves risks and uncertainties at a large scale at various stages and activates of a project. The occurrence of uncertainty at various stages of work may affect the critical path and thereby delayed the goal of completion of the project in time. Risk and uncertainty may vary from one to another activity in a project. The most common risk factors involved in a construction industry may be listed as poor work man ship, lack of supervision, inferior quality of material, frequent changes in drawings and designs during construction process, availability of skilled labour, lack of quality control, lack of safety precautions and less experienced staff.

Different techniques of project management have been used from commencement to end stage to encounter the risk involved during the project construction. Although, risk management has been considered as predominate factor in construction project management even less importance is given to it in the construction industry. It becomes very important to overcome these risks otherwise it may lead to increase in the cost of construction, degrade the quality of construction and delay in project handing.

The aim of this chapter is to find out and explore the risks, uncertainties involved within construction industry and high lightening the potential and challenges of BIM for effective risk management in construction industry in India. We can reduce and manage the risk by using BIM which is a unique development of execution and supervision of construction project. It contributes the involvement of every team member together during the whole process of construction and design. India comes under the category of developing countries; there is a necessity for all type of infrastructure. Like UK, USA and all other developed countries the Indian government does not take an initiative to encourage the practice of BIM in the AEC industry. The AEC industry in India is slowly and gradually implementing BIM but still there is a lot of possibility for BIM usage. It may be implemented passing through explore a software module prior to the real project is constructed and afterward during its construction, maintenance of the building, throughout its working life.

RISKS MANAGEMENT IN CONSTRUCTION PROJECTS

The major task in risk management method is the identification of risk involved in the projects. Risk in the construction projects may be consider as a two dimensional quantity. The first dimension is possibility of occurrence, which means the possibility that event, will occur. The other dimension is its harshness of risk (event) impact in case circumstances of risk arises. The harshness may be indicated numerically or verbally on the suitable scale. Both the risk occurrence and harshness leads to increase the possibility of arising of risk level.

The risk matrix is when levels of all identified risks are plotted into a diagram, where two dimensions mentioned are the two diagram axis. During 1990s for risk factor identification many AEC developed rules to analyze risk. In the past, very few exercises have been made to find out risk factors and implement them in the construction projects. Consequently, there remained a lack of adequate process to determine and implement the risk in construction project. Presently, in the direction of evaluating the risks involved in construction projects more complicated software models have been developed.

DIFFERENT RISK IN CONSTRUCTION PROJECTS

In construction work risk may be categories (Tah et al., 1993) into three types such as internal risks such as financial, policy contract, personal. Second category is external risks such as accidental risk coverage, natural disaster, earthquake, fire, flood and storm. New technology, bidding are covered under third category.

BUILDING INFORMATION MODELING (BIM)

Building Information Modelling (BIM) is a parametric 3D modeling process used to generate all of the necessary to document the design of building. It is process that put all the team members together to build virtual design and construction methodologies all through the complete design and also for whole working of life, all the construction process and maintenance of the building come under this process (Azhar et al., 2008). It does not only mean to use three dimensional intelligent models. BIM make considerable change in the project assignment delivery process work flow. Indian industry depends on 2D computer added (CAD) drawing which are prepared individually and there is lack of intelligence between independently created documents. BIM is a procedure that maintain construction plan with the help of putting all team collectively all through the whole design and construction technique. The main focus is to balance the time, economic and energy so now the motive is changing from conventional 2D based to a realistic authenticity. A single database can share with all discipline which is involved with a project. All the members that are involved in construction project like Structural, electrical and mechanical engineer, Architecture and plumber etc. are attached together. At the beginning of designing phase, Energy analysis can be made. Before project construction, cost prediction also can be done. The automatic conventional building documents like plans sectioning, drawings and elevations of a parametric 3D model can be produced with the use of BIM. The interactive representation of a model drawn by the BIM support software, but in traditional 2D method model prepared by manually coordinated lines. If any changes made in this model that automatically coordinate with all over the project which enhance the overall quality of the task and manually coordination also removed. There are several intangible models and software available with tremendous applications, but these models are not so capable to generate to project design document for construction.

BIM is process using intellectual modelling software efficiently, real-time working to get better productivity, time in the design construction phases, to save money and to decrease working costs after construction. All the new skill advancements project can be easily funded by the Indian government, but instead of it, no steps are being taken by the government. All the responsibility of taking initiative of new tools is leave on Private AEC firms. By using BIM risk can be avoided, rework can be reduced. The best final results can be achieved by this software in every project field. So, BIM is an innovative approach to handle risk in construction project. In developing countries, the main aim is to set up system software that improves the performance of construction projects in terms of time, energy and cost.

DIFFERENCE BETWEEN BIM AND 3D MODEL

The model created for BIM is not just 3D geometry; they are data-rich substances which are intelligent, knowledge-based, scalable, and visual. BIM is a process that uses the intelligent software, information model to facilitate coordination, project management and collaboration communication, analysis and simulation, and even asset management, maintenance and operations. There are different uses of BIM in construction industry. These include 3D BIM the shared information model, 4DBIM, 5DBIM and 6D BIM. Apart from 2D and 3D BIM is capable of carrying other multi-dimensional models, 4D (3D + time), and 5D (4D + cost) to get better productivity. Indian designers are ignorant about BIM and its ability (Construction, 2012).

ROLE OF BUILDING INFORMATION MODELING (BIM) IN PROJECT MANAGEMENT

With the advantage of information technology the construction industry (Fischer & Kunz, 2006) has seen improvement in project risk management. BIM has proved to be a boon for AEC industry globally. Developed countries have already implemented it and are taking lead for adopting it in much effective way whereas India is still not at par with developed countries. For this India must establish centers which would work on promoting BIM in industries on a large scale. India must mandate the use of BIM Approval in every construction project. The Government must support to encourage the use of BIM and it should take the initiative as done by Government in other advanced countries. India must bring in action its worldwide recognized Information and Communication Technology (ICT) Leadership to reinforce the huge range implementation of BIM. If taken, a shared approach by Indian Government and private sector firms, then BIM can do wonders for AEC industry as well as for Indian financial system.

Building Information Modeling (BIM) represents the development of models based on software which helps in the overall project planning, design, execution and maintenance. BIM incorporate data and share other important information among architecture and designer for implementing it in construction projects. The role of IT has been improved in the fields of AEC to improve output and thereby reducing the cost of project as compare to the projects which do not use or have limited use of information technology in construction industry.

BIM INTEGRATED SOLUTIONS

There can be several types of BIM integrated solution explain (Figure 1)

Figure 1. BIM integrated solutions

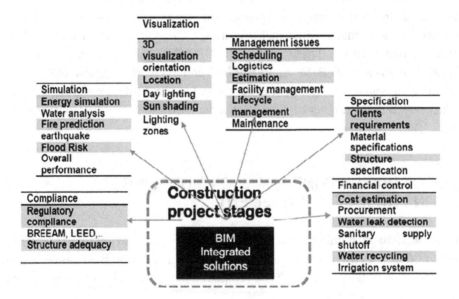

BENEFITS OF IMPLEMENTATION OF BIM IN PROJECT CONSTRUCTION

- **Improved Visualization**: The effective model is provided by the BIM software instead of 2D drawing so there is improvement in visualization.
- **Interoperability:** This is major benefit of using BIM as compare to CAD. Without any loss of information, user can share his own work that is main characteristic of the BIM.
- **Conflict Identification:** Any kind of conflict identification can be visualized by using BIM according to the priority wise. This problem takes a lot of time to solve in country like India, this type of the problem takes lot of time to solve. To save time and money, BIM is most suitable software.
- **Evaluation of Material and Cost**: it is required to describe in advanced the quantity of material before development of BIM model. This is advantageous at the later stage when there is deviancy of quantity of material.
- **Economy of Project**: It will facilitate the calculation of detailed quantity of material and cost estimation and helps in managing the economy of the project.
- **Enhanced Better Understanding**: BIM assist in keeping the updated information by bringing together better understanding between various developers.
- **Concept of Green Buildings**: Green buildings having concepts of energy efficiency is the future demand. BIM helps to give shape to these requirements in a better way.

Reduced Time Delay in Handing Over the Project

BIM helps in proving well organized system development of infrastructure and thereby reduced time delay in handing over the project.

BIM SOFTWARE IN INDUSTRY

BIM models (e.g. Architectural, Structural, MEP etc) can be created through a number of software products. Some of these products are from Autodesk (Revit Architecture, Revit MEP, AutoCAD MEP) Graphisoft (ArchiCAD, ArchiCAD MEP) and Bentley (BIM) (Brewer, Gajendran, & Le Goff, 2012). The associated functions (e.g. 4D scheduling or 5Dcosting) can be interoperable software. The following table (Table 1) describes list of the most common BIM software available from different companies worldwide:

Table 1. BIM software to create models

Software	Website
Solibri Model Viewer	http://www.solibri.com/
DDS-CAD Viewer	http://www.dds-cad.net
Nemetschek IFC Viewer	http://www.nemetschek.co.uk/ifc
IFC Engine Viewer	http://www.ifcbrowser.com/ifcengineviewer.html
IFC File Analyzer:	http://ciks.cbt.nist.gov/cgi-bin/ctv/ifa_request.cgi
ArchiCAD (Graphisoft ArchiCAD 16 EDU:	http://www.graphisoft.com/
Vectorworks (Nemetschek Vectorworks)	http://www.nemetschek.net/
Revit (Autodesk Revit 2014 *student Version*	http://usa.autodesk.com/adsk/servlet/pc/index?siteID=123112&id=6861034

BIM IN PROJECT RISK MANAGEMENT

There are internal and external risks involved in the construction projects. These may be categories into two phases. These are execution period and post execution period. The project risks differ on the basis of

amount of execution at different levels of construction. In the market where BIM is not common used, the innovation risks which need to be managed are much larger, concerning both threats and opportunities. Successful innovation risk management is crucial. When BIM is used, it should have positive impact on risk management, i.e. it mitigates threats and raises opportunities. It is usual that every innovation carries risks, but "the risk of implementing BIM technology is far lower than implementing CAD". It is advised to take a proactive approach to manage risks and to share these risks Factors (Pejman Rezakhani, 2012).

CHALLENGES IN IMPLEMENTATION OF BIM IN CONSTRUCTION INDUSTRY

Among Indian AEC there is a need for focused development, corporation of information skill, bringing together, bridge the communication gap, contribution in information sharing to maintain planning and execution. At present, there is a lack of defined guidelines and regularity for the process of execution of BIM for AEC firms in India. Associated General Contractors (AGC) of America also feels the necessity of single document which provides specific guidelines for BIM application in various firms. Indian government should also realise the problem that instruct BIM application for firms in the country.

BIM AND INDUSTRY FOUNDATION CLASSES (IFC)

ACE vigorously inclining towards the implementation of BIM in the construction industry. There has been a growing trend in the building construction/FM industry to use BIM tools. The data created by BIM tools is saved in various formats. The BIM information which is created by these BIM tools comes in different formats. A large number of data formats are of commercial types and have proprietary writes. Now days there are so many non - proprietary data formats exist in the market. Industry Foundation Classes (IFC) is one of them. Industry Foundation Classes (IFC) is one of them (Thein, V., 2011), IFC an open international standard to exchange BIM data between different software applications used for building construction. Industry professional can use IFC to share data in spite of of what software application they use to get their job done. Likewise, data from one stage of the building lifecycle can be utilized in a later phase without the need for data re- entry.

IFC DATA FILE FORMATS AND ICONS

There are different types of file formats available to store IFC data. The default format is in an ASCII file format according to the IFC-EXPRESS specification, using the file suffix ".ifc". The format is also called SPF format. The IFC-EXPRESS data can also be generated as an XML document using the ifcXML specification, with the file ".ifcXML" normally 300-400% larger than .ifc file. Finally, the two file formats exist in a compressed version with the file suffix ".ifcZIP" and .ifcZIP files usually compress an .ifc down by 60-80% and an .ifcXML file by 90-95%.

FRAMING OF IFC

The IFC structure modeling (Figure 2) for IFC 2x have different layers as described below:

- **Resource Layer:** This layer contains the basic fundamentals articulated component types such as geometry, topology geometric model.
- **Core Layer:** This layer establishes a check that is specific by above mentioned layer. There are intangible ideas such as entity, cluster, method, assets definition, connection or root. There is no occurrence of any firm type of object.
- **Interoperability Layer**: The basic fundamentals of interoperability are characterized between this layer characterize basic concepts for interoperability

Figure 2. Layer structure of Industry Foundation Classes

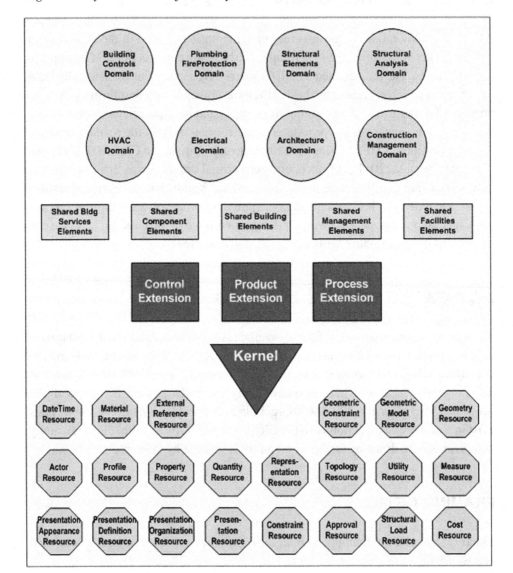

between different domain extension by this layer. Various structural elements such as column, beam, wall, slab, and ventilator are defined in this layer.

- **Domain Layer**: The body of domain layer enlarges the idea of the interoperability layer. The component of one domain is not permitted to point of reference elements of any further domain.

STATE OF THE ART OF WORLD-WIDE IFC BASED MODEL CHECKING PLATFORMS

There are various standalone applications for model checking (Figure 3) such as Solibri Model Checker, SMART codes, ePlan Check, AEC3 Compliance or EDM Model Server.

- **Solibri Model Checker:** The Solibri-Model Checker (SMC) is a software application from company Solibri Inc. that analyses (Khemlani, 2002). Building Information Models (BIM) using the open IFC format.
- **SMART Codes:** SMART codes (Norway, 2009) is a joint project with the International Code Council (ICC), AEC3 and Digital Alchemy to automate code compliance checking in the U.S.
- **EDM Model Server:** The Express Data Manager (EDM) model server provide comprehensive validation of any data- set based on the EXPRESS data Modelling language (ISO 10303-Part 11). EDM Model Server is a very powerful platform for building rules.
- **E –Plan Check:** e-Plan Check is a project started in 2000 for code checking in Singapore. e-PlanCheck presently (Khemlani, 2005) cover code-checking for particular aspects of Architecture and Building services which includes building control regulations, barrier free access, adherence to fire code etc.
- **Design Check:** CSIRO initiated and lead the Design Check project. It was funded by stralia's Cooperative Research Centre for Construction Innovation. Design Check assesses building designs against complex building codes (Ding & Drogemuller, 2006).

In order to fully enable collaboration among BIM tools users, data exchange standards have been developed. The establishment of these standards in the form of Industry Foundation Classes (IFC) for construction objects was led by building SMART. The operative definition of an IFC is "a neutral and open specification that

Figure 3. State of the Art of World-wide IFC checking platforms

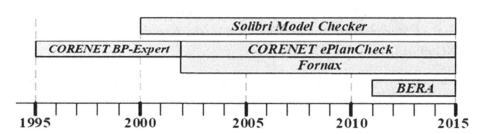

is not controlled by a single vendor or group of vendors". IFCs have been a major step forward in organizing the BIM development process.

CONCLUSION

The presented chapter examined and explained the topic of risks and which can be eliminate with the help of BIM implementation process. Change is required in the method of completion of construction project using BIM to save money, energy and time during the implementing stage and even after the completion stage of bulging. There is a need of set up of principles and defined approach within construction industry in India which can be done with the help of BIM. Practically, there should be an investigated data collection report for the willingness of investors to implement BIM. BIM brings together all the associated groups during the whole process of execution of a project by explore a software model before the real project came into existence and afterward in its execution and completion of project, operation and maintenance, during its working life use of BIM can play major role.

FUTURE SCOPE

Infrastructure development is considered as the back bone for the increase of nation economy. Hence, capital money is invested for the execution of the projects. These projects involve a large quantity of investment to carry out. Wastage of resources, time, and money would lead to the huge financial losses. Sometimes these losses occur due to various risks involved in big projects as they play a crucial role for the completion of project within the stipulated time and budget. By using BIM risk can be reduced and transferred to other parts of the project in order to attain the final results.

REFERENCES

Akinci, B., & Fischer, M. (1998). Actors affecting contractors risk of cost overburden. *Journal of Management Engineering*, *14*(1), 67–76. doi:10.1061/(ASCE)0742-597X(1998)14:1(67)

Azhar, S., Hein, M., and Sketo, B. (2008). Building information modeling: Benefits, risks and challenges. In *Proc., 44th Associated Schools of Construction National Conference*, Auburn, AL.

Bhullar, R. K., Pawar, L., Bajaj, R., & Manocha, A. K. (2017). Intelligent stress calculation and scheduling in segmented processor systems using buddy approach. *Journal of Intelligent & Fuzzy Systems, 32*(4), 3129–3142. doi:10.3233/JIFS-169256

Birnie, J., & Yates, A. (1991). Cost predictions using decision/ risk analysis methodologies. *Construction Management and Economics, 9*(2), 171–186. doi:10.1080/01446199100000015

Brewer G., Gajendran T., & Le Goff R. (2012). Building Information Modelling (BIM): an Introduction and International Perspectives

M.H. Construction, (2012). The business value of BIM in North America: multi-year trend 1analysis and user ratings.

Ding, L., Drogemuller, R., Rosenman, M. A., Marchant, D., & Gero, J. S. (2006). Automating code checking for building designs- DesignCheck. In *Proc of the CRC for Construction Innovation*, Brisbane, Australia

Fischer, M., & Kunz, J. (2006, November 12). The scope and role of information technology in construction.

Khemlani, L. (2002, November 21). Solibri Model Checker. CADENCE AEC Tech News, 87. Retrieved from http://www.epmtech.jotne.com

Khemlani, L. (2005). CORENET e-PlanCheck: Singapore's automated code checking system, AECBytes. *IFC Java Toolbox library.* Retrieved from http://www.ifctoolsproject.com

Norway. (2009). Standardised Computable Rules.

Rezakhani; P. (2012). *Classifying key risk factors in construction Projects. Buletinul Institutului Politrhnic Din Iasi, 58(2).*

Tah, J. H. M., Thorpe, A., & McCaffer, R. (1993). Contractor project risks contingency allocation using linguistic approximation. *Journal of Computing Systems in Engineering, 4*(2-3), 281–293. doi:10.1016/0956-0521(93)90052-X

Thein, V. (2011). *Industry Foundation Classes (IFC) BIM Interoperability through a Vendor-Independent File Format.* Bentley Systems.

Compilation of References

Agarwal, H., Renaud, J., Preston, E., & Padmanabhan, D. (2004). Uncertainty quantification using evidence theory in multidisciplinary design optimization. *Reliability Engineering & System Safety, 85*(13), 281–294.

Aho, A.-M. & Uden, L. (2013). Customer knowledge in value creation for software engineering process. In *Proceedings of the 7th International Conference on Knowledge Management in Organizations: Service and Cloud Computing.* Springer. 10.1007/978-3-642-30867-3_13

Ajay Kumar Jena., Santosh Kumar Swain, & Durga Prasad Mohapatra, A. (2014). A novel approach for test case generation from UML activity diagrams. In *Proceedings of the International Conference on Issues and Challenges in Intelligent Computing Techniques.* IEEE.

Akinci, B., & Fischer, M. (1998). Actors affecting contractors risk of cost overburden. *Journal of Management Engineering, 14*(1), 67–76. doi:10.1061/(ASCE)0742-597X(1998)14:1(67)

Alamgir, M. & Quaddus, M. (2012). Customer Relationship Management Success Model: A Conceptual Framework. In *Proceedings of the 26th Australian and New Zealand Academy of Management Conference (ANZAM)*, Dec 5- 7.

Alam, M. (2010). Software Security Requirements Checklist. *Int. J. of Software Engineering, 3*(1), 53-62.

Alberts, C. J., & Dorofee, A. (2002). *Managing information security risks: the Octave approach.* Boston, MA: Addison-Wesley Longman Publishing Co., Inc.

Al-Busaidi, K. A. (2013). Empowering Organizations through Customer Knowledge Acquisition: A pilot investigation.

Al-Fedaghi, S., & Alrashed, A. A. (2010, Feb. 26–28). Threat risk modeling. In *Proc. 2nd ICCSN* (pp. 405–411).

Allan, D., Hahn, T., Szakal, A., Whitmore, J., & Buecker, A. (2010). Security in development: The IBM secure engineering framework. *IBM Corporation.*

Al-Shammari, M. & Global, I. (2009). Customer knowledge management: People, processes, and technology.

Antunes, R., & Gonzalez, V. (2015). A Production Model for Construction: A Theoretical Framework. *Buildings.*, *5*(1), 209–228. doi:10.3390/buildings5010209

Arshadi Khamseh, A., & Mahmoodi, M. (2014). A new fuzzy TOPSIS-TODIM hybrid method for green supplier selection using fuzzy time function. *Adv. Fuzzy Syst.*

Attafar, A., Sadidi, M., Attafar, H., & Shahin, A. (2013). The Role of Customer Knowledge Management (CKM) in Improving Organization-Customer Relationship. *Middle East Journal of Scientific Research*, *13*(6), 829–835.

Aven, T. (2016). Risk assessment and risk management: Review of recent advances on their foundation. *European Journal of Operational Research.*

Azhar, S., Hein, M., and Sketo, B. (2008). Building information modeling: Benefits, risks and challenges. In *Proc., 44th Associated Schools of Construction National Conference*, Auburn, AL.

Baars, H., Hintzbergen, J., Hintzbergen, K., & Smulders, A. (2010). Foundations of Information Security Based on Iso27001 and Iso27002. Van Haren Publishing.

Bagheri, S., Kusters, R. J., & Trienekens, J. (2015, September). The Customer Knowledge Management lifecycle in PSS Value Networks: Towards process characterization.

Barati, S., & Mohammadi, S. (2008, September). Enhancing risk management with an efficient risk identification approach. In *Proceedings of the 4th IEEE International Conference on Management of Innovation and Technology ICMIT '08* (pp. 1181-1186). IEEE. 10.1109/ICMIT.2008.4654537

Bartle, R. (1996). Hearts, clubs, diamonds, spades: Players who suit MUDs. *Journal of MUD research, 1*(1), 19.

Beasley, D., Bull, D. R., & Martin, R. R. (1993). An overview of genetic algorithms: Part 1, Fundamentals. University Computing. Department of Computing Mathematics.

Belkahla, W., & Triki, A. (2011). Customer knowledge enabled innovation capability: Proposing a measurement scale. *Journal of Knowledge Management*, *15*(4), 648–674.

ben Othmane L, Weffers H, Klabbers M. (2013). Using attacker capabilities and motivations in estimating security risk. In *Workshop on risk perception in it security and privacy*, Newcastle, UK. Retrieved from http://cups.cs.cmu.edu/soups/2013/risk/Cap.-Based-risk.pdf

Bhatia, M. P. S., Kumar, A., & Beniwal, R. (2016). Ontologies for software engineering: Past, present and future. *Indian Journal of Science and Technology*, *9*(9). doi:10.17485/ijst/2016/v9i9/71384

Bhullar, R. K., Pawar, L., & Kumar, V. (2016, October). A novel prime numbers based hashing technique for minimizing collisions. In *Proceedings of the 2016 2nd International Conference on Next Generation Computing Technologies (NGCT)* (pp. 522-527). IEEE.

Bhullar, R. K., Pawar, L., & Kumar, V. (2016, October). A novel prime numbers based hashing technique for minimizing collisions. In *Proceedings of the 2016 2nd International Conference on Next Generation Computing Technologies (NGCT)* (pp. 522-527). IEEE. 10.1109/NGCT.2016.7877471

Bhullar, R. K., Pawar, L., & Kumar, V. (2016, October). A novel prime numbers based hashing technique for minimizing collisions. In *Proceedings of the 2016 2nd International Conference on Next Generation Computing Technologies (NGCT), (pp. 522-527). IEEE.*

Bhullar, R. K., Pawar, L., Bajaj, R., & Manocha, A. K. (2017). Intelligent stress calculation and scheduling in segmented processor systems using buddy approach. *Journal of Intelligent & Fuzzy Systems, 32*(4), 3129–3142. doi:10.3233/JIFS-169256

Birnie, J., & Yates, A. (1991). Cost predictions using decision/ risk analysis methodologies. *Construction Management and Economics, 9*(2), 171–186. doi:10.1080/01446199100000015

Boardman, J., & Sauser, B. (2008). *Systems thinking: Coping with 21st century problems.* CRC Press. doi:10.1201/9781420054927

Boehm, B. W. (1978). *Characteristics of software quality.* North Holland.

Boehm, B. W. (1991). Software risk management: Principles and practices. *IEEE Software, 8*(1), 32–41. doi:10.1109/52.62930

Boukhris, S., Andrews, A., Alhaddad, A., & Dewri, R. (2016). A Case Study of Black Box Fail-Safe Testing in Web Applications. *Journal of Systems and Software.*

Brewer G., Gajendran T., & Le Goff R. (2012). Building Information Modelling (BIM): an Introduction and International Perspectives

Brucker, P., Drexl, A., Möhring, R., Neumann, K., & Pesch, E. (1999). Resource-constrained project scheduling: notation, classification, models and methods. *European Journal of Operational Research, 112*(3-4).

Buchnowska, D. (2011). Customer Knowledge Management Models: Assessment and Proposal. Research in Systems Analysis and Design: Models and Methods 25-38, Springer.

Bucko, M. (2008). Short review of modern vulnerability research.

Bueren, A., Schierholz, R., Kolbe, L., & Brenner, W. (2004). Customer knowledge management improving performance of customer relationship management with knowledge management. In *Proceedings of the 2013 46th Hawaii International Conference on System Sciences.* IEEE Computer Society.

Burg, A., Borgmann, M., Wenk, M., Zellweger, M., Fichtner, W., & Bolcskei, H. (2005). VLSI implementation of MIMO detection using the sphere decoding algorithm. *IEEE Journal of Solid-State Circuits, 40*(7), 1566–1577. doi:10.1109/JSSC.2005.847505

Buriol, R., Resende, M. G. C., Ribeiro, C. C., & Thorup, M. (2005). A hybrid genetic algorithm for the weight setting problem in OSPF/IS-IS routing. *Networks*, *46*(1), 36–56. doi:10.1002/net.20070

Burke, B. (2016). *Gamify: How gamification motivates people to do extraordinary things*. Routledge.

Byers, D., & Shahmehri, N. (2008). A Cause-Based Approach to Preventing Software Vulnerabilities. In *Proceedings of the Third International Conference on Availability, Reliability and Security* (pp. 276-283). 10.1109/ARES.2008.12

Caldern, C., & Marta, E. (2007). A Taxonomy of Software Security Requirements. *Avances en Sistemas e Informtica*, *4*(3), 47–56.

Campbell, A. J. (2003). Creating customer knowledge competence: Managing customer relationship management programs strategically. *Industrial Marketing Management*, *32*(5), 375–383. doi:10.1016/S0019-8501(03)00011-7

Cavusoglu, H., Mishra, B., & Raghunathan, S. (2002). *The Effect of Internet Security Breach Announcements on Market Value of Breached Firms and Internet Security Developers* (tech. report). Univ. of Texas at Dallas, School of Management. Retrieved from www.utdallas.edu/~huseyin/breach.pdf

Chang, Y. Y., Zavarsky, P., Ruhl, R., & Lindskog, D. (2012). Trend Analysis of the CVE for Software Vulnerability Management.

Chan, J. O. (2009). Integrating Knowledge Management and Relationship Management in an Enterprise Environment. *Communications of the IIMA.*, *9*(4), 37.

Charette, R. N. (2005). Why software fails? *IEEE Spectrum*, *42*(9), 42–49. doi:10.1109/MSPEC.2005.1502528

Charland, A., & Leroux, B. (2011). Mobile application development: Web vs. native. *Communications of the ACM*, *54*(5), 49–53. doi:10.1145/1941487.1941504

Chen, Y., Boehm, B., & Sheppard, L. (2007, Jan). Value driven security threat modeling based on attack path analysis. In Proc. 40th Annu. HICSS (pp. 280a–288a).

Choi, S. and Ryu, I. (2013). Leveraging Customer Knowledge in Electronic Knowledge Repositories for Service Expertise. In *PACIS 2013 Proceedings* (pp. 132-145).

Cho, W., Subramanyam, R., & Xia, M. (2013). Vendors' incentives to invest in software quality in enterprise systems. *Decision Support Systems*, *56*, 27–36. doi:10.1016/j.dss.2013.04.005

Chow, W. S., & Chan, L. S. (2008). Social network, social trust and shared goals in organizational knowledge sharing. *Information & Management*, *45*(7), 458–465. doi:10.1016/j.im.2008.06.007

Christian, T. (2010). Security Requirements Reusability and the SQUARE Methodology (no. cmu/sei- 2010-tn-027). Carnegie-Mellon Univ.

Cooper, D. F. (2005). *Project risk management guidelines: managing risk in large projects and complex procurements. John Wiley & Sons, Inc.*

Cooper, D. F. (2005). *Project risk management guidelines: Managing risk in large projects and complex procurements*. John Wiley & Sons, Inc.

Cranor, L. F. (2008). Framework for Reasoning about the Human in the Loop. In *Proceedings of the Symposium on Usable Privacy and Security*, Pittsburgh, PA.

Crockford, N. (1986). *An Introduction to Risk Management*. Cambridge, UK: Woodhead-Faulkner.

Danielle. (2007). Top Ten Risks to Your Website Project. Retrieved May 31, 2007, from http://becircle.com/top_ten_risks

Davenport, T. H., Harris, J. G., & Kohli, A. K. (2001). How do they know their customers so well? *MIT Sloan Management Review, 42*(2), 63–73.

David, T. H. (2004). *Integrated Cost / Schedule Risk Analysis*. PMI Paper.

Deb, K. (2012). Optimization for engineering design-Algorithms and examples. New Delhi: PHI learning Private Limited.

Deepti, V., Ramanamurthy, N., & Balasubramanian, K. U. (2004). Effective Risk Management: Risk Analysis Using an Enhanced FMEA Technique. In *Proceedings of Annual Project Management Leadership Conference, India*.

DeMarco, T., & Lister, T. (2003, October). Risk Management during Requirements. *IEEE Software, 20*(5).

DeMarco, T. (1997). *The Deadline – A novel about project management*. Dorset House Publishing.

Deterding, S., Dixon, D., Khaled, R., & Nacke, L. (2011, September). From game design elements to gamefulness: defining gamification. In *Proceedings of the 15th international academic MindTrek conference: Envisioning future media environments* (pp. 9-15). ACM. 10.1145/2181037.2181040

Dhillon, D. (2011, July/August). Developer-driven threat modeling: Lessons learned in the trenches. *IEEE Security and Privacy, 9*(4), 41–47. doi:10.1109/MSP.2011.47

Dignan, A. (2011). *Game frame: Using games as a strategy for success*. Simon and Schuster.

Ding, L., Drogemuller, R., Rosenman, M. A., Marchant, D., & Gero, J. S. (2006). Automating code checking for building designs- DesignCheck. In *Proc of the CRC for Construction Innovation*, Brisbane, Australia

Dorfman, M. S. (2007). *Introduction to Risk Management and Insurance*. Englewood Cliffs, N.J: Prentice Hall.

Dous, M., Salomann, H., Kolbe, L. and Brenner, W. (2005). Knowledge Management Capabilities in CRM: Making Knowledge For, From, and About Customers Work. In *AMCIS 2005 Proceedings*.

Dubois, E., Heymans, P., Mayer, N., & Matulevicius, R. (2010). A systematic approach to define the domain of nformation system security risk management. In S. Nurcan, C. Salinesi, C. Souveyet et al. (Eds.), Intentional perspectives on information systems engineering (pp. 289-306). Springer.

Duffy, T. (2012). *Programming with mobile applications: Android, iOS, and Windows Phone 7.* Boston, MA: CengageLearning.

Durmuşoğlu, S. S., & Barczak, G. (2011). The use of information technology tools in new product development phases: Analysis of effects on new product innovativeness, quality, and market performance. *Industrial Marketing Management, 40*(2), 321–330. doi:10.1016/j.indmarman.2010.08.009

Durst, S., & Runar Edvardsson, I. (2012). Knowledge management in SMEs: A literature review. *Journal of Knowledge Management, 16*(6), 879–903. doi:10.1108/13673271211276173

Eaton, J. W. (2012). GNU Octave and reproducible research. *Journal of Process Control, 22*(8), 1433-1438.

Eisenhardt, K. M., & Santos, F. M. (2002). Knowledge-based view: A new theory of strategy. In Handbook of strategy and management (Vol. 1, pp. 139-164).

Ellison, C. (2005, January 24). *Ceremony Analysis. Microsoft Think Week paper.*

El-Nasr, M. S., Drachen, A., & Canossa, A. (2016). *Game analytics.* Springer London Limited.

Fairbanks, G. (2010). *Just-enough software architecture: A risk-driven approach.* Boulder, CO: Marshall &Brainerd.

Fan, Z. P., Zhang, X., Chen, F. D., & Liu, Y. (2013). Extended TODIM method for hybrid multiple attribute decision making problems. *Knowledge-Based Systems, 42*, 40–48. doi:10.1016/j.knosys.2012.12.014

Feher, P., & Gabor, A. (2006). The role of knowledge management supporters in software development companies. *Software Process Improvement and Practice, 11*(3), 251–260. doi:10.1002pip.269

Fernandes, J. M., & Machado, R. J. (2015). *Requirements in engineering projects.* Springer; doi:10.1007/978-3-319-18597-2

Fidel, P., Cervera, A., & Schlesinger, W. (2015a). Customer's role in knowledge management and in the innovation process: Effects on innovation capacity and marketing results. *Knowledge Management Research and Practice, 9*(1), 132–146.

Fidel, P., Schlesinger, W., & Cervera, A. (2015b). Collaborating to innovate: Effects on customer knowledge management and performance. *Journal of Business Research, 68*(7), 1426–1428. doi:10.1016/j.jbusres.2015.01.026

Fiksel, J. (2006). Sustainability and resilience: toward a systems approach. *Sustainability: Science, Practice, & Policy, 2*(2).

Firesmith, D. (2003). Engineering security requirements. *Journal of Object Technology, 2*(1), 53–68. doi:10.5381/jot.2003.2.1.c6

Firesmith, D. (2004). Specifying Reusable Security Requirements. *Journal of Object Technology*, *3*(1). Retrieved from http://www.jot.fm

Fischer, M., & Kunz, J. (2006, November 12). The scope and role of information technology in construction.

Franco, E. G., Zurita, F. L., & Delgadillo, G. M. (2006). A genetic algorithm for the resource constrained project scheduling problem. School of Industrial Engineering, University dad de La Sabena.

Frederiksen, H. D., & Iversen, J. H. A. (2003). Implementing Software Metric Programs: A Survey of Lessons and Approaches. Hershey, PA: IGI Global.

Frost and Sullivan. (2016). Analysis of the Global Public Vulnerability Research Market.

Fugini, M., Teimourikia, M., & Hadjichristofi, G. (2016). A web-based cooperative tool for risk management with adaptive security. *Future Generation Computer Systems*, *54*, 409–422.

Gabbard, J. L., Fitch, G. M., & Hyungil, K. (2014). Behind the glass: Driver challenges and opportunities for AR automotive applications. *Proceedings of the IEEE*, *102*(2), 124–136. doi:10.1109/ JPROC.2013.2294642

Ganguly, A., & Mansouri, M. (2011, April). Evaluating risks associated with extended enterprise systems (EES). In *Proceedings of the 2011 IEEE International Systems Conference (SysCon)* (pp. 422-427). IEEE. 10.1109/SYSCON.2011.5929075

Ganguly, A., Mansouri, M., & Nilchiani, R. (2010, April). A risk assessment framework for analyzing risks associated with a systems engineering process. In *Proceedings of the 2010 4th Annual IEEE Systems Conference* (pp. 484-489). IEEE. 10.1109/SYSTEMS.2010.5482460

Ganguly, A., Nilchiani, R., & Farr, J. V. (2011). Identification, classification, and prioritization of risks associated with a disruptive technology process. *International Journal of Innovation and Technology Management*, *8*(02), 273–293. doi:10.1142/S0219877011002313

García, F., Pedreira, O., Piattini, M., Cerdeira-Pena, A., & Penabad, M. (2017). A Framework for Gamification in Software Engineering. *Journal of Systems and Software*, *132*, 21–40. doi:10.1016/j.jss.2017.06.021

Garrido-Moreno, A., Lockett, N., & García-Morales, V. (2014). Paving the way for CRM success: The mediating role of knowledge management and organizational commitment. *Information & Management*, *51*(1), 1031–1042. doi:10.1016/j.im.2014.06.006

Garrido-Moreno, A., & Padilla-Meléndez, A. (2011). Analyzing the impact of knowledge management on CRM success: The mediating effects of organizational factors. *International Journal of Information Management*, *31*(5), 437–444. doi:10.1016/j.ijinfomgt.2011.01.002

Gebert, H., Geib, M., Kolbe, L., & Riempp, G. (2002). Towards customer knowledge management: Integrating customer relationship management and knowledge management concepts. *In Proceedings of the Second International Conference on Electronic Business (ICEB '02).*

George, S. (2008). *Schedule risk analysis - part 2: The six-step process.* Finance Week.

Ghobadi, S. (2015). What drives knowledge sharing in software development teams: A literature review and classification framework. *Information & Management, 52*(1), 82–97. doi:10.1016/j. im.2014.10.008

Gibbert, M., Leibold, M., & Probst, G. (2002). Five styles of customer knowledge management, and how smart companies use them to create value. *European Management Journal, 20*(5), 459–469. doi:10.1016/S0263-2373(02)00101-9

Gopal, J., Sangaiah, A.K., Basu, A., & Gao, X.Z. (2015). Integration of fuzzy DEMATEL and FMCDM approach for evaluating knowledge transfer effectiveness with reference to GSD project outcome. *Int. J. Mach. Learning cybernetics.* doi:.10.1007/s13042-015-0370-5

Grabowski, M., & Roberts, K. H. (1998). Risk mitigation in virtual organizations. *Journal of Computer-Mediated Communication, 3*(4).

Grady, R., & Caswell, D. (1987). *Software metrics: Establishing a company-wide program.* Upper Saddle River, NJ: Prentice Hall.

Grant, R. M. (1996). Toward a knowledge-based theory of the firm. *Strategic Management Journal, 17*(S2), 109–122. doi:10.1002mj.4250171110

Gray, A. (2003). An historical perspective of software vulnerability management.

Guo, Z. X., Wong, W. K., Leung, S. Y., Fan, J. T., & Chan, S. F. (2008). Genetic optimization of order scheduling with multiple uncertainties. *Expert Systems with Applications, 35*(4), 1788–1801. doi:10.1016/j.eswa.2007.08.058

Haimes, Y. Y. (2004). *Risk Modeling, Assessment, and Management* (2nd ed.). Hoboken, NJ: John Wiley and Sons, Inc. doi:10.1002/0471723908

Hair, J. F., Hult, G. T. M., Ringle, C., & Sarstedt, M. (2013). *A primer on partial least squares structural equation modeling (PLS-SEM).* Sage Publications.

Hammami, S. M., & Triki, A. (2011). Exploring the information technology contribution to service recovery performance through knowledge based resources. *Vine, 41*(3), 296–314. doi:10.1108/03055721111171627

Hartmann, S. (2008). A competitive genetic algorithm for resource-constrained project scheduling. *Naval Research Logistics.*

Haupt, R. L., & Haupt, S. E. (2004). Practical genetic algorithms (2nd ed.). New Jersey: John Wiley and Sons, Inc.

Heitkötter, H., Hanschke, S., & Majchrzak, T. A. (2013). Evaluating cross-platform developmentap-proachesfor mobile applications. In *Proceedings of the 8th International Conference on Web Information Systems and Technologies, LNBIP* (Vol. 140, pp. 120–138). Springer.10.1007/978-3-642-36608-6_8

Hernan, S., Lambert, S., Ostwald, T., & Shostack, A. (2006). Uncover security design flaws using the stride approach. *MSDN Magazine*. Retrieved from http://msdn.microsoft.com/en-us/magazine/cc163519.aspx.

Hernan, S., Lambert, S., Ostwald, T., & Shostack, A. (2006, November). Uncover Security Design Flaws Using, the STRIDE Approach. *MSDN magazine.*

Herzog, P. (2001, May 5). Open-Source Security Testing Methodology Manual (Version 1.5).

Hoffman, L., Burley, D., & Toregas, C. (2012, March/April). Holistically building the cyberSecurity workforce. *IEEE Security and Privacy, 10*(2), 33–39. doi:10.1109/MSP.2011.181

Hoglund, G., & McGraw, G. (2004). *Exploiting Software.* Addison-Wesley.

Hong, J., Suh, E., & Kim, S. J. (2009). Context-aware systems: A literature review and classification. *Expert Systems with Applications, 36*(4), 8509–8522. doi:10.1016/j.eswa.2008.10.071

Hopkin, P. (2017). *Fundamentals of risk management: understanding, evaluating and implementing effective risk management.* Kogan Page Publishers.

Howard, M., & LaBlanc, D. (2003). Writing Secure Code (2nd ed.). Microsoft Press.

Huang, C. D., Behara, R. S., & Hu, Q. (2008). Managing risk propagation in extended enterprise networks. *IT Professional, 10*(4), 14–19. doi:10.1109/MITP.2008.90

Hubbard, D. (2009). *The Failure of Risk Management: Why It's Broken and How to Fix It.* John Wiley & Sons.

IBM. (2014). Managing security risks and vulnerabilities.

Ifinedo, P. (2011). Examining the influences of external expertise and in-house computer/IT knowledge on ERP system success. *Journal of Systems and Software, 84*(12), 2065–2078. doi:10.1016/j.jss.2011.05.017

International Organization for Standardization (ISO). (1989). ISO 7498-2 Information Processing Systems - Open Systems Interconnection – Basic Reference Model, Part 2: Security Architecture.

International Organization for Standardization. (2009). ISO/DIS 31000 Risk management — Principles and guidelines on implementation.

International Organization for Standardization. (2009). ISO/IEC Guide 73 Risk management — Vocabulary.

Ismail, M. B. M., & Aboobucker, I. (2014). Risk Assessment (RA) in Transaction Processing System (TPS).

IZenbridge. (2014). Difference between Qualitative and Quantitative Risk Analysis. Retrieved February 11, 2014, from https://www.izenbridge.com/blog/differentiating-quantitative-risk-analysis-and-qualitative-risk-analysis

Jamil, M. A., Arif, M., Normi, S. A. A., & Ahmad, A. A. (2016). Software Testing Techniques: A Literature Review. In *Proceedings of the 2016 6th International Conference on Information and Communication Technology for The Muslim World (ICT4M)*. IEEE.

Juárez-Ramírez, R., Licea, G., Barriba, I., Izquierdo, V., & Angeles, A. (2012). Orchestrating mobile applications: A software engineering view. In R. Aquino-Santos & A.E. Block (Eds.), Embedded systems and wireless technology: Theory and practical applications (pp. 41–72). Boca Raton, FL: CRC Press. doi:10.1201/b12298-3

Kahneman, D., & Tversky. A. (1979). Prospect theory: an analysis of decision under risk. *Econometrica: J, Econ. Soc.*, 263–91.

Kannabiran, G., & Sankaran, K. (2011). Determinants of software quality in offshore development–An empirical study of an Indian vendor. *Information and Software Technology*, *53*(11), 1199–1208.

Kasap, D., & Kaymak, M. (2007, August). Risk identification step of the project risk management. Portland International Center for Management of Engineering and Technology. doi:10.1109/PICMET.2007.4349543

Kaur, D., Kumar, R.V.K.M., Brar, S.S., & Kumaresan, K. (2015). Named entity recognition, extraction and classification using conditional random field with kernel approach. *International Journal of Applied Engineering Research*.

Keith, C. (2010). *Agile Game Development with Scrum (Adobe Reader)*. Pearson Education.

Khemlani, L. (2002, November 21). Solibri Model Checker. CADENCE AEC Tech News, 87. Retrieved from http://www.epmtech.jotne.com

Khemlani, L. (2005). CORENET e-PlanCheck: Singapore's automated code checking system, AECBytes. *IFC Java Toolbox library*. Retrieved from http://www.ifctoolsproject.com

Khodakarami, F. and Chan, Y. E. (2014). Exploring the role of customer relationship management (CRM) systems in customer knowledge creation. *Information & Management*, *51*(1), 27–42.

Khosravi, A., Ab Razak, C.H. & Minaei-Bidgoli, B. (2017). Customer Knowledge Management in Software Development: A Descriptive Field Survey. *Journal of Theoretical and Applied Information Technology*, *96*(1).

Khosravi, A., Ismail, M. A. B., & Najaftorkaman, M. (2014). A Taxonomy of Knowledge Management Outcomes for SMEs. In PACIS 2014 Proceedings.

Kim, G., Oh, J., Seo, D., & Kim, J. (2013). The Design of Vulnerability Management System. *International Journal of Computer Science and Network Security*, *13*(4).

Ko, D.-G., Kirsch, L. J. and King, W. R. (2005). Antecedents of knowledge transfer from consultants to clients in enterprise system implementations. *Management Information Systems Quarterly*, 59–85.

Kokcharov, I. (n.d.). What Is Risk Management? Retrieved from http://www.slideshare.net/igorkokcharov/what-is-project-risk-management

Koren, I., & Krishna, C. M. (2010). *Fault-tolerant systems*. San Francisco, CA: Morgan Kaufmann.

Korhonen-Sande, S., & Sande, J. B. (2016). Improving customer knowledge transfer in industrial firms: How does previous work experience influence the effect of reward systems? *Journal of Business and Industrial Marketing*, *31*(2), 232–246. doi:10.1108/JBIM-03-2014-0048

Kosanke, K., Vernadat, F., & Zelm, M. (1999). CIMOSA: Enterprise engineering and integration. *Computers in Industry*, *40*(2), 83–97. doi:10.1016/S0166-3615(99)00016-0

Kruse, P. (2013a). Customer Involvement in Organizational Innovation–Toward an Integration Concept. In *Proceedings of the Nineteenth Americas Conference on Information Systems, Chicago*, IL, August 15- 17.

Kruse, P. (2013b). External knowledge in organisational innovation-toward an integration concept. In *Proceedings of the 21st European Conference on Information Systems*.

Kumar, R. (2017). DOS Attacks on Cloud Platform: Their Solutions and Implications. *Critical Research on Scalability and Security Issues in Virtual Cloud Environments, 167*.

Kumar, J. (2013, July). Gamification at work: Designing engaging business software. In *Proceedings of the International Conference of Design, User Experience, and Usability* (pp. 528-537). Springer. 10.1007/978-3-642-39241-2_58

Kumar, R. (2012). *Research Methodology: A Step-by-Step Guide for Beginners*. SAGE Publications.

Kumar, R. (2018). *DOS Attacks on Cloud Platform Their Solutions and Implications*. In *Critical Research on Scalability and Security Issues in Virtual Cloud Environments*. doi:10.4018/978-1-5225-3029-9.ch008

Kumar, R., Kumari, N., & Bajaj, R. (2018). Energy Efficient Communication Using Reconfigurable Directional Antenna in MANET. *Procedia Computer Science*.

Kung, S. Y. (1988). *VLSI array processors*. Englewood Cliffs, NJ: Prentice Hall.

Kupsch, J. A., Miller, B. P., Heymann, E., & César, E. (2009). First Principles Vulnerability Assessment.

Kwon, M., Jacobs, M., Cullinane, D., Ipsenand, C., & Foley, J. (2012, March/April). Educating cyber professionals: A view from academia, the private sector, and government. *IEEE Security and Privacy*, *10*(2), 50–53. doi:10.1109/MSP.2012.36

Lasheras, J., Valencia-Garca, R., Fernndez-Breis, J. T., & Toval, A. (2009). Modelling Reusable Security Requirements based on an Ontology Framework. *Journal of Research and Practice in Information Technology*, *41*(2).

Leonidas, S. G. F. (2006). Optimization of Resource Constrained Project Schedules by Genetic Algorithm Based on the Job Priority List. *Information Technology and Control*, *35*(4).

Liao, S.-H., & Wu, C. (2010). System perspective of knowledge management, organizational learning, and organizational innovation. *Expert Systems with Applications*, *37*(2), 1096–1103. doi:10.1016/j.eswa.2009.06.109

Lin, H.-F. (2007). Knowledge sharing and firm innovation capability: An empirical study. *International Journal of Manpower*, *28*(3/4), 315–332. doi:10.1108/01437720710755272

Lin, T. C., Wu, S., & Lu, C. T. (2012). Exploring the affect factors of knowledge sharing behavior: The relations model theory perspective. *Expert Systems with Applications*, *39*(1), 751–764. doi:10.1016/j.eswa.2011.07.068

Lin, Y., Su, H.-Y., & Chien, S. (2006). A knowledge-enabled procedure for customer relationship management. *Industrial Marketing Management*, *35*(4), 446–456. doi:10.1016/j.indmarman.2005.04.002

Liu, B., & Qu, G. (2016). VLSI supply chain security risks and mitigation techniques: a survey. *Integration, the VLSI Journal, 55*, 438-448.

Liu, Y., Zhao, S. L., Du, X. K., & Li, S. Q. (2005, August). Optimization of resource allocation using genetic algorithms. In *Proceedings of the Fourth International Conference on Machine Learning and Cybernetics*, Guangzhou.

Li, X., & He, K. (2008, Apr.). BA unified threat model for assessing threat in web applications. In *Proc. Int. Conf. Inf. Sec. Assurance* (pp. 142–145).

Lohan, G., Lang, M., & Conboy, K. (2011). Having a customer focus in agile software development. In Information Systems Development (pp. 441-453). Springer. doi:10.1007/978-1-4419-9790-6_35

Lorenzo-Romero, C., Constantinides, E., & Brünink, L. A. (2014). Co-creation: Customer Integration in Social Media Based Product and Service Development. *Procedia: Social and Behavioral Sciences*, *148*, 383–396. doi:10.1016/j.sbspro.2014.07.057

Lund, M. S., Solhaug, B., & Stlen, K. (2011). *Model-Driven Risk Analysis–The CORAS Approach*. Berlin, Germany: Springer-Verlag. doi:10.1007/978-3-642-12323-8

Lyu, J.-J., Yang, S.-C., & Chen, C. (2009). Transform customer knowledge into company value— case of a global retailer. In *Proceedings of the 6th International Conference on Service Systems and Service Management ICSSSM '09*. IEEE.

M.H. Construction, (2012). The business value of BIM in North America: multi-year trend 1analysis and user ratings.

Macmillan dictionary. (n.d.). Capability. Retrieved Feb. 2014. from http://www.macmillandictionary.com/us/dictionary/american/capability

Mahdi, M., & Gelayol, S.F. (2014). A new fuzzy DEMATEL-TODIM hybrid method for evaluation criteria of knowledge management in supply chain. *Int. J. Manag. Value Supply Chains*, *5*(2), 29–42. doi:10.5121/ijmvsc.2014.5204

Maletic, J. I., Howald, A., & Marcus, A. (2001). Incorporating PSP into a traditional software engineering course: an experience report. In *Proceedings of the 14th Conference on Software Engineering Education and Training* (pp. 89-97). IEEE. 10.1109/CSEE.2001.913825

Mansouri, M., & Mostashari, A. (2010, April). A systemic approach to governance in extended enterprise systems. In *Proceedings of the 2010 4th Annual IEEE Systems Conference* (pp. 311-316). IEEE. 10.1109/SYSTEMS.2010.5482432

Mansouri, M., Mostashari, A., & Ganguly, A. (2009). Evaluating Agility for an Extended Enterprise Systems: The New York City Transportation Network Case. In *Proceedings of the 1st Annual Global Conference on Systems and Enterprises.*

Marcu, M., Tudor, D., & Fuicu, S. (2010). A view on power efficiency of multimedia mobile applications. In K. Elleithy (Ed.), Advanced Techniques in Computing Sciences and Software Engineering (pp. 407–412). Springer. doi:10.1007/978-90-481-3660-5_70

Markus, M. L. (2000). Paradigm shifts-E-business and business/systems integration. *Communications of the Association for Information Systems, 4*(1), 10.

McGraw, G. (2004) Software Security. *IEEE Security and Privacy, 2*(2), 80–83. doi:10.1109/MSECP.2004.1281254

McGraw, G., Chess, B., & Migues, S. (2010). *Building security in maturity model*. BSIMM.

Mead, C., & Ismail, M. (Eds.). (2012). *Analog VLSI implementation of neural systems* (Vol. 80). Springer Science & Business Media.

Mead, N. R., & Hough, E. D. (2005). *Security Quality Requirements Engineering (SQUARE)*. Carnegie-Mellon Univ. doi:10.21236/ADA443493

Meland, P. H., & Jensen, J. (2008, March 4-7). Secure software design in practice. In *Proc. 3rd Int. Conf. ARES* (pp. 1164–1171).

Mendes, J. J. M., Goncalves, J. F., Resende, M. G. C. (2006, November). A random key based genetic algorithm for the resource-constrained project scheduling problem (Technical Report: TD-6DUK2C, Revised). *AT&T Labs Research.*

Menoni, S., Molinari, D., Parker, D., Ballio, F., & Tapsell, S. (2012). Assessing multifaceted vulnerability and resilience in order to design risk-mitigation strategies. *Natural Hazards, 64*(3), 2057–2082. doi:10.100711069-012-0134-4

Meyer, B. (2019). *Touch of class: Learning to program well with objects and contracts*. Berlin: Springer.

Modarres, M. (2006). *Risk analysis in engineering: techniques, tools, and trends*. CRC press.

Mukherji, S. (2012). A framework for managing customer knowledge in retail industry. *IIMB Management Review, 24*(2), 95–103. doi:10.1016/j.iimb.2012.02.003

Nagati, H., & Rebolledo, C. (2012). The role of relative absorptive capacity in improving suppliers' operational performance. *International Journal of Operations & Production Management, 32*(5), 611–630. doi:10.1108/01443571211226515

Naidu, K. (2005, January 30). How to Check Compliance with your security policy.

Nejatian, H., Sentosa, I., Piaralal, S. K., & Bohari, A. M. (2011). The influence of customer knowledge on CRM performance of Malaysian ICT companies: A structural equation modeling approach. *International Journal of Business and Management, 6*(7), 181. doi:10.5539/ijbm.v6n7p181

Nonaka, I., Von Krogh, G., & Voelpel, S. (2006). Organizational knowledge creation theory: Evolutionary paths and future advances. *Organization Studies, 27*(8), 1179–1208. doi:10.1177/0170840606066312

Norway. (2009). Standardised Computable Rules.

Okada, I., Zhang, F., Yang, H. Y., & Fujimura, S. (2008). A random key-based Genetic algorithm approach for resource-constrained project scheduling problem with multiple modes. In *Proceedings of the international multi-conference of engineers and computer scientists.*

Parker, D., & Mobey, A. (2004). Action Research to Explore Perceptions of Risk in Project Management. *International Journal of Productivity and Performance Management, 53*(1), 18–32. doi:10.1108/17410400410509932

Pfleeger, C. P., & Pfleeger, S. L. (2003). *Security in Computing* (3rd ed.). Upper Saddle River, NJ: Prentice Hall PTR.

Physical Measurement Laboratory of NIST. (2000). The NIST reference on constant, units, and uncertainty of measurement results. Retrieved from http://physics.nist.gov/cuu/Uncertainty/international1.html

Prabhu, N. A., Latha, R., Sankaran, K., & Kannabiran, G. (2011). Impact of knowledge management on offshore software development: An exploratory study. In *Proceedings of the 2011 Third International Conference on Advanced Computing (ICoAC).* IEEE.

Prechelt, L., & Unger, B. (2001). An experiment measuring the effects of personal software process (PSP) training. *IEEE Transactions on Software Engineering, 27*(5), 465–472. doi:10.1109/32.922716

Ramirez, E., David, M. E., & Brusco, M. J. (2013). Marketing's SEM based nomological network: Constructs and research streams in 1987–1997 and in 1998–2008. *Journal of Business Research, 66*(9), 1255–1260. doi:10.1016/j.jbusres.2012.02.022

Ranjan, J., & Bhatnagar, V. (2011). Role of knowledge management and analytical CRM in business: Data mining based framework. *The Learning Organization, 18*(2), 131–148. doi:10.1108/09696471111103731

Rasmussen, J. (1997). Risk management in a dynamic society: A modelling problem. *Safety Science, 27*(2), 183–213. doi:10.1016/S0925-7535(97)00052-0

Rathi, P., & Mehra, V. (2015). Analysis of Automation and Manual Testing Using Software Testing Tool. *International Journal of Innovations & Advancement in Computer Science, 4.*

Rawat, M. S., Mittal, A., & Dubey, S. K. (2012). Survey on Impact of Software Metrics on Software Quality. *International Journal of Advanced Computer Science and Applications, 3*(1).

Raytheon. (2002, January 02). Risk Management and Security, Analysis of the Risk Assessment Process.

Rekha, J. H., & Parvathi, R. (2015). Survey on Software Project Risks and Big Data Analytics. *Procedia Computer Science, 50*, 295–300. doi:10.1016/j.procs.2015.04.045

Rezakhani; P. (2012). *Classifying key risk factors in construction Projects. Buletinul Institutului Politrhnic Din Iasi, 58(2).*

Risk Communication Primer—Tools and Techniques. Navy and Marine Corps Public Health Center.

Rjaibi, N., & Rabai, L. B. A. (2015a). Developing a Novel Holistic Taxonomy of Security Requirements, In *Proceedings of the 2015 International Conference on Soft Computing and Software Engineering.* Elsevier.

Rjaibi, N., & Rabai, L. B. A. (2015b). Expansion and practical implementation of the MFC cybersecurity model via a novel security requirements taxonomy. *International Journal of Secure Software Engineering, 6*(4), 32–51. doi:10.4018/IJSSE.2015100102

Robertson, S., & Robertson, J. C. (2006). *Mastering the requirements process* (2nd ed.). Boston, MA: Addison-Wesley.

Rollins, M., & Halinen, A. (2005). Customer knowledge management competence: towards a theoretical framework. In *Proceedings of the 38th Annual Hawaii International Conference on System Sciences HICSS '05.* IEEE. 10.1109/HICSS.2005.180

Rollins, M., Bellenger, D. N., & Johnston, W. J. (2012). Does customer information usage improve a firm's performance in business-to-business markets? *Industrial Marketing Management, 41*(6), 984–994. doi:10.1016/j.indmarman.2012.01.004

Roman, G. (1985). A taxonomy of current issues in requirements engineering. *IEEE Computer, 18*(4), 14–23. doi:10.1109/MC.1985.1662861

Ross, R., McEvilley, M., & Oren, J. C. (2016, November). Systems Security Engineering. NIST.

Rouse, W. B. (2005). Enterprises as systems: Essential challenges and approaches to transformation. *Systems Engineering, 8*(2), 138–150. doi:10.1002ys.20029

Saghee, M., Sandle, T., & Tidswell, E. (Eds.). (2011). *Microbiology and Sterility Assurance in Pharmaceuticals and Medical Devices* (1st ed.). Business Horizons.

Salojärvi, H., Saarenketo, S., & Puumalainen, K. (2013). How customer knowledge dissemination links to KAM. *Journal of Business and Industrial Marketing*, *28*(5), 383–395. doi:10.1108/08858621311330236

Salojärvi, H., & Sainio, L.-M. (2015). CRM Technology and KAM Performance: The Mediating Effect of Key Account-Related Knowledge. *Journal of Business Marketing Management.*, *8*, 435–454.

Salojärvi, H., Sainio, L.-M., & Tarkiainen, A. (2010). Organizational factors enhancing customer knowledge utilization in the management of key account relationships. *Industrial Marketing Management*, *39*(8), 1395–1402. doi:10.1016/j.indmarman.2010.04.005

Salvi, O., & Debray, B. (2006). A global view on ARAMIS, a risk assessment methodology for industries in the framework of the SEVESO II directive. *Journal of Hazardous Materials*, *130*(3), 187–199. doi:10.1016/j.jhazmat.2005.07.034 PMID:16236437

Sangaiah, A.K., Gopal, J., Basu, A., & Subramaniam, P.R. (2015). An integrated fuzzy DEMATEL, TOPSIS, and ELECTRE approach for evaluating knowledge transfer effectiveness with reference to GSD project outcome. *Neural computing and applications.* doi:.10.1007/ s00521-015-2040-7

Sapna PG, & Arunkumar, A. (2015). An approach for generating minimal test cases for regression testing. *Procedia computer science*, *47*, 188-196.

Sarigiannidis, L., & Chatzoglou, P. D. (2011). Software Development Project Risk Management: A New Conceptual Framework. *Journal of Software Engineering and Applications*, *4*(05), 293–305. doi:10.4236/jsea.2011.45032

Schaarschmidt, M., Bertram, M., Walsh, G. and von Kortzfliesch, H. F. (2015). Customer Knowledge and Requirements Engineering in Customization Projects: A Multi-Method Case Study. *ICIS 2015 Proceedings*, *12*(1), 111-126.

Schiffrin, D. (2004). *Approaches to Discourse*. Oxford, England: Blackwell, OCTAVE Operationally Critical Threat, Asset and Vulnerability Evaluation.

Schneier, B. (1999, December). Attack Trees: Modeling Security Threats. *Dr. Dobb's Journal*.

Sekaran, K. C. (2007). Requirements Driven Multiple View Paradigm for Developing Security Architecture. In *Proceedings of World Academy of Science* (pp. 156–159). Engineering and Technology PWASET.

Shieh, C.-J. (2011). Study on the relations among the customer knowledge management, learning organization, and organizational performance. *Service Industries Journal*, *31*(5), 791–807. doi:10.1080/02642060902960818

Shostack, A. (2008, July). Reinvigorate your Threat Modeling Process. *MSDN Magazine*.

Simmons, L. F. (2002). Project Management-Critical Path Method (CPM) and PERT Simulated with Process Model. In *Proceedings of the 2002 Winter Simulation Conference*. 10.1109/ WSC.2002.1166468

Simon, P. & Hillson; D. (2012). *Practical Risk Management: The ATOM Methodology*. Vienna, VA: Management Concepts.

Sindre, G. & Opdahl, A.L. (2005). *Eliciting Security Requirements by Misuse Cases. In* Proc. 37th Technology of Object-Oriented Languages and Systems(TOOLS-37). IEEE CS Press.

Singh, V. (2008, January). A simulation-based approach to software project risk management. *Asia Pacific Business Review*.

Skotis, A., Katsanakis, I., Macris, A., & Sfakianakis, M. (2013). *Creating Knowledge within a C-Business Context: A Customer Knowledge Management View. In Collaborative, Trusted and Privacy-Aware e/m-Services (pp. 264- 277)*. Springer.

Slade, A. J., & Bokma, A. F. (2002, January). Ontologies within extended enterprises. In *Proceedings of the 35th Annual Hawaii International Conference on System Sciences HICSS '02* (pp. 541-550). IEEE.

Smith, H. A., & McKeen, J. D. (2005). Developments in practice XVIII-customer knowledge management: Adding value for our customers. *Communications of the Association for Information Systems, 16*(1), 36.

Sodiya, A. S., Onashoga, S. A., & Oladunjoye, B. A. (2007, January). Threat modeling using fuzzy logic paradigm. *In Sci. Int. J. Emerging Transdisc., 4*(1), 53–61.

Sofianti, T., Suryadi, K., Govindaraju, R., & Prihartono, B. (2010). Customer Knowledge Co-creation Process in New Product Development. In *Proceedings of the World Congress on Engineering*.

Spielberg, R. F. (2009). *Handbook of reliability, availability, maintainability and safety in engineering design*. London: Springer.

Spiliotopoulos, T., Papadopoulou, P., Martakos, D., & Kouroupetroglou, G. (2010). *Integrating usability engineering for designing the Web experience: Methodologies and principles*. Hershey, PA: IGI Global. doi:10.4018/978-1-60566-896-3

Spriestersbach, A., & Springer, T. (2004). Quality attributes in mobile web application development. In Product Focused Software Process Improvement, *LNCS* (Vol. *3009*, pp. 120-130). doi:10.1007/978-3-540-24659-6_9

Stefanou, C. J., Sarmaniotis, C., & Stafyla, A. (2003). CRM and customer-centric knowledge management: An empirical research. *Business Process Management Journal, 9*(5), 617–634. doi:10.1108/14637150310496721

Steinberg, A. (2007). Open interaction network model for recognizing and predicting threat events. In *Proc* (pp. 285–290). Inf. Decision Control. doi:10.1109/IDC.2007.374564

Stephanou, T. (2001, March 13). Assessing and Exploiting the Internal Security of an Organization.

Steven, J. (2010, May/June). Threat modeling–Perhaps it's time. *IEEE Security and Privacy, 8*(3), 83–86. doi:10.1109/MSP.2010.110

Stewart, M. G. (2008). Cost effectiveness of risk mitigation strategies for protection of buildings against terrorist attack. *Journal of Performance of Constructed Facilities, 22*(2), 115–120. doi:10.1061/(ASCE)0887-3828(2008)22:2(115)

Stoneburner, G., Goguen, A., & Feringa, A. (2002). Gaithersburg, MD: National Institute of Standards and Technology. In Risk Management Guide for Information Technology Systems (Special Publication 800-30).

Stoneburner, G., Goguen, A., & Feringa, A. (2002). *Risk management guide for information technology systems.* NIST. doi:10.6028/NIST.SP.800-30

Stoneburner, G., Hayden, C., & Feringa, A. (2001). *Engineering principles for information technology security (a baseline for achieving security).* Mclean VA: Booz-Allen and Hamilton Inc . doi:10.6028/NIST.SP.800-27

Sundararajan, S., Bhasi, M., & Pramod, K. V. (2013). An Empirical Study of Industry Practice in Software Development Risk Management. *International Journal of Scientific and Research Publications, 3*(6).

Sun, M. T., Chen, T. C., & Gottlieb, A. M. (1989). VLSI implementation of a 16*16 discrete cosine transform. *IEEE Transactions on Circuits and Systems, 36*(4), 610–617. doi:10.1109/31.92893

Sutton, S. G., Khazanchi, D., Hampton, C., & Arnold, V. (2007). Risk analysis in extended enterprise environments: Identification of critical risk factors in B2B e-commerce relationships.

Sutton, S. G. (2006). Extended-enterprise systems' impact on enterprise risk management. *Journal of Enterprise Information Management, 19*(1), 97–114. doi:10.1108/17410390610636904

Swiderski, F., & Snyder, W. (2004). *Threat Modeling.* Microsoft Press.

Tah, J. H. M., Thorpe, A., & McCaffer, R. (1993). Contractor project risks contingency allocation using linguistic approximation. *Journal of Computing Systems in Engineering, 4*(2-3), 281–293. doi:10.1016/0956-0521(93)90052-X

Taivalsaari, A., & Systä, K. (2012). Cloudberry: An HTML 5 cloud phone platform for mobile devices. *IEEE Software, 29*(4), 40–45. doi:10.1109/MS.2012.51

Talet, A. N. (2012). KM Process and CRM to manage Customer Knowledge Relationship Management. *International Proceedings of Economics Development & Research IPEDR., 29,* 60–67.

Tan, W., Xue, J., & Wang, J. (2006, October). A service-oriented virtual enterprise architecture and its applications in Chinese tobacco industrial sector. In *Proceedings of the IEEE International Conference on e-Business Engineering ICEBE'06* (pp. 95-101). IEEE. 10.1109/ICEBE.2006.13

Taneja, K., Taneja, H., & Bhullar, R. K. (2016, March). Cross-platform application development for smartphones: Approaches and implications. In *Proceedings of the 2016 3rd International Conference on Computing for Sustainable Global Development (INDIACom)* (pp. 1752-1758). IEEE.

Taneja, K., Taneja, H., & Kumar, R. (2017). Multi-channel medium access control protocols: review and comparison. *Journal of Information and Optimization Sciences*.

Tao, Y.-H., Wu, Y.-L., & Li, J.-K. (2006). A taxonomy of knowledge maps in business application. In *Proceedings of the Thirty-Fifth Annual Meeting of Western Decision Institute*, Big Island, Hawaii, April 11-14 (pp. 72-81).

Taur, Y., & Ning, T. H. (2013). *Fundamentals of modern VLSI devices*. Cambridge university press.

Taylor, C., & VanMarcke, E. (Eds.). (2002). Acceptable Risk Processes: Lifelines and Natural Hazards. Reston, VA: ASCE, TCLEE.

Telang, R., & Wattal, S. (2007). An Empirical Analysis of the Impact of Software Vulnerability Announcements on Firm Stock Price. IEEE Transactions on software engineering, 33(8).

Thein, V. (2011). *Industry Foundation Classes (IFC) BIM Interoperability through a Vendor-Independent File Format*. Bentley Systems.

Theriou, G. N., & Chatzoglou, P. D. (2008). Enhancing performance through best HRM practices, organizational learning and knowledge management. *European Business Review*, 20(3), 185–207. doi:10.1108/09555340810871400

Tillquist, J. (2002). Strategic Connectivity in Extended Enterprise Networks. *Journal of Electronic Commerce Research*, 3(2), 77–85.

Tiwana, A., & Keil, M. (2004). The one-minute risk assessment tool. *Communications of the ACM*, 47(11), 73–77. doi:10.1145/1029496.1029497

Tseng, S. (2016). The effect of knowledge management capability and customer knowledge gaps on corporate performance. *Journal of Enterprise Information Management*, 29(1), 34–71. doi:10.1108/JEIM-03-2015-0021

Tseng, S. M., & Fang, Y. Y. (2015). Customer Knowledge Management Performance Index. *Knowledge and Process Management*, 22(2), 68–77. doi:10.1002/kpm.1463

Tseng, S.-M., & Wu, P.-H. (2014). The impact of customer knowledge and customer relationship management on service quality. *International Journal of Quality and Service Sciences*, 6(1), 77–96. doi:10.1108/IJQSS-08-2012-0014

Vaezitehrani, S. (2013). Customer Knowledge Management in Global Software Projects [Master thesis]. Northumbria University Gothenburg, Sweden.

Van Den Brink, P. (2001). Measurement of conditions for Knowledge Sharing. In *Proceedings 2nd European Conference on Knowledge Management*, Bled.

Verdon, D., & McGraw, G. (2004). Risk analysis in software design. *IEEE Security & Privacy, 2*(4), 79-84.

Verma, V. & Sona Malhotra, A. (2011). Applications of Software Testing Metrics in Constructing Models of the Software Development Process. *Journal of Global Research in Computer Science, 2*(5).

Viega, J., & McGraw, G. (2000). *Building Secure Software: How to Avoid Security Problems the Right Way.* Addison Wesley.

Wall, M.B. (1996). A Genetic Algorithm for Resource-Constrained Scheduling.

Wallmüller, E. (2011), Risk Management for IT and Software Projects. In *Business Continuity* (pp. 165-178). Springer.

Wanderleya, M., Menezes, J. Jr, Gusmão, C., & Lima, F. (2015). Proposal of risk management metrics for multiple project software development. *Procedia Computer Science, 64,* 1001–1009. doi:10.1016/j.procs.2015.08.619

Wang, Y.J. (2008). Applying FMCDM to evaluate financial performance of domestic airlines in Taiwan. *Expert Syst. Applic., 34*(3), 1837-1845.

Wang, H., Mylopoulos, J., & Liao, S. (2002). Intelligent agents and financial risk monitoring systems. *Communications of the ACM, 45*(3), 83–88. doi:10.1145/504729.504733

Wang, H., & Yu, Z. (2010). The Research of Customer Knowledge Management in CRM. In *Proceedings of the 2010 International Conference on Intelligent Computation Technology and Automation (ICICTA),* May 11-12.

Wang, M.-L. (2015). Learning climate and customer-oriented behaviors: The mediation of customer knowledge. *Journal of Managerial Psychology, 30*(8), 955–969.

Wasserman, A. I. (2010). Software engineering issues for mobile application development. *FSE/SDP Workshop on Future of Software Engineering Research* (pp. 397-400). doi:10.1145/1882362.1882443

Watro, R. J., & Shirley, R. W. (2001, June 12-14). Mapping Mission-Level Availability Requirements to System Architectures and Policy Abstractions. In *Proceedings of DARPA Information Survivability Conference & Exposition II* (Vol. 1, pp. 189-199). 10.1109/DISCEX.2001.932215

Webster, L. R. (2016). Risk Mitigation Strategies. In *Controlled Substance Management in Chronic Pain* (pp. 163–180). Springer International Publishing.

Westfall, L. (2000, January). Software risk management. In *ASQ World Conference on Quality and Improvement Proceedings* (p. 32). American Society for Quality.

Wheeler, E. (2011). Security risk management: building an information security risk management program from the ground up. Waltham, MA: Elsevier.

Wilde, S. (2011). *Customer Knowledge Management.* Springer.

Wu Qianqian,Liu Xianqjun(2014), Research and design on Web application vulnerability scanning service. In *Proceedings of the Software Engineering and Service Science (ICSESS '14)*.

Wu, D. D., & Olson, D. (2010). Enterprise risk management: A DEA VaR approach in vendor selection. *International Journal of Production Research, 48*(16), 4919–4932. doi:10.1080/00207540903051684

Wu, J., Guo, B., & Shi, Y. (2013). Customer knowledge management and IT-enabled business model innovation: A conceptual framework and a case study from China. *European Management Journal, 31*(4), 359–372. doi:10.1016/j.emj.2013.02.001

Xu, D., & Nygard, K. (2013, October). BA threat-driven approach to modeling and verifying secure software. In *Proc. 20th IEEE/ACM Int. Conf. ASE, 2005, pp. 342–346.*

Yadav, M., & Kumar, K. (2014). CMM or CMMI, which is more appropriate for a software industry? *International Journal in IT & Engineering, 2*(1), 24–33.

Yang, L.-R., Huang, C.-F., & Hsu, T.-J. (2014). Knowledge leadership to improve project and organizational performance. *International Journal of Project Management, 32*(1), 40–53. doi:10.1016/j.ijproman.2013.01.011

Ye, N., Chen, X., Jiang, P., Ding, W., & Li, X., A. (2011). Automatic Regression Test selection based on activity diagrams. In *Proceedings of the Fifth International Conference on Secure Software Integration And Reliability Improvement*. IEEE. 10.1109/SSIRI-C.2011.31

Yeung, A. H. W., Lo, V. H. Y., Yeung, A. C. L., & Cheng, T. C. E. (2008). Specific customer knowledge and operational performance in apparel manufacturing. *International Journal of Production Economics, 114*(2), 520–533. doi:10.1016/j.ijpe.2007.06.011

Zhang, Z. J. (2011). Customer knowledge management and the strategies of social software. *Business Process Management Journal, 17*(1), 82–106. doi:10.1108/14637151111105599

Zibula, A., & Majchrzak, T. (2013). Cross-platform development using HTML5, jQuery Mobile, and Phone Gap: Realizing a smart meter application. In Web Information Systems and Technologies, *LNBIP* (Vol. *140*, pp. 16-33). doi:10.1007/978-3-642-36608-6_2

Zichermann, G., & Cunningham, C. (2011). *Gamification by design: Implementing game mechanics in web and mobile apps*. O'Reilly Media, Inc.

Zimmermann, R. (1999). Efficient VLSI implementation of modulo (2/sup n//spl plusmn/1) addition and multiplication. In *Proceedings of the 14th IEEE Symposium on Computer Arithmetic* (pp. 158-167). IEEE.

Zogaj, S. & Bretschneider, U. (2012). Customer integration in new product development-a literature review concerning the appropriateness of different customer integration methods to attain client information. *ECIS 2012 Proceedings, 15*(2), 12-18.

About the Contributors

Rohit Bajaj is a distinguished scholar, having rich Industrial experience as well as varied experience in teaching and Research. He has academic experience of over 10 years with renowned universities He is having PhD in computer science as well as M. Tech. in computer science with specialization in Information Security. His area of interest includes Computer networks, Pattern Recognition, Information Security, Soft Computing etc. He served in several research projects in different profile of researcher funded by DST.

Latifa Ben Arfa Rabai is a University Associate Professor in the Department of Computer Science at the Tunis University in the Higher Institute of Management (ISG). She received the Computer Science Engineering diploma in 1989 from the Sciences Faculty of Tunis and a PhD from the Sciences Faculty of Tunis in 1992. Her research interest includes software engineering trends quantification, quality assessment in education and e-learning, and security measurement and quantification. Her research has been published in Information Sciences Journal, IEEE Technology and Engineering Education magazine. She has participated in several international conferences covering topics related to computer science, E-learning, quality assessment in education, and cyber security.

Deepshikha Chhabra works as Assistant professor since last two years in Chandigarh University Gharuan, Mohali. Prior to this she has worked for Accenture services private limited where she has worked on number of software projects. She has published number of research papers in reputed journals and conferences. She has completed her M tech CSE from Jamia Hamdard New Delhi (2013-2016).

Rimsy Dua received her M.Tech degree from Kurukshetra university in 2016. she is currently working as an Assistant Professor in Chandigarh University and her research interest includes network security and software engineering.

Jasleen Kaur has done Master of engineering in Computer Science and Engineering from University Institute of Engineering and Technology, Panjab University Chandigarh, India. She did her Bachelor of Technology in Computer Science and Engineering from Guru Nanak Dev Engineering College, Ludhiana, India in 2015. Her current research work is based on networks, hardware calibration, modeling and simulation, Risk Analysis etc. She has published many papers in international journals like(Scopus and SCI indexed) and international conferences like WS4, ICSICCS, etc.

Manjot Kaur Sidhu is Associate Professor and Coordinator in Department of Computer Science and Engineering at Chandigarh University. From 2009 to 2013 she served as Assistant Professor in CSE, department at Rayat & Bahra Engg. College, Mohali. During 2006-2009 she was a Lecturer at Indo Global Engg. Colleges, Mohali. From 2003-2006 she worked as lecturer in CSE dept at GGS, College Ludhiana. She has received her M.Tech.&B.Tech. in Computer Science from Punjab Technical University in 2010 & 2003 respectively. Her research interests span both computer networking and Data Mining. Much of her work has been on improving the understanding, design, and performance of Wireless sensor Networks and networked computer systems, mainly through the application of data mining, statistics, and performance evaluation. She has explored the presence and implications of self-similarity and heavy-tailed distributions in network traffic in real time Scenario. She has also investigated the implications of Sensor nodes workloads for the design of scalable and cost-effective Web servers. In addition he has made numerous contributions to measurement and modeling; and she has examined the impact of network properties on the design of protocols and the construction of statistical models. In the Data mining arena, she has focused on the analysis of social, biological, and data networks.

Rajinder Kaur has completed her postgraduate degree of Masters of Engineering in Computer Science & Engineering field from depatment of University Institute of Engineering & Technology, Panjab University Chandigarh. She has done her research work in Data mining. Her topic was text classification. After that she is working as Assistant Professor in Chnadigarh University Gharuan, Punjab. She has one chapter in Springer book on Advs in intelligent System and computing published in January 2018. Also she has added two research papers in Indian Journal of Science and Technology and two papers in International Journal of Computer Science Engineering and Information Research.

Yadwinder Kaur did her B.Tech. in Computer Science and Engineering from Kurukshetra University in 2005. She completed her Masters in 2010 from Guru Nanak Dev Engineering College, Ludhiana, affiliated to Punjab Technical University. Her area of research is Digital Image Processing. She is holding more than 12 years of teaching experience. She has published more than 20 papers in reputed journals and conferences. Currently, she is working as an Assistant Professor with Chandigarh University, Gharuan, Punjab.

K. S. Mann is Professor & Head, Department of Information Technology Guru Nanak Dev Engineering College, Ludhiana-141006, Punjab (India). His research interests include Medical Informatics.

Nitish Ojha is a distinguished scholar, having rich Industrial experience as well as varied experience in teaching and Research. He has academic experience of over 4 years with renowned universities along with 5 years industrial experience. He is having PhD in Information Technology as well as M. Tech. in Information Technology with specialization in Information Security from Indian Institute of Information Technology Allahabad India.His area of interest includes Computer Vision, Pattern Recognition, Information Security, Image Processing, Soft Computing etc. He served in several research projects in different profile of researcher funded by DST/ MCIT/MOHFW Govt. Of India having National and International importance at IIT Delhi and in AIIMS New Delhi, India. He had two international level collaboration based research project in his credit under Indian-Russian DST-RFBR joint research program in the field of computer vision.

Vipin Pal has completed Ph.D from Malaviya National Institute of Technology, Jaipur, India. He has completed B.E. in 2005 from Chhotu Ram State College of Engineering, Murthal, India in Computer Science and Engineering and M.Tech. in 2008 from Guru Jambheshwar University of Science and Technology, Hisar, India in Computer Science and Engineering. He is member of reviewer committee of various Journals of repute, like IEEE Internet of Things Journal, IEEE Access, IEEE Sensors, Elsevier Journal on Simulation Modeling Practice and Theory, IET Wireless Sensor Systems, International Journal of Parallel, Emergent and Distributed Systems, Asian Journal of Mathematics and Computer Research, and various International/National conferences.

Lokesh Pawar is an Assistant Professor in Computer Science and Engineering wing and also the founder member of Technical Training Team at Chandigarh University, Mohali, Punjab. He is a recipient of Outstanding Faculty Research Award in 2016. The author's current interest is in the field of Risk analysis and mitigation, Manet, WSN, Delay tolerant Networks. He has published more than 50 research papers in these areas. He holds two Indian Patents in Hardware Security and easy learning of programming language. He has written several books on data structures and on testing your skills in C language.

Hardeep Singh Rai is Professor in Department of Civil Engineering at Guru Nanak Dev Engineering College, Ludhiana-141006, Punjab (India). He has done Ph.D. in Structural Engineering from IIT Roorkee India. His interests include computer Programming and RCC structures.

Neila Rjaibi is a University Assistant of Computer Science at the Faculty of Law, Economics and Management of Jendouba, Tunisia since 2015. She graduated from the University of Tunis, Higher Institute of Management (ISG) in 2007, then she received her Master's Diploma in 2010 and obtained her PhD degree in 2016. Her research interests include Software Engineering, Cyber Security Measurement and Quantification, Security Risk Management, and E-learning Systems. She has participated in International Conferences and served as a technical program committee member for several of the conferences. Also, she has published papers in international journals and served on several review boards. She has authored several book chapters.

Sumeet Kaur Sehra is Assistant Professor at Guru Nanak Dev Engineering College, Ludhiana. She completed Master of Technology in Computer Science and Engineering from Punjab Agricultural University, Ludhiana in 2005 and Bachelor of Technology in Electronics and Communication from Beant College of Engineering and Technology, Gurdaspur in 2002. She is a member of various professional bodies at National and International forum and has published 54 research articles.

Abhishek Sharma is an Assistant Professor at Chandigarh University in Computer Science and Engineering Department. He completed his masters M.Tech in CSE from MDU Rohtak. He completed his B.Tech in Information Technology from Kurukshetra University. His research area is in the Database Security, Compiler Design, Data Mining and Machine Learning and Information Security. He is also a member of CSI, ACM and IAENG. He published two papers in National Conferences, two papers in International Conferences, and three papers in International Journal. He has five years of teaching experience and two years of corporate experience.

Ankita Sharma is an Assistant Professor in department of computer science and engineering at Chandigarh University, India. She has worked in the field of computer graphics and image processing as her post graduation project and research work. She also worked on Analyzing and Generating Realistic Crack patterns of images. She has obtained her master of technology degree from Punjabi University, Patiala, India. She has published number of research papers in area of image processing, computer graphics and software engineering.

Anu Priya Sharma is an Assistant Professor and Event coordinator of Computer Science & Engineering at Chandigarh University, Gharuan. Ms. Sharma has around 8 years of experience. She has worked as a senior graphic designer in a multinational company for 2.5 years and for the last 5.5 years working as an Assistant Professor. Her current research interest includes NLP, Signal Processing, Software Engineering, Data Mining, Big Data and Analytics. She has published various research papers in the field of Natural language processing and Signal Processing. Ms. Anu Priya Sharma has been appointed as one of the first Charter Members of an Oracle Academy Educator Community.

Anurag Sharma is an Assistant Professor of Electronics and Communication Engineering wing in Chandigarh University at Chandigarh University, Mohali, Punjab. The authors current interest is in the field of software risk analysis and mitigation in accordance to the VLSI Supply Chain, Wireless Sensor Networks, Delay Tolerant Networks and Manet. He has published more than 30 research papers in these areas.

Isha Sharma received B. Tech degree in Information Technology from Seth Jai Parkash Mukand Lal Institute of Engg. & Tech.in 2008 and received M.Tech degree in Computer Science & Engg. from Department of Computer Science & Applications, Kurukshetra University, Kurukshetra in 2011.She has 7 years of teaching experience in field of Computer Science & Engineering . Her core area of interest and research is Software Risk Management, Simulation, Genetic Algorithm an Programming in C, Java, C++.

Samiksha Sharma received her B.Tech degree in Computer Science and Engineering from Beant College of Engineering and Technology, Gurdaspur, Punjab, India in 2014 and completed M.Tech degree in Computer Science and Engineering from DAV Institute of Engineering and Technology, Jalandhar, Punjab, India. She is currently working as Assistant Professor in Chandigarh University. Her research areas includes Cryptography and Network Security.

Arshpreet Sidhu is assistant professor in department of computer science at Chandigarh University, India. She has research area of testing of web applications using UML. She is a member of ISTE and has done projects for improving the quality of educational websites. Also she worked on the area of wearable computers.

Satvir Singh is working as Assistant Professor at CEC, Landran, Mohali, Punjab. He did his bachelor's degree in Electronics and Communication Engineering (ECE) from Chandigarh College of Engineering and Technology, Chandigarh, India under Punjab University, Chandigarh and Master's degree from Punjab Technical University. His area of research is Embedded Systems. He has 5 publications in journals of International repute.

Bhupinder Kaur Srao is a Ph.D scholar at the Computer Science & Engineering Department, Punjab Technical University, Jalandhar Punjab (India). She received her Bachelor degree and Master degree in Computer Science & Engineering from Novosibirsk State Technical University, Russia.

Rajshree Srivastava is an Assistant Professor at Chandigarh University in Computer Science and Engineering Department. She completed her masters M.Tech in CSE-IS from Jaypee Institute of Information Technology, Noida. Her research area is in the Database Security, data mining and Machine Learning and Information Security. She is a member of CSI, ACM, IAENG and Internet Society. Further, she is TPC member in ICAST-2018 and TPC member in RTESD-2018.

Vikas Thukral is working as Technical System Analyst, SaaS (Software as a Service) Operations in Charles River Development at Boston, USA where his responsibilities include managing global operations for SaaS clients, working on batch automation and devise process improvement strategies such as automation tools to ensure efficiency and reliability, assisting with the ongoing implementation\ upgrades, and refinement of operational procedures. Previously he was working as Technology Lead at Bank of America, USA and Infosys Limited, Chandigarh, India (from 2011- 2016) as part of Integration Engineering and Technical Environment support team. His responsibilities include preparing environment for integrated and independent releases. Effectively applying ITIL methodologies and enforced project standards for productivity improvements, managing risks and issues impacting project deliverable. He has B-Tech in computer science and Engineering from Kurukshetra University and Executive MBA in Project management from Sikkim Manipal University.

Shiv Kumar Verma is a distinguished professor and a researcher in the field of computer science. He has obtained his PhD degree from IIT, Roorkee, India. He also obtained is MCA degree from IIT, Roorkee, India in 2003. He has more than 20 years of experience in teaching and research. He is a member of IEEE, ACM, Senior member of Universal Association of Computer and Electronics Engineers, Senior member of Computer Science Teacher Association, CSTA, Reviewer JESTEC, Scopus Index Journal, Editorial board member of International Scientific Committee, World Academy of Science- Engineering and Technology. He has published more than 30 publications in peer reviewed in referred journal and conferences. He also has one patent to his credit. His core area of research are computational science and image processing.

Index

A

Activity diagram 209, 213-214
Activity graph 214-215
Attacker capability 244, 248-251, 254

B

Building Information Modeling 268-270

C

CAD 257, 261, 268, 272
Client Information Administration 150, 152
CMM 219-221
CMMI 220-221
Construction 40-41, 68, 266-273, 275-276
Construction Projects 267-270, 272
Countermeasures 49, 59, 117
CWE 70-72, 74-76, 79
Cyber Security 78, 101, 110, 115, 248

D

DEMATEL 235-236, 238, 241-242
Design Phase 53, 56, 204-205, 212, 231
documentation 2, 5, 8, 18-19, 26, 63, 72,
    75-76, 84, 171, 234
DOI 217
DOS 75

E

EDA 256-258, 265
E-learning 100-101

Estimation of Threats 117
Extended Enterprise System 119, 128

F

Financial risk 122, 131
FMCDM 235-238, 241-242
framework 5, 42-43, 53, 56, 58, 62-65, 69,
    75, 77, 80, 87, 105, 117, 126-127, 150,
    152-155, 157, 176-177, 179, 221-222,
    224, 229-231, 234, 241

G

Gamification 219, 221-224, 226-231
Genetic Algorithm 136-137, 139-142, 147

I

IC 256-265
Identification of Assets 117
IFC 273, 275
Impact 3, 8-10, 23-24, 28, 34-36, 44, 48-49,
    54-56, 59, 65, 70, 75, 84, 111, 114, 117,
    138, 156, 162, 178, 188-189, 198-200,
    246, 248, 254, 267, 272
Information Administration 150, 152
IP 256, 259-262, 265

L

Large Scale System 117
LCOM 217

M

Meta Heuristic 139, 142
Methodology 46-48, 51, 105, 117, 156, 172-173, 222, 224, 227, 230-231, 237, 261
Metrics 21, 28, 39-40, 100-101, 106, 110, 204, 209-211, 214, 216-217
Mitigation 1-3, 11-13, 15, 28, 34-35, 37, 51, 55, 58, 65, 71, 76, 97, 119-120, 123, 125, 127, 131-132, 244-248, 251, 254, 256, 260
Mutation 139-140

N

NDepend simulator 204, 210
NOC 217

O

OCTAVE 69, 245, 248
Ontology 105, 220, 222-223, 230-231
Optimization 136-137, 139, 141, 147, 258

P

Performance Of The Project 238
prioritization 84, 129, 188
Probability 9-10, 12, 22, 28, 30, 48-49, 55, 59, 65, 84, 110-111, 115, 121, 129, 136, 188-189, 197-201, 209, 244
Project risk 25-26, 28, 84, 87, 136, 234-235, 237, 266, 269, 272

Q

Quality Assurance 28, 205, 207-208, 220
Quantification 105

R

Regression testing 204-205, 207-212, 214
Risk Assessment 8, 18, 24-26, 30, 46, 49, 51, 53-54, 56, 59, 63, 65, 69, 79, 84, 100, 115, 117, 190, 201, 236, 238, 246, 251-252, 266
Risk estimation 50-51, 53, 55, 58, 244-248, 251, 254

Risk Evaluation 26, 54, 69, 126-128, 132, 235
Risk Factors 50, 84-85, 87-88, 92, 99, 132, 190, 234-238, 241-243, 267-268
Risk Identification 2-4, 24-26, 28, 84, 121, 126-127, 132
Risk Management 2-3, 18, 21-25, 28, 32, 52, 58, 83-85, 87, 93, 95, 97, 99, 101, 115, 117, 120-123, 132, 188-192, 196, 201-202, 241, 243, 256, 267, 269, 272
Risk Mitigation 1-3, 11-13, 28, 37, 119-120, 123, 127, 132, 244-247, 251, 254
Risk Mitigation Implementation 2-3, 12-13
Risk Mitigation Planning 1-3, 11
Risk Mitigation Progress Monitoring 2
Risk Monitoring 28, 122-123
Risk-analysis 55-56

S

Secure Engineering 62-63, 65, 69, 71-72, 79
Security Assets 117
Security Policy 248
Security Risk Analysis Process 117
SEDA 71-75, 77, 80
Software Development 26, 32, 47, 51, 59, 61-62, 64-66, 79-80, 88, 95, 152, 190, 195, 204, 220, 229, 235, 242
Software Engineering 69, 77, 79, 219-221, 230-231, 237
Software Quality 53, 152, 169, 207, 217
Software Risk 25, 56, 85, 92, 190, 234, 236-237, 241-242
Software Risks 25, 237
STEP 8, 10-14, 17, 44, 51, 75-76, 80, 123, 141, 147, 170, 192, 222, 224, 238, 276
Strategies 12-13, 21, 24, 52-53, 55, 58-59, 64, 85, 120, 122-123, 126, 178, 192, 202, 235
STRIDE 53, 65, 74

T

Tamper 257, 262-264
Taxonomy 65, 103-104, 106, 108, 110, 114-115
The ISO 117

Theft 250, 256-257, 259-260

Threat 1, 21-22, 48-50, 53, 55, 58-59, 62-69, 71-72, 76-79, 84, 97, 111, 118-119, 122-123, 131, 244-249, 251-253, 265

Threat Analysis 62-67, 71-72, 76-78

Threat Modeling 63-65, 68-69

Threats 1-2, 8, 22, 30, 32, 34, 43, 46-49, 51, 56, 58-59, 61, 64-65, 78, 95, 101, 105, 117, 123, 128, 130-131, 196, 227, 245, 272

TODIM 235-237, 239, 241-242

V

VLSI 256, 258-260, 264-265

Vulnerability 34-44, 46-47, 49-50, 55, 59, 66, 69, 119, 249

Ensure Quality Research is Introduced to the Academic Community

Become an IGI Global Reviewer for Authored Book Projects

Premier Reference Source

Emerging GIS Applications for Emergency and Disaster Management

Premier Reference Source

Managerial Strategies and Green Solutions for Project Sustainability

Premier Reference Source

Comparative Approaches to Using R and Python for Statistical Data Analysis

Premier Reference Source

Solutions for High-Touch Communications in a High-Tech World

The overall success of an authored book project is dependent on quality and timely reviews.

In this competitive age of scholarly publishing, constructive and timely feedback significantly expedites the turnaround time of manuscripts from submission to acceptance, allowing the publication and discovery of forward-thinking research at a much more expeditious rate. Several IGI Global authored book projects are currently seeking highly qualified experts in the field to fill vacancies on their respective editorial review boards:

Applications may be sent to:
development@igi-global.com

Applicants must have a doctorate (or an equivalent degree) as well as publishing and reviewing experience. Reviewers are asked to write reviews in a timely, collegial, and constructive manner. All reviewers will begin their role on an ad-hoc basis for a period of one year, and upon successful completion of this term can be considered for full editorial review board status, with the potential for a subsequent promotion to Associate Editor.

If you have a colleague that may be interested in this opportunity, we encourage you to share this information with them.

Information Resources Management Association

Advancing the Concepts & Practices of Information Resources Management in Modern Organizations

Become an IRMA Member

Members of the **Information Resources Management Association (IRMA)** understand the importance of community within their field of study. The Information Resources Management Association is an ideal venue through which professionals, students, and academicians can convene and share the latest industry innovations and scholarly research that is changing the field of information science and technology. Become a member today and enjoy the benefits of membership as well as the opportunity to collaborate and network with fellow experts in the field.

IRMA Membership Benefits:

- **One FREE Journal Subscription**
- **30% Off Additional Journal Subscriptions**
- **20% Off Book Purchases**
- Updates on the latest events and research on Information Resources Management through the IRMA-L listserv.
- Updates on new open access and downloadable content added to Research IRM.
- A copy of the Information Technology Management Newsletter twice a year.
- A certificate of membership.

IRMA Membership $195

Scan code or visit **irma-international.org** and begin by selecting your free journal subscription.

Membership is good for one full year.